KV-027-488

500

PLACES TO STAY
WITH YOUR DOG
in Britain

AA

This edition published in 2007
© Automobile Association Developments
Limited 2007

The Automobile Association Development Limited
retains the copyright in the current
edition © 2007 and in all subsequent
editions, reprints and amendments to editions.

The information contained in this directory is
sourced entirely from the AA's information resources.

Assessments of AA inspected establishments are
based on the experience of the Hotel and Restaurant
Inspectors on the occasion(s) of their visit(s) and
therefore descriptions given in this guide necessarily
dictate an element of subjective opinion which may
not reflect or dictate a reader's own opinion on
another occasion. See AA website www.theAA.com
for a clear explanation of how, based on our
Inspector's inspection experiences, establishments
are graded. If the meal or meals experienced during
an inspection fall between award levels the restaurant
concerned may be awarded the lower of any award
levels applicable.

Cover photo: AA
All photographs in this guide: 1 AA/T Souter; 3
AA/J Wood; 5 AA/M Hayward
Typeset by Jamie Wiltshire
Printed in Italy by G.Canale & C.S.p.A.

Published by AA Publishing, which is a
trading name of Automobile Association
Developments Limited, whose registered office is
Fanum House, Basing View, Basingstoke, Hampshire
RG21 4EA. Registered number 1878835.

A CIP catalogue record for this book is
available from the British Library.

ISBN 13: 978-0-7495-5316-6
ISBN 10: 0-7495-5316-2

A03198

Welcome to the Guide

This pocket guide is perfect for dog owners looking for suitable accommodation for themselves and their pets. We have included hotels and bed and breakfasts that have told us they welcome dogs with their owners, and that the dogs can stay for free. Virtually all of these establishments have dog exercising facilities on site or within a very short distance; most of them allow pets to stay unaccompanied in guests' bedrooms, while others offer kennels or separate accommodation, and many accept dogs in public rooms as well. Some provide welcome packs, comfortable baskets, water bowls, special blankets and home-made treats. Do remember to mention your dog when you book.

Contents:

How to use this Guide

① WINDSOR

② Clarence Hotel ★★★ 63% GA

9 Clarence Road SL4 5AE

☎ 01753 864436 🖷 01753 857060

email: enquiries@clarence-hotel.co.uk

www.clarence-hotel.co.uk

③ Dir: *M4 junct 6, dual-carriageway to Windsor,
left at 1st rdbt onto Clarence Rd*

④ Dogs: Bedrooms Garden Exercise Area
(100yds)

This Grade II listed Victorian house is in the
heart of Windsor. Space in some rooms is
limited, but all are well maintained and offer
excellent value for money. Facilities include a
lounge with a well-stocked bar, and a steam
room. Breakfast is served in the dining room
overlooking attractive gardens.

⑤ Rooms: 20rms en suite (6 fmly) (2 GF) dble
room £55 - £79

⑥ Facilities: TV Modem/Fax Licensed TVL
Cen ht Parking 4

① **Locations** The guide is divided into
country order, then county order, then by
town/village alphabetically. The county
name appears down the side of the page.

② **AA Stars and Diamonds** Every
establishment in this Guide has been
inspected and rated by the AA. The star
system ranges from 1 to 5, with a quality
percentage score to differentiate between
places with the same star rating. Under the
Common Standards system, we now use
stars for B&Bs and Hotels. Each
establishment has a designator, to indicate
what kind of accommodation it is. These
designators are explained on page 6,
Some B&Bs still have diamonds which
range between 1 and 5. An AA Rosette
award is shown where the food is
particularly good. For a more in-depth
explanation of the AA's ratings please see
the website **www.theAA.com**

Directions appear where supplied by proprieters.

Dog facilities All establishments mentioned in this guide should allow your dog to stay for free. We indicate whether your dog can be left unattended in the bedroom, as well as any special provisions made for pets. These include exercise areas, and food or bowls provided, among others.

Rooms The total number of letting bedrooms is followed by the number of those that are en suite, family (fmly) and/or ground floor (GF) rooms where applicable, and then by the price for a double room per night.

Facilities For symbols and abbreviations please see page 6.

Symbols & Abbreviations

AA Awards, Ratings & Other Accommodation Categories

★   Star Classification

%   Quality Percentage Score

B&Bs Only

♦   Diamond Classification

Hotels and B&Bs

⊛   AA Rosette Award for food

Rooms and Prices

dble   Double Room

Facilities

TV   Television in bedrooms (B&Bs only)
Colour television is provided in all hotel rooms unless otherwise stated

TVL   TV in lounge

STV   Satelite television

Cen ht   Full central heating

⌇   Indoor swimming pool

⌇   Outdoor swimming pool

RS   Restricted service, e.g. RS Jan-Mar; Closed Xmas / New Year

ACCOMMODATION DESIGNATORS

All accommodation inspected under the new Common Standards is given one of 12 descriptive designators to help you see at a glance, the different types of accommodation available in Britain. For more detailed information go to:

www.theAA.com/travel/accommodation _restaurants_grading.html

B&B: Private house managed by owner

GH: Guest house, a larger B&B

GA: Guest accommodation

INN: Traditional inn with pub atmosphere

FH: B&B on a working farm

HL: Hotel

SHL: Small hotel managed by owner

RN: Restaurant with Rooms

THH: Town House Hotel

CHH: Country House Hotel

MH: Metro Hotel

BUD: Budget Hotel

ASPLEY GUISE
Best Western Moore Place Hotel

★★★ 70% HL

The Square MK17 8DW

☎ 01908 282000 📠 01908 281888

email: manager@mooreplace.com

www.mooreplace.co.uk

Dir: *M1 junct 13, take A507 signed Aspley Guise & Woburn Sands. Hotel on left in village square*

Dogs: Bedrooms Public Areas (lounge only)
This impressive Georgian house, set in delightful gardens in the village centre, is very conveniently located for the M1. Bedrooms do vary in size, but consideration has been given to guest comfort, with many thoughtful extras provided. There is a wide range of meeting rooms and private dining options.

Rooms: 62rms en suite (16 GF) dble room £85 - £145*

Facilities: TV Modem/Fax Licensed Parking 70 Last d order 9.30pm

BEDFORD
The Barns Hotel ★★★ 73% HL

Cardington Road MK44 3SA

☎ 0870 609 6108 📠 01234 273102

email: bedford@corushotels.com

www.corushotels.com

Dir: *From M1 junct 13, A421, approx 10m to A603 Sandy/Bedford exit, hotel on right at 2nd rdbt*

Dogs: Bedrooms (Unattended) Public Areas (except restaurant) Garden Exercise Area (on site, must be on lead) Pet Bowls
A tranquil location on the outskirts of Bedford, friendly staff and well-equipped bedrooms are the main attractions here. Cosy day rooms and two informal bars add to the appeal, while large windows in the restaurant make the most of the view over the river. The original barn now houses the conference and function suite.

Rooms: 48rms en suite (18 GF)

Facilities: TV STV Modem/Fax Licensed Parking 90

BEDFORDSHIRE

BERKSHIRE

HUNGERFORD

Beacon House ★★★ 59% BB

Bell Lane Upper Green Inkpen RG17 9QJ

☎ 01488 668640 📄 01488 668640

email: l.g.cave@classicfm.net

www.beaconhouseinkpen.com

Dir: *4m SE of Hungerford. Off A4 S into Kintbury, left onto Inkpen Rd, 1m over x-rds, right to common, 3rd left after Crown & Garter pub*

Dogs: Bedrooms (Unattended - may be left in Bedrooms at meal times) Garden Exercise Area (adjacent) Pet Food/Bowls

Resident Pets: Bilbo & Sevie (Cocker Spaniels), Jennie & Clare (donkeys)

This large house is set in peaceful countryside. Dinner is available in the winter months. Bedrooms are comfortably furnished and overlook fields. As well as the lounge, there is usually an art exhibition and sale featuring watercolours, textiles, printmaking and pottery in the adjoining Gallery.

Rooms: 3rms 0 en suite dble room £56

Facilities: TV TVL Cen ht Parking 6

MEMBURY

Days Inn Membury ⇧ BUD

Membury Service Area RG17 7TZ

☎ 01488 72336 📄 01488 72336

email: membury.hotel@welcomebreak.co.uk

www.welcomebreak.co.uk

Dir: *M4 between junct 14 & 15*

Dogs: Bedrooms Public Areas (only for access to bedrooms) Garden Exercise Area (adjacent)

This modern building offers accommodation in smart, spacious and well-equipped bedrooms, suitable for families and business travellers, and all with en suite bathrooms. Continental breakfast is available and other refreshments may be taken at the nearby family restaurant.

Rooms: 38rms en suite (32 fmly) (17 GF) dble room £35 - £55*

Facilities: TV STV Modem/Fax TVL Parking 200 Last d order 10.15pm

READING

Courtyard by Marriott Reading

★ ★ ★ 74% HL

Bath Road Padworth RG7 5HT

☎ 0870 400 7234 📄 0870 400 7334

www.courtyardreading.co.uk

Dir: *M4 junct 12 onto A4 towards Newbury. Hotel 3.5m on left, after petrol station*

Dogs: Bedrooms Exercise Area (canal walk)

This purpose-built hotel combines the benefits of a peaceful rural location with the accessibility afforded by good road links. Modern comforts include air-conditioned bedrooms and rooms with easy access for less mobile guests. A feature of the hotel is its pretty courtyard garden, which can be seen from the restaurant.

Rooms: 50rms en suite (25 GF) dble room £72 - £160*

Facilities: TV STV Modem/Fax Licensed Parking 200

WINDSOR

Clarence Hotel ★ ★ ★ 63% GA

9 Clarence Road SL4 5AE

☎ 01753 864436 📄 01753 857060

email: enquiries@clarence-hotel.co.uk

www.clarence-hotel.co.uk

Dir: *M4 junct 6, dual-carriageway to Windsor, left at 1st rdbt onto Clarence Rd*

Dogs: Bedrooms Garden Exercise Area (100yds)

This Grade II listed Victorian house is in the heart of Windsor. Space in some rooms is limited, but all are well maintained and offer excellent value for money. Facilities include a lounge with a well-stocked bar, and a steam room. Breakfast is served in the dining room overlooking attractive gardens.

Rooms: 20rms en suite (6 fmly) (2 GF) dble room £55 - £79

Facilities: TV Modem/Fax Licensed TVL Cen ht Parking 4

BERKSHIRE

BRISTOL

BRISTOL

Washington Hotel ★★★ 64% GH

11-15 St Pauls Road Clifton BS8 1LX

☎ 0117 973 3980 📠 0117 973 4740

email: washington@cliftonhotels.com

www.cliftonhotels.com/washington

Dir: *A4018 into city, right at lights opp BBC, house 200yds on left*

Dogs: Bedrooms (Unattended) Garden Exercise Area (Victoria Square nearby) This large terrace house is within walking distance of the city centre and Clifton village. The bedrooms, many refurbished, are well equipped for business guests. Public areas include a modern reception lounge and a bright basement breakfast room. The property has secure parking and a rear patio garden.

Rooms: 46rms 40 en suite (4 fmly) (10 GF) dble room £57 - £84

Facilities: TV STV Licenced Cen ht Parking 20 Last d order 10pm

BRISTOL

Berkeley Square Hotel

★★★ 77% HL

15 Berkeley Square Clifton BS8 1HB

☎ 0117 925 4000 📠 0117 925 2970

email: berkeley@cliftonhotels.com

www.cliftonhotels.com/chg.html

Dir: *M32 follow Clifton signs. 1st left at traffic lights by Nills Memorial Tower University into Berkeley Sq*

Dogs: Bedrooms (Unattended) Public Areas (except restaurant/bar) Garden Exercise Area (in front of hotel) Pet Bowls Close to the university, art gallery and Clifton Village, this smart, elegant Georgian hotel has modern bedrooms that feature many welcome extras. There is a cosy lounge and stylish restaurant on the ground floor and a smart bar in the basement. There is a small garden at the rear of the hotel.

Rooms: 43rms en suite (4 GF) dble room £105 - £155*

Facilities: TV STV Modem/Fax Lift Parking 20

GAYHURST

Mill Farm ♦♦♦ 65%

Newport Pagnell MK16 8LT

☎ 01908 611489 & 07714 719640

🖷 01908 611489

email: adamsmillfarm@aol.com

Dir: *B526 trom Newport Pagnell, 2.5m left onto Haversham Rd, Mill Farm 1st on left*

Dogs: Bedrooms Sep Accom (pen, kennel) Garden Exercise Area (500 acres with river)

Resident Pets: Peter (Terrier), Hector (Dachshund), Alfie (Labrador)

Within easy reach of Newport Pagnell and the M1, this historic farmhouse has a peaceful setting with wonderful views over farmland. Bedrooms are decorated in a homely style and have a host of thoughtful extras. The sumptuous lounge-dining room is enhanced with fine antiques.

Rooms: 4rms 3 en suite (1 fmly) (1 GF) dble room £45 - £55

Facilities: TV TVL Cen ht Parking 13 Last d order 10pm

MILTON KEYNES

Swan Revived Hotel ★★ 72% HL

High Street Newport Pagnell MK16 8AR

☎ 01908 610565 🖷 01908 210995

email: info@swanrevived.co.uk

www.swanrevived.co.uk

Dir: *M1 junct 14 onto A509 then B526 into Newport Pagnell for 2m. Hotel on High St*

Dogs: Bedrooms (Unattended) Public Areas (except restaurant) Garden Exercise Area (100yds)

Once a coaching inn, this hotel dates from the 17th century, occupying a prime location in the centre of town. Well-appointed bedrooms are mostly spacious, individually styled and have good levels of comfort. Public areas include a popular bar and a restaurant offering a variety of freshly prepared dishes.

Rooms: 42rms en suite (2 fmly) dble room £74 - £95*

Facilities: TV STV Lift Licensed Parking 18

BUCKINGHAMSHIRE

BUCKINGHAMSHIRE

MILTON KEYNES
Welcome Lodge Newport Pagnell
⌂ BUD
Newport Pagnell MK16 8DS
☎ 01908 610878 📄 01908 216539
email: newport.hotel@welcomebreak.co.uk
www.welcomebreak.co.uk
Dir: *M1 junct 14-15. In service area - follow signs to Barrier Lodge*
Dogs: Bedrooms (Unattended) Garden Exercise Area (adjacent)
This building offers accommodation suitable for families and business travellers, and all with en suite bathrooms. Continental breakfast is available and other refreshments may be taken at the nearby family restaurant.
Rooms: 90rms en suite (54 fmly) dble room £45 - £60*
Facilities: TV STV Licensed Parking 70 Last d order 9.30pm

MILTON KEYNES
Campanile ⌂ BUD
40 Penn Road Fenny Stratford Bletchley MK2 2AU
☎ 01908 649819 📄 01908 649818
email: mk@campanile-hotels.com
www.campanile.com
Dir: *M1 junct 14, follow A4146 to A5. Southbound on A5. 4th exit at 1st rdbt to Fenny Stratford. Hotel 500yds on left*
Dogs: Bedrooms (Unattended) Public Areas (except bar & restaurant) Garden Exercise Area (riverside walk)
This modern building offers accommodation in smart, well-equipped bedrooms, all with en suite bathrooms. Refreshments may be taken at the informal Bistro.
Rooms: 80rms en suite
Facilities: TV STV Licensed Parking 80 Last d order 10pm

TAPLOW

Cliveden ★★★★★ 88% @@@ CHH

SL6 0JF

☎ 01628 668561 📄 01628 661837

email: reservations@clivedenhouse.co.uk

www.vonessenhotels.co.uk

Dir: *M4 junct 7, follow A4 towards Maidenhead for 1.5m, turn onto B476 towards Taplow, 2.5m, hotel on left*

Dogs: Bedrooms (Unattended) Public Areas (except restaurant) Garden Exercise Area (in grounds) Pet Food/Bowls dog menu, dog sitting

Visitors are treated as house-guests at this wonderful stately home. Both restaurants here are awarded AA rosettes - The Terrace has two rosettes, and the luxurious Waldo's has three. Leisure facilities include cruises along Cliveden Reach and massages in the Pavilion.

Rooms: 39rms en suite (8 GF) dble room £335 - £950*

Facilities: TV STV Modem/Fax Lift Licensed Parking 60 Last d order 9.30pm

CAMBRIDGE

Best Western The Gonville Hotel

★★★ 77% HL

Gonville Place CB1 1LY

☎ 01223 366611 & 221111 📄 01223 315470

email: all@gonvillehotel.co.uk

www.bw-gonvillehotel.co.uk

Dir: *M11 junct 11, on A1309 follow city centre signs. At 2nd mini rdbt right into Lensfield Rd, over junct with lights. Hotel 25yds on right*

Dogs: Bedrooms Garden Exercise Area (park opposite)

This hotel is situated on the inner ring road, a short walk across the green from the city centre. It's popular for its relaxing, informal atmosphere. The air-conditioned public areas are cheerfully furnished, and include a lounge bar and brasserie; bedrooms are well appointed and appealing, with good facilities.

Rooms: 73rms en suite (1 fmly) (5 GF) dble room £99 - £170*

Facilities: TV Modem/Fax Lift Licensed Parking 80 Last d order 9pm

CAMBRIDGESHIRE

ELY

Lamb Hotel ★★★ 72% HL

2 Lynn Road CB7 4EJ

☎ 01353 663574 📠 01353 662023

email: lamb.ely@oldenglishinns.co.uk

www.oldenglish.co.uk

Dir: *from A10 into Ely, hotel in town centre*

Dogs: Bedrooms Public Areas (except restaurant) Exercise Area (200yds) Pet Bowls
This 15th-century former coaching inn is situated in the heart of this popular market town. The hotel offers a combination of light, modern and traditional public rooms, whilst the bedrooms provide contemporary standards of accommodation. Food is available throughout the hotel - the same menu provided in the bar and restaurant areas.

Rooms: 31rms en suite (6 fmly) dble room £75 - £95*

Facilities: TV STV Modem/Fax Licensed Parking 20 Last d order 9.30pm

HUNTINGDON

Huntingdon Marriott Hotel

★★★★ 75% HL

Kingfisher Way

Hinchingbrooke Business Park PE29 6FL

☎ 01480 446000 📠 01480 451111

email:
reservations.huntingdon@marriotthotels.com

www.huntingdonmarriott.co.uk

Dir: *1m from Huntington centre on A14, close to Brampton racecourse*

Dogs: Bedrooms (Unattended) Public Areas Garden Exercise Area (park nearby)
With its excellent road links, this purpose-built hotel is a popular venue for business meetings, and is convenient for Huntingdon, Cambridge and racing at Newmarket. Spacious bedrooms offer modern comfort and air conditioning. Impressive leisure facilities.

Rooms: 150rms en suite (45 GF) dble room £94 - £180

Facilities: TV STV Modem/Fax Lift Licensed Parking 200 Last d order 9.30pm

SIX MILE BOTTOM
Swynford Paddocks Hotel
★★★ 82% ◉ HL
CB8 0UE
☎ 01638 570234 ▤ 01638 570283
email: info@swynfordpaddocks.com
www.swynfordpaddocks.com
Dir: *M11 junct 9, take A11 towards Newmarket, then onto A1304 to Newmarket, hotel 0.75m on left*

Dogs: Bedrooms Public Areas (bar only) Garden
This smart country house is set in attractive grounds, within easy reach of Newmarket. Bedrooms are comfortably appointed, thoughtfully equipped and include some delightful four-poster rooms. Imaginative, carefully prepared food is served in the elegant restaurant; service is friendly. Meeting and conference facilities are available.
Rooms: 15rms en suite (1 fmly) dble room £135 - £195*
Facilities: TV STV Licensed Parking 180 Last d order 9pm

WISBECH
Elme Hall Hotel ★★★ 73% HL
Elm High Road PE14 0DQ
☎ 01945 475566 ▤ 01945 475666
email: elme@paktel.co.uk
www.paktel.co.uk
Dir: *off A47 onto A1101 towards Wisbech. Hotel on right*

Dogs: Bedrooms Garden Exercise Area
An imposing, Georgian-style property conveniently situated on the outskirts of the town centre just off the A47. Individually decorated bedrooms are tastefully furnished with quality reproduction pieces and equipped to a high standard. Public rooms include a choice of attractive lounges, as well as two bars, meeting rooms and a banqueting suite.
Rooms: 7rms en suite (3 fmly) dble room £68 - £220*
Facilities: TV FTV Modem/Fax Licensed TVL Parking 200 Last d order 9.30pm

CHESHIRE

BURWARDSLEY

The Pheasant Inn ★★ 81% ◉ HL

Higher Burwardsley CH3 9PF

☎ 01829 770434 📠 01829 771097

email: info@thepheasantinn.co.uk

www.thepheasantinn.co.uk

Dir: *from A41, left to Tattenhall, right at 1st junct and left at 2nd to Higher Burwardsley. At post office left, hotel signed*

Dogs: Bedrooms (Unattended) Public Areas (at manager's discretion) Garden Exercise Area (surrounding countryside)

This delightful 300-year-old inn sits high on the Peckforton Hills and enjoys spectacular views over the Cheshire Plain. Well-equipped, comfortable bedrooms are housed in an adjacent converted barn. Creative dishes are served either in the stylish restaurant or in the traditional, beamed bar. Real fires are lit in the winter months.

Rooms: 12rms en suite (2 fmly) (5 GF) dble room £80 - £130

Facilities: TV Licensed Parking 80 Last d order 9.30pm

CHESTER

Hoole Hall Hotel ★★★ 71% HL

Warrington Road Hoole Village CH2 3PD

☎ 0870 609 6126 & 01244 408800

📠 01244 320251

email: hoolehall@corushotels.com

www.corushotels.com

Dir: *M53 junct 12, A56 for 0.5m towards city centre, hotel 500yds on left*

Dogs: Bedrooms (Unattended) Garden Pet Food/Bowls

Situated in extensive gardens on the outskirts of the city, part of this hotel dates back to the 18th century. The newly refurbished reception lounge now offers BT Openzone. Meetings, banquets and conferences are well catered for and ample parking space is available.

Rooms: 97rms en suite (4 fmly) (33 GF) dble room £85 - £110

Facilities: TV STV Modem/Fax Lift Licensed TVL Parking 200 Last d order 9.30pm

GLAZEBROOK
The Rhinewood Country House Hotel ★★★ 75% HL

Glazebrook Lane Glazebrook WA3 5BB

☎ 0161 775 5555 📠 0161 775 7965

email: info@therhinewoodhotel.co.uk

www.therhinewoodhotel.co.uk

Dir: *M6 junct 21, follow A57 towards Irlam. Turn left at Glazebrook sign, hotel 0.25m left handside.*

Dogs: Bedrooms Garden Exercise Area (5 mins walk)

A warm welcome and attentive service are assured at this privately owned and personally run hotel. It stands in spacious grounds and gardens and is located between Warrington and Manchester. Facilities here include conference and function rooms and the hotel is also licensed for civil wedding ceremonies.

Rooms: 32rms en suite (4 fmly) (16 GF) dble room £75 - £115*

Facilities: TV STV Modem/Fax Licensed TVL Parking 120 Last d order 10pm

NANTWICH
Best Western Crown Hotel & Restaurant ★★ 71% HL

High St CW5 5AS

☎ 01270 625283 📠 01270 628047

email: info@crownhotelnantwich.com

www.crownhotelnantwich.com

Dir: *A52 to Nantwich, hotel in centre of town*

Dogs: Bedrooms Public Areas

Resident Pets: Buttons (dog)

Ideally set in the heart of this historic and delightful market town, The Crown has been offering hospitality for centuries. It has an abundance of original features and the well-equipped bedrooms retain an old world charm. There is also a bar with live entertainment throughout the week and diners can enjoy Italian food in the atmospheric brasserie.

Rooms: 18rms en suite (2 fmly) dble room £82

Facilities: TV Modem/Fax Licensed Parking 18 Last d order 9.45pm

CHESHIRE

CHESHIRE

NORTHWICH

The Floatel, Northwich

★★★ 64% HL

London Road CW9 5HD

☎ 01606 44443 📄 01606 42596

email: enquiries@hotels-northwich.com

www.hotels-northwich.com

Dir: *M6 junct 19, follow A556 for 4m, take right turn & follow signs for town centre*

Dogs: Bedrooms (Unattended) Garden Exercise Area (on site)

A first in the UK, this floating hotel has been built on the River Weaver in the town centre and is proving a very successful concept. The bedrooms are modern and well equipped, and there is a pleasant restaurant that overlooks the river.

Rooms: 60rms en suite (2 fmly)

dble room £40 - £91*

Facilities: TV STV Modem/Fax Lift Licensed TVL Parking 110

Last d order 9.30pm

RUNCORN

Campanile ⭐ BUD

Lowlands Road WA7 5TP

☎ 01928 581771 📄 01928 581730

email: runcorn@envergure.co.uk

www.campanile.com

Dir: *M56 junct 12, take A557, then follow signs for Runcorn rail station/Runcorn College*

Dogs: Bedrooms Garden Exercise Area (5 min walk to park & canal)

This modern building offers accommodation in smart, well equipped bedrooms, all with en suite bathrooms. Refreshments may be taken at the informal Bistro.

Rooms: 53rms en suite (18 GF)

Facilities: TV STV Modem/Fax Licensed TVL Parking 50 Last d order 9.30pm

TARPORLEY

Willington Hall ★★★ 78% HL

Willington CW6 0NB

☎ 01829 752321 📄 01829 752596

email: enquiries@willingtonhall.co.uk

www.willingtonhall.co.uk

Dir: *3m NW off unclass road linking A51 & A54, at Clotton turn off A51 at Bulls Head, then follow signs*

Dogs: Bedrooms (Unattended) Garden Exercise Area Pet Food/Bowls

Situated in 17 acres of parkland and built in 1829, this attractively furnished country-house hotel offers spacious bedrooms, many with views over open countryside. Service is courteous and friendly, and freshly prepared meals are offered in the dining room or in the bar and drawing room. A smart function suite confirms the popularity of this hotel as a venue for weddings and conferences.

Rooms: 10rms en suite

dble room £110 - £120*

Facilities: TV STV Modem/Fax Licensed Parking 60

TARPORLEY

Hill House Farm ★★★★ 70% FH

Rushton CW6 9AU

☎ 01829 732238 📄 01829 733929

email: rayner@hillhousefarm.fsnet.co.uk

www.hillhousefarm.info

Dir: *1.5m E of Tarporley. Off A51/A49 to Eaton, continue E for Rushton, right onto The Hall Ln, farm 0.5m*

Dogs: Bedrooms Sep Accom (kennels) Public Areas (if well behaved) Garden Exercise Area (surrounding area)

Resident Pets: 2 Springer Spaniels, Labrador, Patterdale Terrier, Wallace & Grommit (cats), 2 ponies

This impressive brick farmhouse stands in attractive gardens within 14 acres of rolling pastureland. The stylish bedrooms have en suite or private facilities. There is a spacious lounge and a traditional breakfast room.

Rooms: 3rms en suite (1 fmly)

dble room £60 - £65*

Facilities: TV TVL Cen ht Parking 6

Last d order 9.30pm

CHESHIRE

WARRINGTON
Paddington House Hotel
★★ 71% HL
514 Old Manchester Road WA1 3TZ
☎ 01925 816767 ▤ 01925 816651
email: hotel@paddingtonhouse.co.uk
www.paddingtonhouse.co.uk
Dir: *1m from M6 junct 21, off A57, 2m from town centre*
Dogs: Bedrooms (Unattended) Garden Exercise Area
This busy, friendly hotel is conveniently situated just over a mile from the M6. Bedrooms are attractively furnished, and include four-poster and ground-floor rooms. Guests can dine in the wood-panelled Padgate restaurant or in the cosy bar. Conference and function facilities are available.
Rooms: 37rms en suite (9 fmly) (6 GF) dble room £60 - £90
Facilities: TV FTV Modem/Fax Lift Licensed TVL Parking 50

BOSCASTLE
Tolcarne House Hotel ◆◆◆◆ 78%
Tintagel Road PL35 0AS
☎ 01840 250654 ▤ 01840 250654
email: crowntolhouse@eclipse.co.uk
www.milford.co.uk/go/tolcarne.html
Dir: *In village at junct B3266 & B3263*
Dogs: Bedrooms Public Areas (except dining room) Garden Exercise Area (400yds)
Resident Pets: William, Candida & Amber (rescue cats)
You are assured of a warm welcome at this substantial Victorian residence, set in delightful grounds and gardens at the top of the village. The stylish bedrooms have many extras, and there is a lounge with an open fire and a separate cosy bar. Evening meals, by arrangement, are served in the elegant dining room.
Rooms: 8rms en suite dble room £66 - £81*
Facilities: TV Parking 15
Last d order 9.30pm

CAMBORNE

Tyacks Hotel ★ ★ ★ 71% HL

27 Commercial Street TR14 8LD

☎ 01209 612424   🖷 01209 612435

email: tyacks@smallandfriendy.co.uk

www.smallandfriendy.co.uk

Dir: *W on A30 past A3047 junct & turn off at*
Camborne West junct. Left & left again at
rdbt, follow town centre signs. Hotel on left

Dogs: Bedrooms (certain Bedrooms only)
Public Areas (except restaurant, must be on
lead) Garden Exercise Area (various walks, 4
beaches within 4m)

This 18th-century former coaching inn has
spacious, well-furnished public areas which
include a smart lounge and bar, the popular
Coach Bar and a restaurant serving fixed-
price and carte menus. The comfortable
bedrooms are attractively decorated and well
equipped; two have separate sitting areas.

Rooms: 15rms en suite (2 fmly)
dble room £75*

Facilities: TV STV Licensed Parking 27

FALMOUTH

The Rosemary ★ ★ ★ ★ 77% GA

22 Gyllyngvase Terrace TR11 4DL

☎ 01326 314669

email: therosemary@tiscali.co.uk

www.therosemary.co.uk

Dir: *A39 Melvill Rd signed to beaches &*
seafront, right onto Gyllyngvase Rd, 1st left

Dogs: Bedrooms Public Areas (except
dining room) Garden Exercise Area (0.25m)

Resident Pets: Rifca (Black Labrador)

Centrally located with splendid views over
Falmouth Bay, this friendly establishment
provides comfortable accommodation. The
attractive bedrooms are thoughtfully equipped;
some with the benefit of the views. Guests
can relax in the lounge with a drink from the
well stocked bar. Also available is a sunny
decking area at the rear in the pretty garden,
facing the sea.

Rooms: 10rms en suite (4 fmly)
dble room £60 - £68*

Facilities: TV Licensed TVL Cen ht
Parking 3 Last d order 10pm

CORNWALL & ISLES OF SCILLY

CORNWALL & ISLES OF SCILLY

FOWEY

Marina Hotel ★★ 84% ◉◉ HL

Esplanade PL23 1HY

☎ 01726 833315 ◷ 01726 832779

email: marina.hotel@dial.pipex.com

www.themarinahotel.co.uk

Dir: *into along down Lostwithiel St, near*
bottom of hill, right into Esplanade

Dogs: Bedrooms (Unattended) Public Areas
Garden Exercise Area

Built in 1815 as a seaside retreat, the Marina
has much style, and from its setting on the
water's edge has glorious views of the river
and the sea. Bedrooms, some with balconies,
are spacious and comfortable - not forgetting
the addition of a host of thoughtful touches
that are provided. Skilled cuisine, using the
freshest local produce, including fish landed
nearby, is the hallmark of the waterside
restaurant.

Rooms: 13rms en suite (1 fmly)
dble room £100 - £200*

Facilities: TV Modem/Fax Licensed
Parking 13

FOWEY

Trevanion Guest House ◆◆◆◆ 71%

70 Lostwithiel Street PL23 1BQ

☎ 01726 832602

email: alisteve@trevanionguesthouse.co.uk

www.trevanionguesthouse.co.uk

Dir: *A3082 into Fowey, down hill, left onto*
Lostwithiel St, Trevanion on left

Dogs: Bedrooms (Unattended) Public Areas
Garden Exercise Area (adjacent) Pet
Food/Bowls food & bowls with prior notice

Resident Pets: Poppy (Hans Macaw)

This 16th-century merchant's house provides
comfortable accommodation within easy
walking distance of the historic town of Fowey
and is convenient for visiting The Eden
Project. A hearty farmhouse-style cooked
breakfast, using local produce, is served in
the attractive dining room and other menu
options are available.

Rooms: 5rms 4 en suite (2 fmly) (1 GF)
dble room £50 - £65*

Facilities: TV Cen ht Parking 5
Last d order 8.30pm

CORNWALL & ISLES OF SCILLY

LAUNCESTON

Eagle House Hotel ★ ★ 69% SHL

Castle Street PL15 8BA

☎ 01566 772036 🖹 01566 772036

email: eaglehousehotel@aol.com

Dir: *from Launceston on Holsworthy Rd follow brown signs for hotel*

Dogs: Bedrooms Garden Exercise Area
Next to the castle, this elegant Georgian house dates back to 1767 and is within walking distance of all the local amenities. Many of the bedrooms have wonderful views over the Cornish countryside. A short carte is served each evening in the restaurant.

Rooms: 14rms en suite (1 fmly)
dble room £62*

Facilities: TV STV Licensed TVL Parking 100 Last d order 9pm

MARAZION

Godolphin Arms ★ ★ 72% SHL

TR17 0EN

☎ 01736 710202 🖹 01736 710171

email: enquiries@godolphinarms.co.uk

www.godolphinarms.co.uk

Dir: *from A30 follow Marazion signs for 1m to hotel. At end of causeway to St Michael's Mount*

Dogs: Bedrooms (Unattended) Public Areas (except restaurant) Exercise Area (100yds)
This 170-year-old waterside hotel is in a prime location where the stunning views of St Michael's Mount provide a backdrop for the restaurant and lounge bar. Bedrooms are colourful, comfortable and spacious. A choice of menu is offered in the main restaurant and the Gig Bar, all with an emphasis on local seafood.

Rooms: 10rms en suite (2 fmly) (2 GF)
dble room £90 - £140*

Facilities: TV STV Licensed Parking 48
Last d order 8.30pm

CORNWALL & ISLES OF SCILLY

NEWQUAY
Whipsiderry Hotel ★★ 76% HL
Trevelgue Road Porth TR7 3LY
☎ 01637 874777 & 876066 ▤ 01637 874777
email: info@whipsiderry.co.uk
www.whipsiderry.co.uk
Dir: *right onto Padstow road B3276 out of*
Newquay, in 0.5m right at Trevelgue Rd
Dogs: Bedrooms (Unattended) Public Areas
(except certain areas inc. restaurant) Garden
Exercise Area (100yds)
Quietly located, overlooking Porth Beach, this
friendly hotel offers bedrooms in a variety of
sizes and styles, many with superb views. A
daily-changing menu offers interesting and
well-cooked dishes with the emphasis on
fresh, local produce. An outdoor pool is
available, and at dusk guests may be able to
watch badgers in the attractive grounds.
Rooms: 20rms 19 en suite (5 fmly) (3 GF)
dble room £106 - £130*
Facilities: TV Licensed TVL Parking 30 🐾

NEWQUAY
Corisande Manor Hotel
★★★★★ 86% ⊛ GA
Riverside Avenue Pentire TR7 1PL
☎ 01637 872042 ▤ 01637 874557
email: relax@corisande.com
www.corisande.com
Dir: *Off A392 in Pentire*
Dogs: Bedrooms Garden Exercise Area
Resident Pets: Treacle (cat)
This attractive manor house has a tranquil
setting tucked away on the side of an estuary.
The friendly proprietors provide attentive and
skilled service. Bedrooms, many with superb
views, are decorated and furnished with great
care, imagination and individuality. Freshly
prepared dishes are offered from a daily
changing menu, supported by a lovingly
compiled wine list of considerable merit.
Rooms: 9rms en suite
dble room £150 - £178*
Facilities: TV Licensed Cen ht Parking 19

PENZANCE

Penmorvah ★ ★ ★ 68% GA

61 Alexandra Road TR18 4LZ

☎ 01736 363711 & 07875 675940

Dir: *A30 to Penzance, at railway station follow road along harbour front onto Promenade Rd. Right onto Alexandra Rd. Penmorvah on right*

Dogs: Bedrooms Public Areas (except dining room) Garden Exercise Area (200yds)

Resident Pets: Paddy (Lhasa Apso), Max (Jack Russell), Shadow, Midnight, Sooty, Smokey & Minky (rabbits)

Situated in a quiet, tree-lined road just a short walk from the seafront and town centre, and convenient for the ferry port, the Penmorvah has a friendly and relaxing atmosphere. Bedrooms are well appointed and equipped with thoughtful extras. Well-cooked breakfasts are served in the attractive dining room.

Rooms: 8rms en suite (2 fmly) (1 GF)

dble room £40 - £54

Facilities: TV TVL Cen ht

Last d order 8.30pm

PENZANCE

Mount View ★ ★ ★ 59% INN

Longrock TR20 8JJ

☎ 01736 710416 📄 01736 710416

Dir: *Off A30 at Marazion/Penzance rdbt. 3rd exit signed Longrock. Hotel on right after pelican crossing*

Dogs: Bedrooms (Unattended) Public Areas (except dining room) Exercise Area (100yds)

Resident Pets: Muppet (Beagle)

The Victorian inn, just a short walk from the beach and 0.5m from the Isles of Scilly heliport, is a good base for exploring west Cornwall. Bedrooms are well equipped, including a hospitality tray, and the bar is a popular with locals. Breakfast is served in the dining room and a dinner menu is available.

Rooms: 5rms 3 en suite (2 fmly)

dble room £40 - £55

Facilities: TV Licensed Parking 8

CORNWALL & ISLES OF SCILLY

CORNWALL & ISLES OF SCILLY

POLPERRO

Penryn House ◆◆◆◆ 73%

The Coombes PL13 2RQ

☎ 01503 272157 📠 01503 273055

email: chrispidcock@aol.com

www.penrynhouse.co.uk

Dir: *A387 to Polperro, at minirdbt left down hill into village ignore restricted access. Hotel 200yds on left*

Dogs: Bedrooms (Unattended) Sep Accom (office) Public Areas (except restaurant) Garden Exercise Area (200yds) Pet Food/Bowls

Resident Pets: Yogi (Weimeraner)

Penryn House has a welcoming atmosphere. Every effort is made to ensure a memorable stay. Bedrooms are neatly presented and reflect the character of the building. After a day exploring, enjoy a drink at the bar and relax in the comfortable lounge.

Rooms: 12rms 11 en suite (3 fmly) dble room £62 - £80

Facilities: TV Licensed Parking 13 Last d order 9.30/10pm Fri/Sat

SALTASH

Crooked Inn ★★★ 68% INN

Stoketon Cross Trematon PL12 4RZ

☎ 01752 848177 📠 01752 843203

email: info@crooked-inn.co.uk

www.crooked-inn.co.uk

Dir: *1.5m NW of Saltash. A38 W from Saltash, 2nd left to Trematon, sharp right*

Dogs: Bedrooms (Unattended) Public Areas Garden Exercise Area (on site) Pet Food/Bowls

Resident Pets: 3 dogs, 1 pig, 1 sheep, 2 horses, 4 cats, geese, ducks

The friendly animals that freely roam the courtyard add to the relaxed country style of this delightful inn. The spacious bedrooms are well equipped, and freshly cooked dinners are available in the bar and conservatory. Breakfast is served in the cottage-style dining room.

Rooms: 18rms 15 en suite (5 fmly) (7 GF)

Facilities: TV Licensed Cen ht Parking 45 Last d order 8.30pm 🐾

ST AGNES
Beacon Country House Hotel

★★ 80% CHH

Goonvrea Road TR5 0NW

☎ 01872 552318 📠 01872 552318

email: info@beaconhotel.co.uk

www.beaconhotel.co.uk

Dir: *from A30 take B3277 to St Agnes. At rdbt left onto Goonvrea Rd. Hotel 0.75m on right*

Dogs: Bedrooms (Unattended) Garden Exercise Area (hotel grounds)

Resident Pets: Hercules (Chocolate Labrador), Piglet & Wellington (cats), Betty & Gus (rabbits)

Set in a quiet and attractive area away from the busy village, this friendly hotel has splendid views over the countryside towards the sea. Now totally upgraded, the public areas and bedrooms are comfortable and well equipped; many benefit from glorious views.

Rooms: 11rms en suite (1 fmly) (2 GF) dble room £74 - £88*

Facilities: TV Licensed Parking 12

ST AUSTELL
Sunnycroft ★★★ 59% GA

28 Penwinnick Road PL25 5DS

☎ 01726 73351 📠 01726 879409

email: info@sunnycroft.net

www.sunnycroft.net

Dir: *600yds SW of town centre on A390*

Dogs: Bedrooms Garden Exercise Area (100yds)

The 1930s house is convenient for The Eden Project and just a short walk from the town centre. Its bright bedrooms offer good levels of comfort, and ground-floor rooms are available. Substantial tasty breakfasts are served in the smart dining room.

Rooms: 7rms en suite (1 fmly) (3 GF) dble room £50 - £65*

Facilities: TV Modem/Fax Cen ht Parking 7

ST IVES

Old Vicarage ★ ★ ★ ★ 76% GH

Parc-an-Creet TR26 2ES

☎ 01736 796124

email: stay@oldvicarage.com

www.oldvicarage.com

Dir: *Off A3074 in town centre onto B3306,*
0.5m right into Parc-an-Creet

Dogs: Bedrooms Public Areas (must be well
behaved) Garden Exercise Area (in grounds)
This former Victorian rectory stands in
secluded gardens in a quiet part of St Ives and
is convenient for the seaside, town and the
Tate. The bedrooms are enhanced by modern
facilities. A good choice of local produce is
offered at breakfast, plus home-made yoghurt
and preserves.

Rooms: 7rms en suite (4 fmly)

Facilities: TV Modem/Fax Licensed TVL
Cen ht Parking 12

ST IVES

Chy Roma Guest House ◆◆◆◆ 75%

2 Seaview Terrace TR26 2DH

☎ 01736 797539 📄 01736 797539

email: jenny@omshanti.demon.co.uk

www.connexions.co.uk/chyroma

Dir: *A3074 into St Ives, fork left at*
Porthminster Hotel, 1st left, 1st right, down
slope 2nd guest house on left

Dogs: Bedrooms Exercise Area (open fields)
Resident Pets: Saorisa (Golden Retriever),
Gypsy Rose Lee (Yorkshire/ Cairn Terrier
cross)
This friendly home is quietly tucked away and
its proprietors offer genuine hospitality. The
smart bedrooms are comfortably appointed,
and some have views of the harbour and St
Ives Bay. Substantial, freshly prepared
breakfasts are served in the lounge-dining
room. Some parking is available.

Rooms: 6rms en suite (2 fmly)
dble room £52 - £90*

Facilities: TV TVL Cen ht Parking 5
Last d order 8.45-9.15pm

ST MAWGAN
The Falcon Inn ♦♦♦♦ 68%

TR8 4EP

☎ 01637 860225   🖷 01637 860884

email:
enquiries@thefalconinn-newquay.co.uk

www.thefalconinn-newquay.co.uk

Dir: *In village centre*

Dogs: Bedrooms   Public Areas (except dining room)   Garden   Exercise Area (50yds)
Resident Pets: Stuart (cat), Saffy (Springer Spaniel)

The delightful early 19th-century inn stands opposite the village church in a quiet wooded valley. It is popular with locals and has a friendly atmosphere, with warming log fires. Bedrooms vary in size and are well equipped. There is a good choice for lunch and dinner, including local fish and cheeses.

Rooms: 2rms en suite dble room £68 - £74*
Facilities: TV   Licensed   Cen ht   Parking 12
Last d order 9.15pm

BORROWDALE
Borrowdale Hotel ★★★ 73% HL

CA12 5UY

☎ 017687 77224   🖷 017687 77338

email: theborrowdalehotel@yahoo.com

www.theborrowdalehotel.co.uk

Dir: *3m from Keswick, on B5289 at S end of Lake Derwentwater*

Dogs: Bedrooms (Unattended)   Sep Accom (kennels) Public Areas (except restaurant, and bar at lunch)   Garden   Exercise Area (50yds)
Pet Food/Bowls

Situated in the beautiful Borrowdale Valley overlooking Derwentwater, this traditionally styled hotel has been family-run for over 30 years. Public areas include a choice of lounges, a stylish dining room, and a lounge bar, plus a popular conservatory. There is a wide variety of bedroom sizes and styles; two are particularly suitable for less able guests.

Rooms: 36rms en suite (9 fmly) (2 GF)
dble room £120 - £190
Facilities: TV   Modem/Fax   Licensed
Parking 100   Last d order 8pm

CORNWALL & ISLES OF SCILLY/CUMBRIA

CUMBRIA

BORROWDALE

Lisdoonie Hotel ★ ★ 64% HL

307/309 Abbey Road LA14 5LF

☎ 01229 827312 📄 01229 820944

email: lisdoonie@aol.com

www.lisdoonie.com

Dir: *on A590, at 1st set of lights in town*
Strawberry pub on left continue for 100yds,
hotel on right

Dogs: Bedrooms Garden

Resident Pets: Peggy (German Wirehaired
Pointer)

This friendly hotel is conveniently located
for access to the centre of the town and is
popular with commercial visitors. The
comfortable bedrooms are well equipped,
and vary in size and style. There are two
comfortable lounges, one with a bar and
restaurant adjacent. There is also a large
function suite.

Rooms: 12rms en suite (2 fmly)

Facilities: TV Licensed TVL Parking 30
Last d order 9.30pm

CARLISLE

The Crown & Mitre ★ ★ ★ 66% HL

4 English Street CA3 8HZ

☎ 01228 525491 📄 01228 514553

email:
info@crownandmitre-hotel-carlisle.com

www.crownandmitre-hotel-carlisle.com

Dir: *A6 to city centre, pass station &*
Woolworths on left. Right into Blackfriars St.
Rear entrance at end

Dogs: Bedrooms Public Areas (except
restaurant)

Located in the heart of the city, this Edwardian
hotel is close to the cathedral and a few
minutes' walk from the castle. Bedrooms vary
in size and style, from smart executive rooms
to more functional standard rooms. Public
rooms include a comfortable lounge area and
the lovely bar with its feature stained-glass
windows.

Rooms: 94rms en suite (4 fmly)

dble room £89 - £120*

Facilities: TV STV Lift Licensed TVL
Parking 42 🐾

COCKERMOUTH
Rose Cottage ★ ★ ★ ★ 75% GH

Lorton Road CA13 9DX

☎ 01900 822189 🖹 01900 822189

email: bookings@rosecottageguest.co.uk

www.rosecottageguest.co.uk

Dir: *A5292 from Cockermouth to Lorton/Buttermere, Rose Cottage on right*

Dogs: Bedrooms Public Areas (except dining room) Exercise Area (200yds) Pet Food/Bowls

Resident Pets: Flynn (Irish Wolfhound)
This former inn is on the edge of town and has been refurbished to provide attractive, modern accommodation. The smart, well-equipped en suite bedrooms include a self-contained studio room with external access. There is a cosy lounge, and a smart dining room where delicious home-cooked dinners are a highlight.

Rooms: 7rms en suite (2 fmly) (3 GF)
dble room £60 - £90

Facilities: TV Licensed Cen ht Parking 12
Last d order 9pm

COCKERMOUTH
Shepherds Hotel ★ ★ ★ 70% HL

Lakeland Sheep & Wool Centre Egremont Road CA13 0QX

☎ 01900 822673 🖹 01900 822673

email: reception@shepherdshotel.co.uk

www.shepherdshotel.co.uk

Dir: *at junct of A66 & A5086 S of Cockermouth, entrance off A5086, 200yds off rdbt*

Dogs: Bedrooms (Unattended) Garden Exercise Area (on site)

Resident Pets: dogs, sheep, geese, cow
This hotel is modern in style and offers thoughtfully equipped accommodation. The property also houses the Lakeland Sheep and Wool Centre, with live sheep shows from Easter to mid November. A restaurant serving a variety of meals and snacks is open all day.

Rooms: 26rms en suite (4 fmly) (13 GF)
dble room £49 - £60*

Facilities: TV FTV Modem/Fax Lift Licensed TVL Parking 100
Last d order 8.30pm

CUMBRIA

CUMBRIA

CROSTHWAITE
Damson Dene Hotel ★★★ 68% HL

Bowness on Windermere LA8 8JE

☎ 015395 68676 📠 015395 68227

email: info@damsondene.co.uk

www.bestlakesbreaks.co.uk

Dir: *M6 junct 36, A590 signed Barrow-in-Furness, 5m right onto A5074. Hotel on right in 5m*

Dogs: Bedrooms (Unattended) Public Areas (except restaurant/leisure club) Garden Exercise Area (in grounds)

A short drive from Lake Windermere, this hotel enjoys a tranquil and scenic setting. Bedrooms include a number with four-poster beds and jacuzzi baths. The spacious restaurant serves a daily-changing menu, with some of the produce coming from the hotel's own kitchen garden. Leisure facilities are available.

Rooms: 37rms en suite (4 fmly) (9 GF) dble room £78 - £118

Facilities: TV Licensed TVL Parking 45 Last d order 5pm 🍴

CROSTHWAITE
Crosthwaite House ★★★★ 73% GH

Kendal LA8 8BP

☎ 015395 68264 📠 015395 68264

email: bookings@crosthwaitehouse.co.uk

www.crosthwaitehouse.co.uk

Dir: *A590 onto A5074, 4m right to Crosthwaite, 0.5m turn left*

Dogs: Bedrooms (Unattended) Garden Exercise Area (100yds)

Resident Pets: Pepper (Labrador), Fidge (Labrador/Collie cross), Bertie (cat)

Having stunning views across the Lyth Valley, this friendly Georgian house is a haven of tranquillity. Bedrooms are spacious and offer a host of thoughtful extras. The reception rooms include a comfortable lounge and a pleasant dining room with polished floorboards and individual tables.

Rooms: 6rms en suite dble room £50 - £55

Facilities: TV Modem/Fax Licensed TVL Cen ht Parking 10

GRANGE-OVER-SANDS

Elton House Bed & Breakfast

★ ★ ★ ★ 70% GH

Windermere Road LA11 6EQ

☎ 015395 32838 ▣ 015395 32838

email: info@eltonprivatehotel.co.uk

www.eltonprivatehotel.co.uk

Dir: *A590 onto B5277 signed Grange-over-Sands, pass railway station, right at T-junct, 100yds on left*

Dogs: Bedrooms (Unattended) Public Areas Garden Exercise Area (adjacent)

Resident Pets: CJ & Poppy (cats)

Friendly, attentive service is assured at this attractive Victorian house, just a stroll from the town. There are well-equipped bedrooms, with two on the ground floor, and the spacious lounge has a stunning feature fireplace.

Rooms: 7rms 5 en suite (1 fmly) (2 GF) dble room £52 - £56

Facilities: TV Licensed TVL Cen ht Parking 5 Last d order 8.30pm

GRIZEDALE

Grizedale Lodge The Hotel in the Forest ★ ★ ★ ★ 75% GA

Hawkshead, Ambleside LA22 0QL

☎ 015394 36532 ▣ 015394 36572

email: enquiries@grizedale-lodge.com

www.grizedale-lodge.com

Dir: *From Hawkshead signs S to Grizedale, Lodge 2m on right*

Dogs: Bedrooms (Unattended) Public Areas (except dining room) Garden Exercise Area (200-300yds) Pet Food breakfast doggy bag

Set in the heart of the tranquil Grizedale Forest Park, this charming establishment provides particularly comfortable bedrooms, some with four-poster beds and splendid views. Hearty breakfasts are served in the attractive dining room, which leads to a balcony for relaxing on in summer.

Rooms: 8rms en suite (1 fmly) (2 GF) dble room £90 - £95*

Facilities: TV Licensed Cen ht Parking 20 Last d order 9.30pm

CUMBRIA

CUMBRIA

HAWKSHEAD

Kings Arms Hotel ★ ★ ★ 66% INN

LA22 0NZ

☎ 015394 36372 📄 015394 36006

email: info@kingsarmshawkshead.co.uk

www.kingsarmshawkshead.co.uk

Dir: *In main square*

Dogs: Bedrooms Public Areas (except
dining room) Garden Exercise Area (on the
doorstep)

A traditional Lakeland inn in the heart of a
conservation area. The cosy, thoughtfully
equipped bedrooms retain much character
and are traditionally furnished. A good choice
of freshly prepared food is available in the
lounge bar and the neatly presented dining
room.

Rooms: 9rms 8 en suite (3 fmly)
dble room £62 - £80

Facilities: TV Modem/Fax Licensed
Cen ht Last d order 9pm

KENDAL

Riverside Hotel Kendal

★ ★ ★ 70% HL

Beezon Road Stramongate Bridge LA9 6EL

☎ 01539 734861 📄 01539 734863

email: info@riversidekendal.co.uk

www.bestlakesbreaks.co.uk

Dir: *M6 junct 36 Sedburgh, Kendal 7m, left
at end of Ann St, 1st right onto Beezon Rd,
hotel on left*

Dogs: Bedrooms (Unattended) Public Areas
(except restaurant & leisure areas) Exercise
Area (100yds)

Centrally located in this market town, and
enjoying a peaceful riverside location, this
17th-century former tannery provides a base
for business travellers and tourists. The
comfortable bedrooms are well equipped, and
open-plan day rooms include the attractive
restaurant and bar. Conference facilities are
available, and the leisure club proves popular.

Rooms: 47rms en suite (18 fmly) (10 GF)

Facilities: TV STV Lift Licensed TVL
Parking 60 🏊

KESWICK

Cragside ★★★★ 72% GH

39 Blencathra Street CA12 4HX

☎ 017687 73344 📠 017687 73344

email: wayne-alison@cragside39blencathra.fsnet.co.uk

http://cragside-keswick.mysite.wanadoo-members.co.uk

Dir: *A591 Penrith Rd into Keswick, under railway bridge, 2nd left*

Dogs: Bedrooms Public Areas (except dining room) Exercise Area (2 mins to park)

Expect warm hospitality at this guest house, located within easy walking distance of the town centre. The attractive bedrooms are well equipped, and many have fine views of the fells. Hearty Cumbrian breakfasts are served in the breakfast room, which overlooks the small front garden. Visually or hearing impaired guests are catered for, with Braille information, televisions with teletext, and a loop system installed in the dining room.

Rooms: 4rms en suite (2 fmly)

Facilities: TV Cen ht

KESWICK

Howe Keld Lakeland Guest House

★★★★ 75% GH

5/7 The Heads CA12 5ES

☎ 017687 72417 📠 017687 72417

email: david@howekeld.co.uk

www.howekeld.co.uk

Dir: *From town centre towards Borrowdale, right opp main car park, 1st on left*

Dogs: Bedrooms Public Areas (except lounge) Exercise Area (200yds to park)

Resident Pets: Lucy (cat)

Modern accommodation is offered at this friendly, well-run property close to the town and lake. Bedrooms are smartly decorated and furnished, and the first-floor lounge has spectacular views of the fells. Breakfast is a highlight, with local and home-made produce featuring on the menu. Dinner is available by arrangement.

Rooms: 15rms en suite (3 fmly) (2 GF)

Facilities: TV Licensed Cen ht Parking 9

CUMBRIA

CUMBRIA

KESWICK

Hazelmere ★★★★ 72% GA

Crosthwaite Road CA12 5PG

☎ 017687 72445 ▤ 017687 74075

email: info@hazelmerekeswick.co.uk

www.hazelmerekeswick.co.uk

Dir: *Off A66 at Crosthwaite rdbt A591 junct for Keswick, Hazelmere 400yds on right*

Dogs: Bedrooms Exercise Area (100yds)
This large Victorian house is only a short walk from Market Square and within walking distance of Derwentwater and the local fells. The attractive bedrooms are comfortably furnished and well equipped. Hearty Cumbrian breakfasts are served at individual tables in the ground-floor dining room, which has delightful views.

Rooms: 6rms en suite (1 fmly)
dble room £56 - £66*

Facilities: TV Cen ht Parking 7

KIRKBY STEPHEN

Southview Farm ★★★ 76% FH

Winton CA17 4HS

☎ 01768 371120 & 07801 432184

▤ 01768 371120

email: southviewwinton@hotmail.com

Dir: *1.5m N of Kirkby Stephen. Off A685 signed Winton*

Dogs: Bedrooms (Unattended) Public Areas (except in dining area) Exercise Area (300yds) Pet Food/Bowls
A friendly family home, Southview lies in the centre of Winton village, part of a terrace with the working farm to the rear. Two well-proportioned bedrooms are available, and there is a cosy lounge-dining room where traditional breakfasts are served around one table.

Rooms: 2rms 0 en suite (2 fmly)

Facilities: TVL Parking 2

KIRKBY STEPHEN
Brownber Hall Country House

★★★★★ 84% GH

Newbiggin-on-Lune CA17 4NX

☎ 01539 623208

email: enquiries@brownberhall.co.uk

www.brownberhall.co.uk

Dir: *6m SW of Kirkby Stephen. Off A685
signed Great Asby. 60yds right through
gatehouse, 0.25m sharp left onto driveway*

Dogs: Bedrooms Public Areas (must be
under supervision) Garden Exercise Area

Resident Pets: Sooty & Polar Bear (cats)

Having an elevated position with superb views
of the surrounding countryside, Brownber
Hall, built in 1860, has been restored to its
original glory. The bedrooms are comfortably
proportioned and well equipped. There are
two lovely reception rooms, and a dining
room where breakfasts, and by arrangement
dinners, are served. There is also a lift.

Rooms: 6rms en suite (1 GF)

dble room £60*

Facilities: TV Lift Cen ht Parking 12

NEAR SAWREY
Ees Wyke Country House

★★★★★ 87% ● GH

Ambleside LA22 0JZ

☎ 015394 36393

email: mail@eeswyke.co.uk

www.eeswyke.co.uk

Dir: *On B5285 on W side of village*

Dogs: Bedrooms Garden Exercise Area
(adjacent) Pet Food/Bowls

Resident Pets: Teddy & Harry (Old English
Sheepdogs)

A warm welcome awaits you at this elegant
Georgian country house with views over
Esthwaite Water and the surrounding
countryside. The bedrooms have been
decorated and furnished with care. There is
a charming lounge with an open fire, and a
splendid dining room where a five-course
dinner is served.

Rooms: 8rms en suite (1 GF)

dble room £160 - £180

Facilities: TV Modem/Fax Licensed
Cen ht Parking 12 Last d order 9pm

CUMBRIA

CUMBRIA

RAVENSTONEDALE

The Fat Lamb ★★ 67% HL

Crossbank CA17 4LL

☎ 015396 23242 📄 015396 23285

email: fatlamb@cumbria.com

www.fatlamb.co.uk

Dir: *on A683, between Kirkby Stephen and Sedbergh*

Dogs: Bedrooms Public Areas (except restaurant) Garden Exercise Area (100yds)

Open fires and solid stone walls are a feature of this 17th-century inn, set on its own nature reserve. There is a choice of dining options with an extensive menu available in the traditional bar or a more formal dining experience in the restaurant. Bedrooms are bright and cheerful and include family rooms and easily accessible rooms for guests with limited mobility.

Rooms: 12rms en suite (4 fmly) (5 GF) dble room £76 - £84*

Facilities: TV Licensed TVL Parking 60

ROSTHWAITE

Royal Oak Hotel ★ 68% HL

Keswick CA12 5XB

☎ 017687 77214 📄 017687 77214

email: info@royaloakhotel.co.uk

www.royaloakhotel.co.uk

Dir: *6m S of Keswick on B5289 in centre of Rosthwaite*

Dogs: Bedrooms Public Areas (except dining room) Garden Exercise Area Pet Food/Bowls

Set in a village in one of Lakeland's most picturesque valleys, this family-run hotel offers friendly and obliging service. There is a variety of accommodation styles, with particularly impressive rooms being located in a converted barn across the courtyard and backed by a stream. Family rooms are available. The bar is for residents and diners only. A set home-cooked dinner is served.

Rooms: 15rms 12 en suite (6 fmly) (4 GF) dble room £68 - £108

Facilities: Licensed TVL Parking 15 Last d order 9pm

TEBAY

The Cross Keys Inn ★ ★ ★ 64% INN

Penrith CA10 3UY

☎ 01539 624240 🖹 01539 629922

email: stay@crosskeys-tebay.co.uk

www.crosskeys-tebay.co.uk

Dir: *0.5m from M6 junct 38 through Tebay Village*

Dogs: Bedrooms Public Areas (except at dining times) Garden Exercise Area Pet Food/Bowls

Situated in the centre of the village, only a short drive from the motorway, this one-time coaching inn has original low-beamed ceilings and open fires. A wide selection of popular dishes is available in the bar and the smart dining room. The bedrooms are comfortably proportioned and traditionally furnished, with three attractive bedrooms in a converted barn at the rear.

Rooms: 9rms 6 en suite (1 fmly) (6 GF) dble room £40 - £65*

Facilities: TV Licensed TVL Cen ht Parking 30

ULVERSTON

Church Walk House ★ ★ ★ ★ 74%

BB

Church Walk LA12 7EW

☎ 01229 582211

email: martinchadd@btinternet.com

Dir: *Follow Town Centre sign at main rdbt, sharp right at junct opp Kings Arms, house opp Stables furniture shop*

Dogs: Bedrooms Public Areas Garden Exercise Area (adjacent) Pet Bowls bowls on request, owners to bring other pet requirements

This Grade II listed 18th-century residence stands in the heart of the historic market town. Stylishly decorated, the accommodation includes attractive bedrooms with a mix of antiques and contemporary pieces. A peaceful atmosphere prevails with attentive service, and there is a small herbal garden and patio.

Rooms: 3rms 2 en suite dble room £55 - £60*

Facilities: TVL Cen ht Last d order 9.30pm

CUMBRIA

CUMBRIA

WINDERMERE
Langdale Chase Hotel
★★★ 81% ◉ HL

Langdale Chase LA23 1LW

☎ 015394 32201 ▤ 015394 32604

email: sales@langdalechase.co.uk

www.langdalechase.co.uk

Dir: *2m S of Ambleside and 3m N of Windermere, on A591*

Dogs: Bedrooms (Unattended) Public Areas (except restaurant/bar) Garden Exercise Area (hotel gardens) Pet Food/Bowls as required, pre-arranged

Resident Pets: Nobby (Boxer), Baggy (Black Labrador), Max (cat)

This imposing country manor enjoys views of Lake Windermere. Public areas feature carved fireplaces, oak panelling and an imposing galleried staircase. Bedrooms have stylish, spacious bathrooms and outstanding views.

Rooms: 27rms en suite (2 fmly) (1 GF) dble room £90 - £158

Facilities: TV Licensed Parking 50 Last d order 9pm

WINDERMERE
Linthwaite House Hotel & Restaurant ★★★ 82% ◉◉◉ CHH

Crook Road LA23 3JA

☎ 015394 88600 ▤ 015394 88601

email: stay@linthwaite.com

www.linthwaite.com

Dir: *A591 towards The Lakes for 8m to large rdbt, take 1st exit B5284, 6m, hotel on left, 1m past Windermere golf club*

Dogs: Sep Accom (kennel) Garden Exercise Area (14-acre grounds) Pet Food/Bowls on request

Linthwaite House is set in 14 acres of hilltop grounds and enjoys stunning views over Lake Windermere. There is a conservatory and adjoining lounge, a smokers' bar and an elegant restaurant. Well equipped bedrooms combine contemporary furnishings with classical styles. Friendly service.

Rooms: 27rms en suite (1 fmly) (7 GF) dble room £170 - £320

Facilities: TV STV Modem/Fax Parking 40 Last d order 8.30pm

WORKINGTON

Hunday Manor Country House Hotel ★★★ 75% HL

Hunday Winscales CA14 4JF

☎ 01900 61798 📄 01900 601202

email: info@hunday-manor-hotel.co.uk

www.hunday-manor-hotel.co.uk

Dir: *off A66 onto A595 towards Whitehaven, hotel is 3m on right, signed*

Dogs: Bedrooms (Unattended) Garden Exercise Area (nearby fields)

Delightfully situated and enjoying distant views of the Solway Firth, this charming hotel has well-furnished rooms with lots of extras. The open-plan bar and foyer lounge boast welcoming open fires, and the attractive restaurant overlooks the woodland gardens. The provision of a function suite makes the hotel an excellent wedding venue.

Rooms: 24rms en suite (1 fmly)
dble room £95 - £125*

Facilities: TV Modem/Fax Licensed Parking 50 Last d order 9pm

BAKEWELL

Rutland Arms Hotel ★★★ 70% ⊛ HL

The Square DE45 1BT

☎ 01629 812812 📄 01629 812309

email: rutland@bakewell.demon.co.uk

www.rutlandarmsbakewell.com

Dir: *M1 junct 28 to Matlock, A6 to Bakewell. Hotel in town centre*

Dogs: Bedrooms (Unattended) Garden Exercise Area (100yds)

This 19th-century hotel lies at the very centre of Bakewell and offers a wide range of quality accommodation. The friendly staff are attentive and welcoming, and The Four Seasons candlelit restaurant offers interesting fine dining in elegant surroundings.

Rooms: 35rms en suite (2 fmly)

Facilities: TV FTV Modem/Fax Licensed Parking 25

CUMBRIA/DERBYSHIRE

DERBYSHIRE

BAKEWELL

Croft Cottages ★★★★ 73% GH

Coombs Road DE45 1AQ

☎ 01629 814101

email: croftco@btopenworld.com

www.visitpeakdistrict.com

Dir: *A619 E from town centre over bridge, right onto Station Rd & Coombs Rd*

Dogs: Bedrooms (Unattended) Garden Exercise Area (50yds) Pet Food/Bowls

Resident Pets: Steffi (Belgian Shepherd)

A warm welcome is assured at this Grade II listed stone building close to the River Wye and town centre. Thoughtfully equipped bedrooms are available in the main house or in an adjoining converted barn suite. Breakfast is served in a spacious lounge dining room.

Rooms: 4rms 3 en suite (1 fmly)

dble room £54 - £64

Facilities: TV Cen ht Parking 2

BUXTON

Wellhead Farm ★★★ 69%

Wormhill SK17 8SL

☎ 01298 871023 📠 0871 236 0267

email: wellhead4bunkntrough@cbits.net

www.bunkntrough.co.uk

Dir: *Between Bakewell and Buxton. Ott A6 onto B6049 signed Millers Dale/Tideswell & left to Wormhill*

Dogs: Bedrooms Public Areas (except dining room) Garden Exercise Area (250yds)

Resident Pets: Zoro (cat), Zack (Retriever), Murphy (Border Terrier)

This 16th-century farmhouse is in a peaceful location, and has low beams and two comfortable lounges. The bedrooms, some with four poster beds, come wlth radios, beverage trays and many thoughtful extras. The proprietors provide friendly and attentive hospitality in their delightful home.

Rooms: 4rms en suite (1 fmly)

dble room £60 - £68

Facilities: TVL Cen ht Parking 4

CALVER

Valley View ★ ★ ★ ★ 80% GA

Smithy Knoll Road Hope Valley S32 3XW

☎ 01433 631407

email: sue@a-place-2-stay.co.uk

www.a-place-2-stay.co.uk

Dir: *A623 from Baslow into Calver, 3rd left onto Donkey Ln*

Dogs: Bedrooms Exercise Area (by open fields, dogs can run off lead)

This detached stone house is in the heart of the village. It is very well-furnished throughout and delightfully friendly service is provided. A hearty breakfast is served in the cosy dining room, which is well-stocked with local guide books.

Rooms: 3rms en suite (1 fmly)

dble room £60 - £90

Facilities: TV Cen ht Parking 6

Last d order 9.30pm

FENNY BENTLEY

Bentley Brook Inn ★ ★ 69% HL

Ashbourne DE6 1LF

☎ 01335 350278 & 07976 614877

🖷 01335 350422

email: all@bentleybrookinn.co.uk

www.bentleybrookinn.co.uk

Dir: *2m N of Ashbourne at junct of A515 & B5056, entrance off B5056*

Dogs: Bedrooms (Unattended) Public Areas (except restaurant) Garden Exercise Area (on site) Pet Food/Bowls

This popular inn is located within the Peak District National Park. It is a charming building with an attractive terrace, lawns, and nursery gardens. A family restaurant dominates the ground floor, where dishes are available all day. The bar serves beer from its own micro-brewery. Bedrooms vary in styles and sizes, but all are well equipped.

Rooms: 12rms en suite (1 fmly) (1 GF)

dble room £76*

Facilities: TV Modem/Fax Licensed

Parking 100

DERBYSHIRE

DERBYSHIRE

GLOSSOP
Kings Clough Head Farm
★ ★ ★ 58%

Back Rowarth SK13 6ED

☎ 01457 862668

email: kingscloughheadfarm@hotmail.com

Dir: *Monks Rd off A624 near Grouse Inn*

Dogs: Bedrooms Sep Accom (barn)
Exercise Area

Situated in the hills with stunning country views, this 18th-century stone house provides thoughtfully furnished bedrooms and a modern efficient bathroom. Breakfast is served at one table in an antique-furnished dining room and a warm welcome is assured.

Rooms: 3rms 0 en suite dble room £46

Facilities: TV TVL Cen ht Parking 4

HOPE
Underleigh House ★ ★ ★ ★ ★ 89%
GA

Off Edale Road S33 6RF

☎ 01433 621372 📠 01433 621324

email: info@underleighhouse.co.uk

www.underleighhouse.co.uk

Dir: *From village church on A6187 onto Edale Rd, 1m left onto lane*

Dogs: Bedrooms (Ground-floor rooms only)
Garden Exercise Area (nearby public footpath)

Resident Pets: Tessa (Border Terrier), Freddie (cat)

Set at the end of a private lane, surrounded by glorious scenery, Underleigh House offers attractive bedrooms with modern facilities. One room has a private lounge and others have access to the gardens. There is a spacious lounge. Breakfasts are served at one large table in the dining room.

Rooms: 6rms en suite (2 GF)
dble room £70 - £90

Facilities: TV Licensed TVL Cen ht
Parking 6

LONGFORD

Russets ★★★★ 75% BB

Off Main Street Ashbourne DE6 3DR

☎ 01335 330874 📄 01335 330874

email: geoffreynolan@btinternet.com

www.russets.com

Dir: *A516 in Hatton onto Sutton Ln,
at T-junct right onto Long Ln, next right into
Longford & right before phone box on
Main St*

Dogs: Bedrooms (Unattended) Public Areas
Garden Exercise Area (200yds)
Pet Food/Bowls

Resident Pets: Honey (Bearded Collie),
Lottie (Miniature Dachshund), Ollie (Blue
Persian)

An indoor swimming pool is available at this
beautifully maintained bungalow, in a peaceful
location near Alton Towers. Bedrooms have
modern bathrooms, and breakfasts are served
at a family table in the dining room.

Rooms: 2rms en suite (1 fmly) (2 GF)

Facilities: TV STV TVL Cen ht Parking 4

MATLOCK

Hearthstone Farm ★★★★ 78% FH

Hearthstone Lane Riber DE4 5JW

☎ 01629 534304 📄 01629 534372

email: enquiries@hearthstonefarm.co.uk

www.hearthstonefarm.co.uk

Dir: *A615 at Tansley 2m E of Matlock, turn
opp Royal Oak towards Riber, at gates to
Riber Hall left onto Riber Rd and 1st left onto
Hearthstone Ln, farmhouse on left*

Dogs: Bedrooms Public Areas Exercise Area
(fields opposite)

Resident Pets: Ben (Labrador)

Situated on a stunning elevated location, this
traditional stone farmhouse retains many
original features and is stylishly decorated
throughout. Bedrooms are equipped with a
wealth of homely extras and comprehensive
breakfasts feature the farm's organic produce.
There is a very comfortable lounge, and the
farm animals in the grounds are an attraction.

Rooms: 3rms en suite dble room £130

Facilities: TV TVL Cen ht Parking 6
Last d order 9pm

DERBYSHIRE

DERBYSHIRE

MATLOCK

The Hollybush Inn ★★★ 61% INN

Grangemill DE4 4HU

☎ 01629 650300 & 07971 584266

Dir: *Off A6 at Cromford onto B5012 for 4m*

Dogs: Sep Accom (lounge in cottage annexe) Public Areas (except dining areas) Garden Exercise Area (on doorstep)

Resident Pets: Buster & Cleo (cats)

A former drovers' inn, popular with locals and walkers, this 18th-century property is being renovated to provide thoughtfully equipped bedrooms, some of which are in converted stable blocks. The character public areas are the setting for wholesome food and real ales.

Rooms: 9rms 2 en suite (4 fmly) (2 GF) dble room £40*

Facilities: TV Licensed TVL Cen ht Parking 48

SWADLINCOTE

Overseale House ★★★ 64% BB

Acresford Road Overseal DE12 6HX

☎ 01283 763741 🖹 01283 760015

email: oversealehouse@hotmail.com

www.oversealehouse.co.uk

Dir: *On A444 between Burton upon Trent & M42 junct 11*

Dogs: Bedrooms Garden Exercise Area

Located in the village, this well-proportioned Georgian mansion, built for a renowned industrialist, retains many original features including a magnificent dining room decorated with ornate mouldings. The period-furnished ground-floor areas include a cosy sitting room, and bedrooms contain many thoughtful extras.

Rooms: 5rms 4 en suite (3 fmly) (2 GF)

Facilities: TV Cen ht Parking 6

TIDESWELL

Poppies ★★★ 62%

Bank Square Buxton SK17 8LA

☎ 01298 871083

email: poptidza@dialstart.net

www.poppiesbandb.co.uk

Dir: *On B6049 in village centre opp NatWest bank*

Dogs: Bedrooms Public Areas Exercise Area (200yds)

A friendly welcome is assured at this non-smoking house, located in the heart of a former lead-mining and textile community, a short walk from the 14th-century parish church. Bedrooms are homely and the excellent breakfast features good vegetarian options.

Rooms: 3rms 1 en suite (1 fmly)

dble room £41 - £50*

Facilities: TV Cen ht Last d order 9.15pm

ASHBURTON

The Rising Sun ★★★★ 70% INN

Woodland TQ13 7JT

☎ 01364 652544 🖷 01364 654202

email: risingsun.hazel@btconnect.com

www.risingsunwoodland.co.uk

Dir: *Off A38 signed Woodland & Denbury, Rising Sun 1.5m on left*

Dogs: Bedrooms (Unattended) Public Areas Garden Exercise Area (50yds)

Pet Food/Bowls

Resident Pets: peacocks

Peacefully situated in scenic south Devon countryside, this inn is just a short drive from the A38. A friendly welcome is extended to all guests, business, leisure and families alike. Bedrooms are comfortable and well equipped. Dinner and breakfast feature much local and organic produce. A good selection of homemade puddings, West Country cheeses, local wines and quality real ales are available.

Rooms: 4rms en suite (1 fmly) (2 GF)

Facilities: TV Licensed Cen ht Parking 40

DERBYSHIRE/DEVON

DEVON

AXMINSTER

Lea Hill ★★★★★ 85%

Membury EX13 7AQ

☎ 01404 881881

email: reception@leahill.co.uk

www.leahill.co.uk

Dir: *A30 W from Chard, 1m left signed Stockland, at x-rds right to Membury, through village, pass church & Trout Farm, Lea Hill signed on right*

Dogs: Bedrooms (Unattended) Public Areas (if other guests are happy) Garden Exercise Area (50yds (fields, footpaths)) Pet Food/Bowls bowls/dried meal for dogs

Resident Pets: Florrie (Collie/Labrador cross), Tiger (cat)

Lea Hill is set in 8 acres. Accommodation is in the annexes to the main house, a thatched Devon longhouse. Bedrooms are furnished to a high standard. Enjoy a game of golf on the six-hole course. Breakfast is a highlight.

Rooms: 4rms en suite dble room £60 - £90*

Facilities: TV Cen ht Parking 20

Last d order 8pm

BARNSTAPLE

Halmpstone Manor

★★★★★ 90% GA

Bishop's Tawton EX32 0EA

☎ 01271 830321 & 831003 ▤ 01271 830826

email: jane@halmpstonemanor.co.uk

www.halmpstonemanor.co.uk

Dir: *3m SE of Barnstaple. Off A377 E of river & rail bridges*

Dogs: Bedrooms (Unattended) Public Areas (except restaurant) Garden Exercise Area (100yds)

Resident Pets: Barley (Cocker Spaniel)

The manor was mentioned in the Domesday Book and parts of the later medieval manor house survive. Halmpstone Manor now provides quality accommodation, personal service and fine cuisine. Delightful day rooms include a spacious lounge, and a creative, daily changing menu is offered in the elegant restaurant.

Rooms: 4rms en suite

dble room £100 - £140*

Facilities: TV Licensed Parking 12

BARNSTAPLE

Cresta Guest House ★ ★ ★ 65% GH

26 Sticklepath Hill EX31 2BU

☎ 01271 374022 🖺 01271 374022

www.crestaguesthouse.com

Dir: *On A3215 0.6m W of town centre, top of hill on right*

Dogs: Bedrooms Garden Exercise Area
Please note this establishment has recently changed hands. Warm hospitality is provided at this detached property on the western outskirts of Barnstaple. The well-equipped bedrooms are comfortable and two are available on the ground floor. A hearty breakfast is served in the dining room.

Rooms: 6rms 4 en suite (2 fmly) (2 GF)

Facilities: TV Cen ht Parking 6

BIDEFORD

The Pines at Eastleigh

★ ★ ★ ★ 76% GA

The Pines Eastleigh EX39 4PA

☎ 01271 860561

email: pirrie@thepinesateastleigh.co.uk

www.thepinesateastleigh.co.uk

Dir: *A39 onto A386 signed East-The-Water. 1st left signed Eastleigh, 500yds next left, 1.5m to village, house on right*

Dogs: Bedrooms Garden Exercise Area (on site (gardens, orchards)) Pet Food/Bowls on request
This hospitable Georgian farmhouse is set in 7 acres of gardens. Two of the comfortable bedrooms are located in the main house, the remainder in converted barns around a charming courtyard, with a pond and well. Breakfast is served in the dining room and a lounge and honesty bar are also available.

Rooms: 6rms en suite (3 fmly) (4 GF)
dble room £75 - £90*

Facilities: TV Modem/Fax Licensed
Cen ht Parking 20 Last d order 9pm

DEVON

DEVON

BISHOPSTEIGNTON
Cockhaven Manor Hotel ★★ 68% HL

Cockhaven Road TQ14 9RF

☎ 01626 775252 📠 01626 775572

email: cockhaven.manor@virgin.net

www.cockhavenmanor.com

Dir: *M5/A380 towards Torquay, then A381 towards Teignmouth. Left at Metro Motors. Hotel 500yds on left*

Dogs: Bedrooms (Unattended) Public Areas (except restaurant) Garden Exercise Area (20yds) Pet Food/Bowls

Resident Pets: Bitsy (dog)

A friendly, family-run inn that dates back to the 16th century. Bedrooms are well equipped and many enjoy views across the beautiful Teign estuary. A choice of dining options is offered, and traditional and interesting dishes along with locally caught fish are popular with visitors and locals alike.

Rooms: 12rms en suite (2 fmly) dble room £60 - £72*

Facilities: TV Licensed Parking 50

BRENDON
Leeford Cottage ★★★★ 72% GA

Lynton EX35 6PS

☎ 01598 741279 📠 01598 741392

email: g.linley@virgin.net

www.leefordcottage.com

Dir: *4.5m E of Lynton. Off A39 at Brendon sign, cross packhorse bridges and village green, over x-rds, Leeford Cottage on left*

Dogs: Bedrooms Public Areas (except dining room) Garden Exercise Area (garden under supervision, large paddock) Pet Food/Bowls

Resident Pets: Benny, Milly & Molly (goats), Meg (Labrador), Smudge (cat), Marcus (cockerel), ducks, chickens

Situated in the hamlet of Brendon, this 400-year-old cottage has great character. The proprietors grow vegetables and rear hens for the breakfast eggs. Cosy bedrooms. Home-cooked dinner by arrangement.

Rooms: 3rms 1 en suite dble room £47 - £49*

Facilities: TVL Cen ht Parking 10 Last d order 8.30pm

BUCKFASTLEIGH

Kings Arms Hotel ★ ★ ★ 63% INN

15 Fore Street TQ11 0BT

☎ 01364 642341

Dir: *In town centre opp tourist office & The Valiant Soldier*

Dogs: Bedrooms Public Areas (except restaurant) Garden Exercise Area (200yds) Pet Food/Bowls

This long-established, friendly and popular inn has been refurbished and now provides a well-appointed base from which to explore this picturesque area. Bedrooms are comfortably furnished, while public areas include a choice of bars, dining area and an attractive patio and garden.

Rooms: 4rms 1 en suite

dble room £50 - £70*

Facilities: TV Licensed Parking 1

CLOVELLY

East Dyke Farmhouse

★ ★ ★ ★ 77% FH

East Dyke Farm Higher Clovelly Bideford EX39 5RU

☎ 01237 431216

email: steve.goaman@virgin.net

Dir: *A39 onto B3237 at Clovelly Cross rdbt, farm 500yds on left*

Dogs: Bedrooms (Unattended) Public Areas Garden Exercise Area (surrounding fields) Pet Food/Bowls towels/blankets, baths can be arranged, dog biscuits

Resident Pets: Winston (Labrador)

Adjoining Clovelly's Iron Age hill fort, the working farm has glorious views. The farmhouse has a friendly atmosphere and attractive bedrooms. Local produce and home-made preserves are served for breakfast at a large table. Helen Goaman was a top-twenty finalist for AA Landlady of the Year 2006. **Rooms:** 3rms 2 en suite

Facilities: TV Modem/Fax Licensed TVL Cen ht Parking 6

DEVON

DEVON

COLYFORD

Lower Orchard ★★★★ 73% BB

Swan Hill Road EX24 6QQ

☎ 01297 553615

email: robin@barnardl.co.uk

Dir: *On A3052 in Colyford, between Lyme Regis & Sidmouth*

Dogs: Bedrooms (Unattended) Public Areas Garden Exercise Area (300yds to water meadows)

Resident Pets: Biene & Sasha (Tibetan Terriers)

This modern ranch-style family home looks over the Axe Valley. The spacious ground-floor bedrooms are very well equipped. Breakfast is served in the lounge-dining room with patio doors leading to a private sun terrace, well-tended gardens and splash pool. The owners are creating a motoring memories museum and a classic car showroom.

Rooms: 2rms 1 en suite (2 GF)

dble room £50 - £60*

Facilities: TV TVL Cen ht Parking 3 🐾

DARTMEET

Brimpts Farm ★★★ 58% GA

PL20 6SG

☎ 01364 631450 📠 01364 631179

email: info@brimptsfarm.co.uk

www.brimptsfarm.co.uk

Dir: *Dartmeet at E end of B3357, establishment signed on right at top of hill*

Dogs: Bedrooms Public Areas Garden Exercise Area (adjacent)

Resident Pets: Billy (Border Collie), Kipper (Jack Russell)

A popular venue for walkers and lovers of the great outdoors, Brimpts is peacefully situated in the heart of Dartmoor and has been a Duchy of Cornwall farm since 1307. Bedrooms are simply furnished and many have wonderful views across Dartmoor. Dinner is served by arrangement. There is a children's play area and sauna and spa.

Rooms: 10rms en suite (2 fmly) (7 GF)

dble room £48 - £60*

Facilities: TV Modem/Fax Licensed TVL Cen ht Parking 50 Last d order 9pm

DAWLISH
Langstone Cliff Hotel
★ ★ ★ 77% HL
Dawlish Warren EX7 0NA
☎ 01626 868000   🖨 01626 868006
email: reception@langstone-hotel.co.uk
www.langstone-hotel.co.uk
Dir: *1.5m NE off A379 Exeter road to Dawlish Warren*

Dogs: Bedrooms (Unattended) Public Areas (except food service areas) Garden Exercise Area (100yds to coastal path; beach in winter)
A family owned and run hotel, the Langstone Cliff offers a range of leisure, conference and function facilities. Bedrooms, many with sea views and balconies, are spacious, comfortable and well equipped. There are a number of attractive lounges and a well stocked bar. Dinner is served, often carvery style, in the restaurant.

Rooms: 66rms en suite (52 fmly) (10 GF) dble room £108 - £150*
Facilities: TV STV FTV Modem/Fax Lift Licensed TVL Parking 200 🐾 🐾

EXETER
Rydon Farm
★ ★ ★ ★ 71% FH
Woodbury EX5 1LB
☎ 01395 232341   🖨 01395 232341
email: sallyglanvill@aol.com
Dir: *A376 & B3179 from Exeter into Woodbury, right before 30mph sign*

Dogs: Bedrooms Garden Exercise Area (adjacent)
Dating from the 16th century, this Devon longhouse has been run by the same family for eight generations. The farmhouse provides spacious bedrooms, which are equipped with many useful extra facilities and one has a four-poster bed. There is a television lounge and a delightful garden in which to relax. Breakfast is served in front of an inglenook fireplace.

Rooms: 3rms 2 en suite (1 fmly) dble room £60 - £66*
Facilities: TVL Cen ht Parking 3

DEVON

DEVON

HONITON

Atwell's At Wellington Farm

♦♦♦♦ 70%

Wilmington EX14 9JR

☎ 01404 831885

email: wilmington@btinternet.com

www.ponyrescue.org

Dir: *3m E of Honiton on A35 towards Dorchester, 500yds through Wilmington on left*

Dogs: Bedrooms (Unattended) Public Areas Garden Exercise Area (100yds)

Resident Pets: Pip (Shetland pony), Trojan (Shire Horse), Holly (sheep)

Convenient for Honiton and the coast, this delightful Grade II listed 16th-century farmhouse is set in 5 acres, which also accommodates a rescue centre for animals. This friendly house offers comfortable accommodation, hearty breakfasts using fresh local produce and cream teas.

Rooms: 3rms 2 en suite (1 GF) dble room £40 - £46*

Facilities: TV TVL Cen ht Parking 10

HONITON

Ridgeway Farm ★★★★ 70% GA

Awliscombe EX14 3PY

☎ 01404 841331 📄 01404 841119

email: jessica@ridgewayfarm.co.uk

www.smoothhound.com/ridgewayfarm

Dir: *3m NW of Honiton. A30 onto A373, through Awliscombe to end of 40mph area, right opp Godford Farm, farm 0.25m up narrow lane*

Dogs: Bedrooms Public Areas Garden Exercise Area (surrounding farmland)

Resident Pets: Crumble (Terrier), Puzzle (Border Terrier),Teazle (lLurcher), 3 horses

This 18th-century farmhouse has a peaceful location on the slopes of Hembury Hill, and is a good base for exploring Honiton and the east Devon coast. Renovations have brought the cosy accommodation to a high standard. The proprietors and their pets assure a warm welcome and relaxed atmosphere.

Rooms: 2rms en suite dble room £52 - £58

Facilities: TV TVL Cen ht Parking 4

ILFRACOMBE
Darnley Hotel ★★ 69% SHL

3 Belmont Road EX34 8DR

☎ 01271 863955 📠 01271 864076

email: darnleyhotel@yahoo.co.uk

www.darnleyhotel.co.uk

Dir: *M5 junct 27 then A361 to Barnstaple/Ilfracombe. Left at Church Hill then first left into Belmont Rd.*

Dogs: Bedrooms (Unattended) Public Areas (except restaurant) Garden Exercise Area (0.25m)

Resident Pets: Pepsi (cat)

Standing within award winning, mature gardens, with a wooded path to the High Street and the beach, about a five minute stroll away, this former Victorian gentleman's residence offers friendly, informal service. The individually decorated bedrooms vary in size. Dinners feature honest home cooking.

Rooms: 10rms 7 en suite (2 fmly) (2 GF) dble room £56 - £85*

Facilities: TV Licensed TVL Parking 10 Last d order 8.25pm

LYNMOUTH
Bath Hotel ★★ 69% HL

Sea Front EX35 6EL

☎ 01598 752238 📠 01598 753894

email: bathhotel@torslynmouth.co.uk

www.torslynmouth.co.uk

Dir: *M5 junct 25, follow A39 to Minehead then Porlock and Lynmouth*

Dogs: Bedrooms (Unattended) Public Areas (except restaurant) Exercise Area (200yds)

Resident Pets: Boadecia & Polyanna (Persian cats)

This well-established, friendly hotel is situated near the harbour and offers lovely views from the attractive, sea-facing bedrooms and an excellent starting point for scenic walks. There are two lounges and a sun lounge. The restaurant menu is extensive and features daily changing specials, making good use of fresh produce and local fish.

Rooms: 22rms en suite (9 fmly) dble room £70 - £130

Facilities: TV Licensed Parking 12

DEVON

DEVON

LYNMOUTH

Countisbury Lodge ★★★ 64% GA

6 Tors Park Countisbury Hill EX35 6NB

☎ 01598 752388

email: paulpat@countisburylodge.co.uk

www.countisburylodge.co.uk

Dir: *Off A39 Countisbury Hill just before Lynmouth centre, signed Countisbury Lodge*

Dogs: Bedrooms (Unattended) Garden Exercise Area (10 mins' walk) Pet Food/Bowls by prior arrangement

Resident Pets: Jessica & Magic (Golden Retrievers), Eric (cat)

From its elevated position high above the town, this former vicarage has spectacular views of the harbour and countryside. The atmosphere is informal but with attentive service. The bedrooms are attractive and comfortable. Breakfast is served in the pleasant dining room. There is a cosy bar.

Rooms: 4rms en suite (1 fmly) dble room £50 - £56*

Facilities: TV Licensed TVL Cen ht Parking 6

LYNMOUTH

The Heatherville ★★★★★ 89% GA

Tors Park EX35 6NB

☎ 01598 752327 📠 01598 752634

www.heatherville.co.uk

Dir: *Off A39 onto Tors Rd, 1st left fork into Tors Park*

Dogs: Bedrooms Public Areas (except dining room) Garden Exercise Area (adjacent)

Having a secluded and elevated south-facing position, the Heatherville has splendid views over Lynmouth and surrounding woodland. Lovingly restored over the last few years to a very high standard, both the bedrooms and the lounge give a feeling of luxury, with the charm of a large country house. By arrangement, enjoyable evening meals feature organic and free-range produce whenever possible. There is also an intimate bar.

Rooms: 6rms en suite dble room £60 - £80

Facilities: TV Licensed Cen ht Parking 7 Last d order 9.30pm

LYNTON
Lynton Cottage Hotel
★★★ 69% ◉ ◉ HL

Northwalk EX35 6ED

☎ 01598 752342 ▤ 01598 754016

email: mail@lyntoncottage.co.uk

www.lyntoncottage.co.uk

Dir: *M5 junct 23 to Bridgewater, then A39 to Minehead & follow signs to Lynton. 1st right after church and right again.*

Dogs: Bedrooms Public Areas Garden Exercise Area (0.5m)

Resident Pets: Chloe & Charlie (cats)

Boasting simply breathtaking views, this wonderfully relaxing and friendly hotel stands some 500 feet above the sea and provides a peaceful hideaway. Bedrooms are individual in style and size, with the added bonus of scenic views, whilst public areas have both charm and character. Accomplished cuisine is also on offer with taste-laden dishes constructed with care and considerable skill.

Rooms: 16rms en suite (1 fmly) (1 GF)

Facilities: TV Licensed Parking 20

OTTERY ST MARY
Fluxton Farm ★★ 48% BB

Fluxton EX11 1RJ

☎ 01404 812818 ▤ 01404 814843

www.fluxtonfarm.co.uk

Dir: *2m SW of Ottery St Mary. B3174 W from Ottery over river, left, next left to Fluxton*

Dogs: Bedrooms (Unattended) Garden Exercise Area (next door) Pet Food/Bowls can provide whatever is required

Resident Pets: The farm is a cat rescue sanctuary. 18 cats, geese, chickens

A haven for cat lovers, Fluxton Farm offers comfortable accommodation with a choice of lounges and a large garden, complete with pond and ducks. Set in peaceful farmland 4m from the coast, this 16th-century longhouse has a wealth of beams and open fireplaces.

Rooms: 7rms 6 en suite (1 fmly)

dble room £50 - £55*

Facilities: TV TVL Cen ht Parking 15

DEVON

PLYMOUTH

The Cranbourne ★★★ 70% GA

278-282 Citadel Road The Hoe PL1 2PZ

☎ 01752 263858 & 224646

🖹 01752 263858

email: cran.hotel@virgin.net

www.cranbournehotel.co.uk

Dogs: Bedrooms Public Areas (except dining room) Garden Exercise Area (100yds - The Hoe)

Resident Pets: Harry (Golden Retriever)

This attractive Georgian terrace house has been extensively renovated, and is located just a short walk from The Hoe, The Barbican and the city centre. Bedrooms are practically furnished and well equipped. Hearty breakfasts are served in the elegant dining room and there is also a cosy bar.

Rooms: 40rms 28 en suite (5 fmly) (1 GF) dble room £44 - £56*

Facilities: TV Licensed TVL Cen ht Parking 14

PLYMOUTH

Four Seasons Guest House

★★★★ 72% GH

207 Citadel Road East The Hoe PL1 2JF

☎ 01752 223591

email: Bobkatecarter@btconnect.com

www.fourseasonsguesthouse.co.uk

Dogs: Bedrooms (Unattended) Public Areas Exercise Area (100yds)

Resident Pets: Edward (West Highland Terrier)

Tucked away on an elegant Victorian terrace, a short stroll from the city centre, The Hoe and Barbican offers comfortable and welcoming accommodation. Bedrooms are tastefully furnished in soft colours and fabrics, resulting in a restful, contemporary style. Breakfast is a showcase for local and organic produce with a few interesting house specialities to tempt the taste buds! Wi-fi access available.

Rooms: 7rms 5 en suite (1 GF) dble room £45 - £60

Facilities: TV Modem/Fax Cen ht Last d order 9pm

PLYMOUTH

The Moorland Hotel ★★ 68% HL

Wotter Shaugh Prior PL7 5HP

☎ 01752 839228 🖺 01752 839153

email: enquiries@moorlandhotel.com

www.moorlandhotel.com

Dir: *From A38 take Lee Mill exit. Through underpass turn right then left, 6m through Cornwood to Wotter*

Dogs: Bedrooms (Unattended) Public Areas (bar only) Garden Exercise Area (adjacent, moorland) Pet Food/Bowls

Resident Pets: Gwennap (Labrador), Winnie (Dalmatian), Jethro (Jack Russell), Aussie (Australian Terrier)

On the southern slopes of Dartmoor National Park, this hotel offers a warm welcome. Bedrooms are well appointed. The bar is popular with both visitors and locals. A range of menus is available in the bar or restaurant.

Rooms: 18rms en suite (2 fmly) dble room £54 - £60*

Facilities: TV Modem/Fax Licensed Parking 40

ROCKBEARE

Lower Allercombe Farm ★★ 52% FH

EX5 2HD

☎ 01404 822519 🖺 01404 822519

email: susie@allercombe.fsnet.co

www.lowerallercombefarm.co.uk

Dir: *A30 at Daisy Mount onto B3180. After 200yds turn right to Allercombe. In 1m at Allercombe x-rds turn right , farm is 50yds on right*

Dogs: Bedrooms Public Areas Garden Exercise Area (adjacent)

Resident Pets: Lizzie (Patterdale Terrier), Daisy (cat)

Lower Allercombe dates from the 17th century and offers comfortable accommodation. The rural location is handy for the A30 and Exeter Airport, and is convenient for visiting local attractions.

Rooms: 3rms 1 en suite (1 fmly) dble room £50 - £65*

Facilities: TV TVL Cen ht

Last d order 10pm

DEVON

DEVON

SALCOMBE
Soar Mill Cove Hotel
★ ★ ★ ★ 78% ◉ ◉ HL

Soar Mill Cove Malborough TQ7 3DS

☎ 01548 561566 📄 01548 561223

email: info@soarmillcove.co.uk

www.soarmillcove.co.uk

Dir: *3m W of town off A381at Malborough.*
Follow 'Soar' signs

Dogs: Bedrooms Garden Exercise Area
(adjacent)

Resident Pets: Rosie (Bichon Fris)

Situated amid spectacular scenery with sea
views, this hotel is ideal for a relaxing stay.
Family-run, it upholds keen standards of
service. Bedrooms are well equipped and
many have private terraces. There are seating
areas where cream teas are served, and a
choice of swimming pools. Local produce and
seafood is used in the restaurant.

Rooms: 22rms en suite (5 fmly) (21 GF)
dble room £150 - £200

Facilities: TV Modem/Fax Licensed
Parking 30 Last d order 9pm 🏊 🏊

SAMPFORD PEVERELL
The Parkway Inn ★ ★ 67% HL

32 Lowertown Tiverton EX16 7BJ

☎ 01884 820255 & 07813 955274

📄 01884 820780

email:
enquiries@parkwayhousehotel-uk.com

www.parkwayhousehotel-uk.com

Dir: *M5 junct 27, follow signs for Tiverton*
Parkway Station. Hotel on right, on entering
village

Dogs: Bedrooms (Unattended) Public Areas
(except restaurant) Garden Exercise Area
(canal walks by hotel)

An ideal choice for both business and leisure
travellers, this hotel is located within a mile of
the M5 and has extensive views across the
Culm Valley. The carvery is a good choice at
dinner in the conservatory style restaurant.
This hotel offers relaxed hospitality.

Rooms: 10rms en suite (2 fmly)
dble room £65*

Facilities: TV Modem/Fax Licensed
Parking 80 Last d order 9pm

TAVISTOCK

The Coach House Hotel & Restaurant ★ ★ ★ 62% GA

Nr TAVISTOCK PL19 8NS

☎ 01822 617515 📠 01822 617515

email: the-coachhouse@otterytavistock.fsnet.co.uk

www.the-coachhouse.co.uk

Dir: *2.5m NW of Tavistock. A390 from Tavistock to Gulworthy Cross, right to Ottery village, 1st on right*

Dogs: Bedrooms Public Areas (in bar only) Garden Exercise Area (20yds)
Dating from 1857, this building was constructed for the Duke of Bedford and converted by the current owners. Some bedrooms are on the ground floor and in an adjacent barn conversion. Dinner is available in the cosy dining room or the restaurant, which leads onto the south-facing garden.

Rooms: 9rms en suite (4 GF)

Facilities: TV Modem/Fax Licensed Cen ht Parking 24

TORQUAY

Hotel Blue Conifer ★ ★ ★ ★ 72% GA

Higher Downs Road The Seafront
Babbacombe TQ1 3LD

☎ 01803 327637

www.torbay.gov.uk/tourism/t-hotels/blueconi.htm

Dir: *Signs for Babbacombe & seafront, premises 500yds from model village*

Dogs: Bedrooms Public Areas (except dining room) Garden Exercise Area (50yds)
Surrounded by neat gardens and having splendid views across beaches to the bay, this attractive property provides a relaxed and friendly atmosphere. Bedrooms, many with sea views, are well-equipped and one is on the ground floor. A relaxing lounge and spacious car park are welcome additions.

Rooms: 7rms en suite (3 fmly) (1 GF)
dble room £46 - £68*

Facilities: TV Cen ht Parking 9

DEVON

DEVON

TORQUAY

Tyndale Guest House ★★★ 56% GA

68 Avenue Road Devon TQ2 5LF

☎ 01803 380888

Dir: *A380 onto A3022, pass Torre station onto Avenue Rd, 1st lights right onto Old Mill Rd & right into car park*

Dogs: Bedrooms Public Areas (except lounge) Exercise Area (100yds)

Resident Pets: Trixie (Terrier/Jack Russell cross)

Close to the seaside attractions and the town centre, this neatly presented house is only a short level walk from the railway station. Bedrooms are brightly decorated in a range of sizes. A comfortable lounge is provided and a freshly cooked, traditional British breakfast is served in the dining room.

Rooms: 3rms en suite (1 GF)

Facilities: TV TVL Cen ht Parking 5

TOTNES

The Red Slipper ★★★★ 77% GA

Stoke Gabriel TQ9 6RU

☎ 01803 782315

email: enquiries@redslipper.co.uk

www.redslipper.co.uk

Dir: *Off A385 S to Stoke Gabriel. Hotel opp Church House Inn*

Dogs: Bedrooms Public Areas (except dining room at meal times) Exercise Area (adjacent)

Resident Pets: Tara & Tico (Siamese cats)

An ideal base for exploring the South Hams or just for a relaxing break, this delightful 1920s house is hidden away in the picturesque village of Stoke Gabriel. The bedrooms have many extra facilities. Well-cooked dinners are served by arrangement, and feature local produce.

Rooms: 3rms en suite dble room £64 - £70

Facilities: TV Licensed TVL Cen ht Parking 4 Last d order 9pm

TWO BRIDGES

Two Bridges Hotel ★ ★ 76% HL

Dartmoor PL20 6SW

☎ 01822 890581 📠 01822 892306

email: enquiries@twobridges.co.uk

www.twobridges.co.uk

Dir: *junct of B3212 & B3357*

Dogs: Bedrooms (Unattended) Public Areas (except restaurant) Garden Exercise Area (Dartmoor nearby)

This wonderfully relaxing hotel is set in the heart of the Dartmoor National Park, in a beautiful riverside location. Three standards of comfortable rooms provide every modern convenience. There is a choice of lounges and fine dining is available in the restaurant, with menus featuring local game and seasonal produce.

Rooms: 33rms en suite (2 fmly) (6 GF) dble room £130 - £180

Facilities: TV STV Modem/Fax Licensed Parking 100 Last d order 8.30pm

TWO BRIDGES

Prince Hall Hotel ★ ★ 83% ◉ CHH

PL20 6SA

☎ 01822 890403 📠 01822 890676

email: info@princehall.co.uk

www.princehall.co.uk

Dir: *on B3357 1m E of Two Bridges road junct*

Dogs: Bedrooms Public Areas (except kitchen & restaurant) Garden Exercise Area (adjacent)

Resident Pets: Cello (Bouvier des Flanders)

Charm, peace and relaxed informality pervade at this small hotel, which has a stunning location at the heart of Dartmoor. Bedrooms, each named after a Dartmoor tour, have been equipped with thoughtful extras. The history of the house and its location are reflected throughout the comfortable public areas. Dogs are welcomed as warmly as their owners. The cooking is memorable.

Rooms: 8rms en suite dble room £185 - £250

Facilities: TV Licensed Parking 13

DEVON

DEVON

UMBERLEIGH
Eastacott Barton ★ ★ ★ ★ ★ 95%

EX37 9AJ

☎ 01769 540545

email: stay@eastacott.com

www.eastacott.com

Dir: *1m E of Umberleigh. Off B3227 signed Eastacott, straight on at stone cross, Eastacott Barton 700yds on left*

Dogs: Bedrooms Public Areas (except dining rooms) Garden Exercise Area (27-acre grounds) Pet Food/Bowls dog towels & biscuits

Resident Pets: Ben (Black Labrador), Meggie & Spencer (Jack Russells)

This large, stone-built former farmhouse has been restored to provide spacious and well-equipped accommodation, including three bedrooms in converted farm buildings. There is also a self-catering cottage. Choice of sitting rooms and access to the grounds.

Rooms: 5rms en suite
dble room £70 - £115*

Facilities: TV STV TVL Cen ht Parking 8

WESTWARD HO!
Culloden House ★ ★ ★ 70% GH

Fosketh Hill EX39 1UL

☎ 01237 479421 📠 08701 334359

email: enquiry@culloden-house.co.uk

www.culloden-house.co.uk

Dir: *S of town centre. Off B3236 Stanwell Hill onto Fosketh Hill*

Dogs: Bedrooms Public Areas (except dining room) Garden Exercise Area (300yds)

This Victorian property stands on a wooded hillside with sweeping views over the beach and coast. A warm welcome is assured in this family friendly house. Guests can relax in the spacious lounge with its log burning fire and enjoy the wonderful sea views.

Rooms: 5rms en suite (3 fmly) (1 GF)
dble room £60 - £70*

Facilities: TV TVL Cen ht Parking 5

WINKLEIGH
The Old Parsonage ★★★★ 72%
Court Walk EX19 8JA

☎ 01837 83772 📄 01837 680074

email: tonypeel@fsbdial.co.uk

www.parsonagebandb.co.uk

Dir: *In village off A3124, behind parish church*

Dogs: Bedrooms Garden Exercise Area (1m)

Resident Pets: Cinders, Max, Jessie, Boots, Cobweb (cats)

The Old Parsonage is a Grade II listed thatched house, dating in part from the 15th century, set in 2 acres of walled Victorian gardens next to the church. The bedrooms are individually designed and well appointed. Delicious breakfasts are served around a grand communal table in the dining room.

Rooms: 3rms en suite (1 GF)

dble room £50 - £60

Facilities: TV Cen ht Parking 4

BRIDPORT
Britmead House ★★★★ 67% GA
West Bay Road DT6 4EG

☎ 01308 422941 & 07973 725243

email: britmead@talk21.com

www.britmeadhouse.co.uk

Dir: *1m S of town centre, off A35 onto West Bay Rd*

Dogs: Bedrooms Public Areas (must be on lead) Exercise Area (adjacent)

Britmead House is located south of Bridport, within easy reach of the town centre and West Bay harbour. Family-run, the atmosphere is friendly and the accommodation well-appointed and comfortable. Suitable for business and leisure, many guests return regularly. A choice of breakfast is served in the light and airy dining room.

Rooms: 8rms en suite (2 fmly) (2 GF)

dble room £54 - £70*

Facilities: TV TVL Cen ht Parking 12

Last d order 9.30pm

DEVON/DORSET

DORSET

BRIDPORT
Bridge House Hotel ★★ 67% HL

115 East Street DT6 3LB

☎ 01308 423371 📠 01308 459573

email: info@bridgehousebridport.co.uk

www.bridgehousebridport.co.uk

Dir: *follow signs to town centre from A35 rdbt, hotel 200yds on right*

Dogs: Bedrooms (Unattended) Public Areas (except restaurant, must be well behaved) Garden Exercise Area (adjacent)

A short stroll from the town centre, this 18th-century Grade II listed property is undergoing a major refurbishment. The well-equipped bedrooms vary in size. In addition to the main lounge, there is a small bar-lounge and a separate breakfast room. An interesting range of home-cooked meals is provided in the restaurant.

Rooms: 10rms en suite (3 fmly)

dble room £79 - £99*

Facilities: TV Licensed TVL Parking 13

CASHMOOR
Cashmoor House ★★★★ 74% FH

Blandford DT11 8DN

☎ 01725 552339

email: spencer@cashmoorhouse.co.uk

www.cashmoorhouse.co.uk

Dir: *On A354 Salisbury to Blandford, 3m S of Sixpenny Handley rdbt just past Inn on the Chase*

Dogs: Bedrooms (with own bed & towels) Public Areas (must be on lead & under control) Garden Exercise Area (adjacent field)

Resident Pets: Holly & Daisy (Springer Spaniels), Grumpy (cat)

Situated halfway between Blandford and Salisbury, parts of Cashmoor House date from the 17th century. The property has a homely ambience. Breakfasts feature home-made bread and preserves, and eggs laid by the owners' hens. Suppers by arrangement.

Rooms: 4rms en suite (2 fmly) (2 GF)

dble room £45.50*

Facilities: TV TVL Cen ht Parking 8

Last d order 8.45pm

CATTISTOCK

Fox & Hounds Inn ★ ★ ★ ★ 70%

Duck Street Dorchester DT2 0JH

☎ 01300 320444 📄 01300 320444

email: info@foxandhoundsinn.com

www.foxandhoundsinn.com

Dir: *Signed from A37 Dorchester to Yeovil*

Dogs: Bedrooms Public Areas Garden
Exercise Area (50yds)

Resident Pets: Widget & Dooley
(Labradors), Sophie (Retriever), Freddie,
Figaro & Pimms (cats)

Under new ownership, this traditional village
inn is quietly located not far from Dorchester
and is a delightful place from which to explore
the varied attractions of Dorset. Bedrooms are
spacious and very well equipped. The public
rooms offer real ales and a good choice of
food in a relaxed atmosphere.

Rooms: 3rms 2 en suite (1 fmly)
dble room £70*

Facilities: TV Licensed Cen ht Parking 10
Last d order 9pm

CHRISTCHURCH

Fishermans Haunt ★ ★ ★ 68%

Winkton BH23 7AS

☎ 01202 477283 📄 01202 478883

email:
fishermanshaunt@accommodating-inns.co.uk

www.accommodating-inns.co.uk

Dir: *Follow B3347*

Dogs: Bedrooms Public Areas Garden

Dating from 1673 and situated close to the
River Avon, this characterful inn is popular
with anglers and country-lovers alike.
Bedrooms, some of which are suitable for
families, offer comfortable accommodation
with many added extras including satellite
television. Real ales and wholesome cuisine
can be enjoyed in the spacious restaurant and
lounge bars, which have log fires in colder
months.

Rooms: 17rms en suite (2 fmly) (6 GF)

Facilities: TV Licensed Cen ht Parking 70
Last d order 9pm

DORSET

DORSET

FONTMELL MAGNA
The Crown Inn ★ ★ 71% ❀ INN

Shaftesbury SP7 0PA

☎ 01747 811441 & 812222

▤ 01747 811145

email: crowninnfm@hotmail.com

www.crowninn.me.uk

Dir: *In village centre*

Dogs: Bedrooms Public Areas (bar area only) Garden Exercise Area (150yds)

A traditional country inn where a friendly welcome is assured. Local real ales are offered in the small bar, while the relaxing restaurant serves a fine selection of carefully prepared dishes, with the emphasis on local produce. Bedrooms vary in size but include some welcome extras.

Rooms: 5rms 3 en suite
dble room £75 - £100*

Facilities: TV Licensed Cen ht Parking 17

MILTON ABBAS
Fishmore Hill Farm ♦♦♦ 71%

Blandford Forum DT11 0DL

☎ 01258 881122 ▤ 01258 881122

email: neal.clarke@btinternet.com

Dir: *Off A354 signed Milton Abbas, 3m left on sharp bend, up steep hill, B&B 1st left*

Dogs: Sep Accom (kennel) Garden Exercise Area Pet Food/Bowls

Resident Pets: dogs, horses, sheep

This working sheep farm and family home is surrounded by beautiful Dorset countryside and is close to historic Milton Abbey and a short drive from the coast. Bedrooms, which vary in size, are comfortable and finished with considerate extras. The atmosphere is friendly and relaxed. Breakfast is served in the smart dining room around a communal table.

Rooms: 3rms en suite dble room £54*

Facilities: TV Cen ht Parking 4 Last d order 8.45pm

POOLE

Arndale Court Hotel ★ ★ ★ 68% HL

62/66 Wimborne Road BH15 2BY

☎ 01202 683746 📠 01202 668838

email: info@arndalecourthotel.com

www.arndalecourthotel.com

Dir: *on A349 close to town centre, opp Poole Stadium*

Dogs: Bedrooms Garden Exercise Area (0.5m)

Ideally situated for the town centre and ferry terminal, this is a small, privately owned hotel. Bedrooms are well equipped, pleasantly spacious and comfortable. Particularly well suited to business guests, this hotel has a pleasant range of stylish public areas and good parking.

Rooms: 39rms en suite (7 fmly) (14 GF) dble room £84 - £89*

Facilities: TV STV Modem/Fax Licensed TVL Parking 40 Last d order 9pm

POWERSTOCK

Three Horseshoes Inn

★ ★ ★ ★ 71% INN

Bridport DT6 3TF

☎ 01308 485328

email: info@threehorseshoesinn.com

www.threehorseshoesinn.com

Dir: *3m from Bridport. Powerstock signed off A3066 Bridport to Beaminster*

Dogs: Bedrooms (Unattended) Public Areas (except restaurant) Garden Exercise Area (surrounding countryside) Pet Food/Bowls

Resident Pets: JJ & Piglet (Springer Spaniels)

This inn overlooks rolling hills. The cosy dining room and unpretentious bar appeal to locals and visitors alike, and a wide range of meals is available, with the emphasis on local and organic produce. The spacious bedrooms have considerate extras.

Rooms: 3rms en suite (1 fmly) (2 GF) dble room £60 - £80*

Facilities: TV FTV Licensed Cen ht Parking 25 Last d order 8.30pm

DORSET

DORSET

SWANAGE

The Pines Hotel ★★★ 71% HL

Burlington Road BH19 1LT

☎ 01929 425211 ▤ 01929 422075

email: reservations@pineshotel.co.uk

www.pineshotel.co.uk

Dir: *A351 to seafront, left then 2nd right. Hotel at end of road*

Dogs: Bedrooms (Unattended) Public Areas (except food areas) Garden Exercise Area (100yds) Pet Food/Bowls by prior request only

Resident Pets: Sid (cat)

Enjoying a peaceful location with spectacular views over the cliffs and sea, The Pines is a pleasant place to stay. Many of the comfortable bedrooms have sea views. Guests can take tea in the lounge, enjoy appetising bar snacks in the attractive bar and interesting and accomplished cuisine in the restaurant.

Rooms: 49rms en suite (26 fmly) (6 GF) dble room £117 - £141*

Facilities: TV Lift Licensed Parking 60 Last d order 9pm

WAREHAM

Worgret Manor Hotel ★★★ 70% HL

Worgret Road BH20 6AB

☎ 01929 552957 ▤ 01929 554804

email: admin@worgretmanorhotel.co.uk

www.worgretmanorhotel.co.uk

Dir: *on A352 from Wareham to Wool, 0.5m from Wareham rdbt*

Dogs: Bedrooms Public Areas (bar & reception only; not restaurant) Garden Exercise Area (300yds)

Resident Pets: Tammy (Golden Retriever)

On the edge of Wareham, with easy access to major routes, this privately owned Georgian manor house offers a friendly, cheerful ambience. The bedrooms come in a variety of sizes. Public rooms are well presented and comprise a popular bar, a quiet lounge and an airy restaurant.

Rooms: 12rms en suite (1 fmly) (3 GF) dble room £100 - £110*

Facilities: TV Modem/Fax Licensed TVL Parking 25

WEYMOUTH

Charlotte Guest House ★★ 50% GH

5 Commercial Road DT4 7DW

☎ 01305 772942 & 07970 798425

email: charlotteGH1@aol.co.uk

Dir: *On A353 Esplanade, turn right at clock onto Kings St. 1st right at rdbt, then right onto Commercial Rd*

Dogs: Bedrooms Public Areas Exercise Area (good dog walks, private beaches nearby) Pet Food/Bowls

A warm welcome is offered at this small renovated guest house within easy walking distance of the town's amienities. The breakfast room is light and airy and the bedrooms vary in size.

Rooms: 6rms en suite (2 fmly) (1 GF) dble room £50 - £60*

Facilities: TV Cen ht Parking 3 Last d order 10pm

DARLINGTON

Hall Garth Hotel, Golf and Country Club ★★★ 73% ⊛ HL

Coatham Mundeville DL1 3LU

☎ 0870 6096131 ᕒ 01325 310083

Dir: *A1M junct 59, A167 towards Darlington. After 600yds left at top of hill, hotel on right*

Dogs: Bedrooms (Unattended) Public Areas (except restaurant) Garden Exercise Area (country lane walks)

Peacefully situated in grounds that include a golf course, this hotel is just a few minutes from the motorway network. The well-equipped bedrooms come in various styles - its worth asking for the trendy, modern rooms. Public rooms include relaxing lounges, a fine-dining restaurant and a separate pub. The extensive leisure and conference facilities are an important focus here.

Rooms: 51rms en suite (5 fmly) dble room £98 - £118*

Facilities: TV STV Modem/Fax Licensed TVL Parking 150 Last d order 9.30pm ᕦ

DORSET/CO DURHAM

CO DURHAM

FIR TREE

Helme Park Hall Hotel ★★ 71% HL

DL13 4NW

☎ 01388 730970 📄 01388 731799

email: enquiries@helmeparkhotel.co.uk

www.helmeparkhotel.co.uk

Dir: *1m N of A689/A68 rdbt between Darlington & Corbridge*

Dogs: Bedrooms (Unattended) Garden Exercise Area (quiet country walks)
Dating back to the 13th century, this welcoming hotel boasts superb panoramic views up the Wear Valley. The bedrooms are comfortably equipped and furnished. The cosy lounge bar is extremely popular for its comprehensive selection of bar meals, and the restaurant offers both table d'hote and carte menus.

Rooms: 13rms en suite (1 fmly)

Facilities: TV STV FTV Licensed TVL Parking 70 Last d order 9pm

MIDDLETON-IN-TEESDALE

The Teesdale Hotel ★★ 65% HL

Market Place DL12 0QG

☎ 01833 640264 📄 01833 640651

email: john@falconer0.wanadoo.co.uk

www.teesdalehotel.com

Dir: *from Barnard Castle take B6278, follow signs for Middleton-in-Teesdale & Highforce. Hotel in town centre*

Dogs: Bedrooms Public Areas (bar only) Exercise Area (50yds)
Located in the heart of the popular village, this family-run hotel offers a relaxed and friendly atmosphere. Bedrooms and bathrooms are well-equipped and offer a good standard of quality and comfort. Public areas include a resident's lounge on the first floor, a lounge bar which is also popular with locals and a spacious restaurant.

Rooms: 14rms en suite (1 fmly)
dble room £70

Facilities: TV Licensed TVL Parking 20 Last d order 9.15pm

STOCKTON-ON-TEES

The Parkwood Hotel ★★★ 68% GA

64-66 Darlington Road Hartburn TS18 5ER

☎ 01642 587933

email: theparkwoodhotel@aol.com

www.theparkwoodhotel.com

Dir: *1.5m SW of town centre. A66 onto A137 signed Yarm & Stockton West, left at lights onto A1027, left onto Darlington Rd*

Dogs: Bedrooms Public Areas (except dining areas) Garden Exercise Area (park nearby) Pet Food/Bowls

Resident Pets: Charlie (Yorkshire Terrier cross)

A very friendly welcome awaits you at this family-run establishment. The well-equipped en suite bedrooms come with many homely extras and a range of professionally prepared meals are served in the cosy bar lounge, conservatory, or the attractive non-smoking dining room.

Rooms: 5rms en suite

Facilities: TV Licensed Cen ht Parking 36

SOUTHEND-ON-SEA

Terrace Hotel ★★★ 64%

8 Royal Terrace SS1 1DY

☎ 01702 348143 📠 01702 348143

email: info@theterracehotel.co.uk

www.theterracehotel.co.uk

Dir: *From pier up Pier Hill onto Royal Ter*

Dogs: Bedrooms Exercise Area (10yds)

Resident Pets: Suzie (Staffordshire terrier)

Set on a terrace above the Western Esplanade, this comfortable guest house has an informal atmosphere. There is a cosy bar, and an elegant sitting room and breakfast room. The spacious, well-planned bedrooms consist of four en suite front and rear-facing rooms, and several front-facing rooms that share two bathrooms.

Rooms: 9rms 6 en suite (2 fmly)

dble room £44.65*

Facilities: TV TVL Cen ht

CO DURHAM/ESSEX

ESSEX/GLOUCESTERSHIRE

STANSTED

Days Inn London Stansted ⬆ BUD

Birchanger Green Bishop Stortford CM23 5QZ

☎ 01279 656477 📄 01279 656590

email:

birchanger.hotel@welcomebreak.co.uk

www.welcomebreak.co.uk

Dir: *M11 junct 8*

Dogs: Bedrooms (Unattended) Public Areas
Garden

This modern building offers accommodation
in smart, spacious and well-equipped
bedrooms, suitable for families and business
travellers, and all with en suite bathrooms.
Continental breakfast is available and other
refreshments may be taken at the nearby
family restaurant.

Rooms: 60rms en suite (57 fmly)

dble room £69 - £99*

Facilities: TV STV Parking 60

Last d order 9.30pm

ALVESTON

Alveston House Hotel ★★★ 78%
HL

Davids Lane Bristol BS35 2LA

☎ 01454 415050 📄 01454 415425

email: info@alvestonhousehotel.co.uk

www.alvestonhousehotel.co.uk

Dir: *M5 junct 14 from N or junct 16 from S,
on A38*

Dogs: Bedrooms (Unattended) Garden
Exercise Area (5 mins' walk)

In a quiet area with easy access to the city and
a short drive from both the M4 and M5, this
smartly presented hotel provides an
impressive combination of good service,
friendly hospitality and a relaxed atmosphere.
Bedrooms are well equipped and comfortable
for business or leisure use. The restaurant
offers carefully prepared fresh food, and the
pleasant bar and conservatory area is perfect
for enjoying a pre-dinner drink.

Rooms: 30rms en suite (1 fmly) (6 GF)

dble room £99.50 - £114.50*

Facilities: TV STV Modem/Fax Licensed
TVL Parking 75 Last d order 9pm

BOURTON-ON-THE-WATER
Chester House Hotel ★★ 79% HL

Victoria Street Cheltenham GL54 2BU

☎ 01451 820286 📄 01451 820471

email: info@chesterhousehotel.com

www.chesterhousehotel.com

Dogs: Bedrooms (Unattended) Public Areas (except lounge & bar) Garden Exercise Area (10yds)

Resident Pets: Poppy (Patterdale Terrier)

Chester House occupies a secluded but central location in this delightful Cotswold village. Rooms, some at ground floor level, are situated in the main house and adjoining coach house. The refurbished public areas are stylish, light and airy. Breakfast is taken in the main building whereas dinner is served in the attractive restaurant just a few yards away. The rear hotel garden provides a pleasant relief from the hustle and bustle of the town. The spacious car park is a bonus.

Rooms: 22rms en suite (8 fmly) (8 GF) dble room £80 - £90*

Facilities: TV Licensed Parking 20

BOURTON-ON-THE-WATER
Strathspey ★★★ 61% BB

Lansdowne GL54 2AR

☎ 01451 810321 & 07889 491993

email: information@strathspey.org.uk

www.strathspey.org.uk

Dir: *Off A429 into Lansdowne, 200yds on right*

Dogs: Bedrooms (Unattended) Public Areas (except dining room) Garden Exercise Area (200yds) Pet Food/Bowls

This friendly Edwardian-style cottage is just a short riverside walk from the charming village centre, perfume factory and the famous model village. Bedrooms, one at ground floor level having its own front door, are well presented with many useful extras, and substantial breakfasts are part of the caring hospitality.

Rooms: 3rms en suite (1 fmly) (1 GF) dble room £50*

Facilities: TV TVL Cen ht Parking 4

Last d order 9.30pm

GLOUCESTERSHIRE

GLOUCESTERSHIRE

CHELTENHAM

Carlton Hotel ★★★ 71% HL

Parabola Road GL50 3AQ

☎ 01242 514453 🖹 01242 226487

email: enquiries@thecarltonhotel.co.uk

www.thecarltonhotel.co.uk

Dir: *Follow signs to town centre, at Town Hall straight on through 2 sets of lights, turn left, then 1st right*

Dogs: Bedrooms (Unattended) Garden Exercise Area

This well-presented family owned and run Regency property is situated just a short walk from the town centre. Bedrooms are located both in the main hotel and also within an annexe building, where rooms are larger and more luxurious. Other features include a choice of bars, lounge and conference facilities.

Rooms: 75rms en suite (2 fmly) (4 GF) dble room £90 - £106*

Facilities: TV STV Modem/Fax Lift Licensed Parking 85 Last d order 7.30pm

CHELTENHAM

Cotswold Grange Hotel ★★ 71% HL

Pittville Circus Road GL52 2QH

☎ 01242 515119 🖹 01242 241537

email: paul@cotswoldgrange.co.uk

www.cotswoldgrange.co.uk

Dir: *from town centre, follow Prestbury signs. Right at 1st rdbt, hotel 200yds on left*

Dogs: Bedrooms Public Areas Garden Exercise Area (10yds)

Built from Cotswold limestone, this attractive Georgian property retains many impressive architectural features. Situated conveniently close to the centre of Cheltenham, this long established, family-run hotel offers well-equipped and comfortable accommodation. The convivial bar is a popular venue, and additional facilities include a spacious restaurant, cosy lounge, pleasant rear garden and ample parking.

Rooms: 25rms en suite (4 fmly) dble room £80 - £95

Facilities: TV Modem/Fax Licensed TVL Parking 20

CHELTENHAM

Hope Orchard ★★★ 68% GA

Gloucester Road Staverton GL51 0TF

☎ 01452 855556 📄 01452 530037

email: info@hopeorchard.com

www.hopeorchard.com

Dir: *A40 onto B4063 at Arlecourt rdbt, Hope Orchard 1.25m on right*

Dogs: Bedrooms (Unattended) Garden
Exercise Area (on site) Pet Food/Bowls
towels & shampoo for dogs on request

Resident Pets: Bertie (Staffordshire Terrier),
Jessie, Jasper & Louis (cats)

Situated midway between Gloucester and
Cheltenham, this is a good base for exploring
the area. The comfortable bedrooms are next
to the main house, all of which are on the
ground floor and have their own separate
entrances. There is a large garden and ample
off-road parking is available.

Rooms: 8rms en suite (2 fmly) (8 GF)

Facilities: TV FTV Modem/Fax Cen ht
Parking 10 Last d order 9.45pm

CHIPPING CAMPDEN

Cotswold House

★★★★ 90% ◉◉◉◉ HL

The Square GL55 6AN

☎ 01386 840330 📄 01386 840310

email: reception@cotswoldhouse.com

www.cotswoldhouse.com

Dir: *A44 take B4081 to Chipping Campden. Right at T-junct into High St. House in The Square*

Dogs: Bedrooms (Unattended) Garden
Exercise Area (The Common)

Relaxation is inevitable at this mellow
Cotswold stone house, set in the centre of the
town. Bedrooms, including spacious suites in
the courtyard, offer a blend of style, quality
and comfort. The restaurant is a stunning
venue to sample the imaginative cuisine
based on local produce. The Hicks Brasserie
and Bar provides more informal dining.

Rooms: 29rms en suite (1 fmly) (5 GF)
dble room £225

Facilities: TV STV Modem/Fax Licensed
TVL Parking 28 Last d order 9.30pm

GLOUCESTERSHIRE

CHIPPING CAMPDEN
Noel Arms Hotel ★★★ 73% HL
High Street GL55 6AT

☎ 01386 840317 ▤ 01386 841136

email: reception@noelarmshotel.com

www.noelarmshotel.com

Dir: *off A44 onto B4081 to Chipping Campden, 1st right down hill into town. Hotel on right opposite Market Hall*

Dogs: Bedrooms (Unattended) Exercise Area (outside hotel)

This historic 14th-century hotel has a wealth of character and charm, and retains some of its original features. Bedrooms are very individual in style, but all have high levels of comfort and interesting interior design. Such distinctiveness is also evident throughout the public areas, which include the popular bar, conservatory lounge and attractive restaurant.

Rooms: 26rms en suite (1 fmly) (6 GF) dble room £125 - £175

Facilities: TV Licensed Parking 26 Last d order 9pm

CHIPPING CAMPDEN
Three Ways House ★★★ 79% ◉ HL
Mickleton GL55 6SB

☎ 01386 438429 ▤ 01386 438118

email: reception@puddingclub.com

www.puddingclub.com

Dir: *in centre of Mickleton, on B4632 Stratford-upon-Avon to Broadway road*

Dogs: Bedrooms (Unattended) Public Areas (except restaurant) Garden Exercise Area (feilds nearby approx 100yds)

Built in 1870, this charming hotel has welcomed guests for over 100 years and is home to the famous Pudding Club, formed in 1985 to promote traditional English puddings. Individuality is a hallmark, as reflected in a number of bedrooms, which have been styled according to a pudding theme. Public areas are stylish and include the air-conditioned restaurant, lounges and meeting rooms.

Rooms: 48rms en suite (7 fmly) (14 GF) dble room £130 - £195*

Facilities: TV Modem/Fax Lift Licensed Parking 37

CHIPPING SODBURY

The Moda Hotel ★ ★ ★ ★ 72% GA

1 High Street BS37 6BA

☎ 01454 312135 🖹 01454 850090

email: enquiries@modahotel.com

www.modahotel.com

Dir: *In town centre*

Dogs: Bedrooms (Unattended) Garden
Exercise Area Pet Food/Bowls

Resident Pets: Sky (Black Labrador)

This popular Grade II listed Georgian house
has an imposing position at the top of High
St. It has been refurbished to provide modern
bedrooms of varying shapes and sizes and
comfortable public areas while retaining many
original features. Room facilities include
satellite televisions and phones.

Rooms: 10rms en suite (1 fmly) (3 GF)
dble room £75 - £98*

Facilities: TV STV Modem/Fax Licensed
TVL Cen ht

COLEFORD

Dryslade Farm ★ ★ ★ ★ 77% FH

English Bicknor GL16 7PA

☎ 01594 860259 🖹 01594 860259

email: daphne@drysladefarm.co.uk

www.drysladefarm.co.uk

Dir: *3m N of Coleford. Off A4136 onto B4432,
right towards English Bicknor, farm 1m*

Dogs: Bedrooms Public Areas Exercise Area
(grounds)

Resident Pets: Kay (Spaniel)

You are warmly welcomed at this 184-acre
working farm, which dates from 1780 and has
been in the same family for almost 100 years.
The en suite bedrooms are attractively
furnished in natural pine and are well
equipped. The lounge leads onto a
conservatory where hearty breakfasts are
served. Daphne Gwilliam was a top-twenty
finalist for AA Landlady of the Year 2006.

Rooms: 3rms en suite (1 GF)
dble room £52 - £64

Facilities: TV TVL Cen ht Parking 6
Last d order 9.30pm

GLOUCESTERSHIRE

GLOUCESTERSHIRE

CORSE LAWN
Corse Lawn House Hotel
★★★ 85% ◉◉ HL
GL19 4LZ
☎ 01452 780479 & 780771 📄 01452 780840
email: enquiries@corselawn.com
www.corselawn.com
Dir: *on B4211 5m SW of Tewkesbury*
Dogs: Bedrooms (Unattended) Public Areas
Garden Exercise Area (adjacent)
Pet Food/Bowls
Resident Pets: Sugar & Spice (Black
Labradors), Donna & Gigi (horses)
This gracious Grade II listed Queen Anne
house has been home to the Hine family since
1978. Aided by a committed team, the family
presides over all aspects, creating a relaxed
environment. Bedrooms offer a mix of comfort
and quality. Impressive cuisine is based upon
excellent produce, much of it locally sourced.
Rooms: 19rms en suite (2 fmly) (5 GF)
dble room £140
Facilities: TV STV Modem/Fax Licensed
Parking 62 Last d order 9pm 🍲

DUMBLETON
Dumbleton Hall Hotel
★★★ 73% HL
Evesham WR11 7TS
☎ 01386 881240 📄 01386 882142
email: dh@pofr.co.uk
www.dumbletonhall.co.uk
Dir: *M5 junct 8 follow A46 for Evesham. 5m
S of Evesham take right signed Dumbleton.
Hotel is set back at S end of village.*
Dogs: Bedrooms (Unattended) Exercise Area
(grounds)
Originally constructed in the 16th century,
and re-built in the mid-18th century this
establishment is set in 19 acres of landscaped
gardens and parkland. Spacious public
rooms make this an ideal venue for weddings,
conferences or a hideaway retreat - the
location makes an ideal touring base.
Panoramic views of the Vale of Evesham can
be seen from every window.
Rooms: 34rms en suite (9 fmly)
dble room £160 - £260*
Facilities: TV FTV Lift Licensed Parking
60 Last d order 9.30pm

GLOUCESTER
Macdonald Hatherley Manor
★ ★ ★ 70% HL

Down Hatherley Lane GL2 9QA

☎ 0870 1942126 📄 01452 731032

email: hatherleymanor@macdonaldhotels.co.uk

www.macdonaldhotels.co.uk

Dir: *off A38 into Down Hatherley Lane,*
signed. Hotel 600yds on left

Dogs: Bedrooms (Unattended) Garden
Exercise Area (two fields at rear of hotel)
Within easy striking distance of the M5,
Gloucester, Cheltenham and the Cotswolds,
this stylish 17th-century manor remains
popular with both business and leisure
guests. Bedrooms have undergone a
substantial refurbishment and all offer
contemporary comforts. A range of meeting
and function rooms is available.

Rooms: 52rms en suite

dble room £80 - £120*

Facilities: TV Modem/Fax Licensed
Parking 250 Last d order 9.30pm

GUITING POWER
The Hollow Bottom ★ ★ ★ 65% INN

Winchcombe Road Cheltenham GL54 5UX

☎ 01451 850392 📄 01451 850945

email: hello@hollowbottom.com

www.hollowbottom.com

Dir: *In village centre*

Dogs: Bedrooms (Unattended) Public Areas
(except restaurant) Garden Exercise Area (on
site) Pet Food/Bowls

Resident Pets: Lassie (Collie)

Original features have been retained at this
inn, located on the edge of this unspoiled
Cotswold village and popular with followers of
National Hunt racing. Rustic furniture and
racing memorabilia all add to the atmosphere.
A range of real ales and good food is
complemented by warm hospitality.

Rooms: 4rms 4 en suite (1 fmly) (1 GF)

dble room £70*

Facilities: TV Licensed Cen ht Parking 12

GLOUCESTERSHIRE

GLOUCESTERSHIRE

LONGHOPE

The Old Farm ★★★★ 71% BB

Barrel Lane GL17 0LR

☎ 01452 830252

email: lucy@the-old-farm.co.uk

www.the-old-farm.co.uk

Dir: *1m N of Longhope. Off A40 N onto Barrel Ln, B&B 300yds on right*

Dogs: Bedrooms Public Areas Garden Exercise Area (20yds)

Resident Pets: Donna & Charlie (Golden Retrievers), Cassie, Toffee, Fudge (cats), Woody, Zac, Juniper (horses)

This former cider farm, off the A40 between Gloucester and Ross-on-Wye, offers some bedrooms in the main house and self-catering cottages in converted barns. The house has lots of character. There is a lounge, and breakfast is served in the cosy dining area. Pubs serving food within walking distance.

Rooms: 3rms en suite (1 GF)

dble room £54 - £65*

Facilities: TV Modem/Fax Cen ht Parking 6

MICHAEL WOOD MOTORWAY SERVICE AREA (M5)

Days Inn Michaelwood ⭐ BUD

Michael Wood Service Area

Lower Wick GL11 6DD

☎ 01454 261513 🖷 01454 269150

email: michaelwood.hotel@welcomebreak.co.uk

www.welcomebreak.co.uk

Dir: *M5 northbound between junct 13 and 14*

Dogs: Bedrooms (Unattended) Public Areas (must be kept on lead) Garden Exercise Area (adjacent) welcome snack pack on arrival

This modern building offers accommodation in smart, spacious and well-equipped bedrooms, suitable for families and business travellers, and all with en suite bathrooms. Continental breakfast is available and other refreshments may be taken at the nearby family restaurant.

Rooms: 38rms en suite (34 fmly)

dble room £45 - £55*

Facilities: TV STV TVL Parking 40

NAILSWORTH

Aaron Farm ★ ★ ★ 66% BB

Nympsfield Road GL6 0ET

☎ 01453 833598   🖷 01453 833626

email: aaronfarm@aol.com

www.aaronfarm-bedandbreakfast.co.uk

Dir: *Off A46 at Nailsworth minirdbt onto
Spring Hill & Nympsfield Rd. Farm 1m on left
at top of hill*

Dogs: Bedrooms   Garden   Exercise Area

Resident Pets: Brooke (dog)

Located on the outskirts of town, this mellow-stone former farmhouse has been extended to provide spacious bedrooms. A traditional English breakfast, featuring local produce, is served in the dining room at separate tables. There is a lounge for guest use.

Rooms: 3rms en suite dble room £50 - £55

Facilities: TV   Cen ht   Parking 6

STOW-ON-THE-WOLD

Limes Guest House ★ ★ ★ 65% BB

Evesham Road GL54 1EJ

☎ 01451 830034   🖷 01451 830034

email: thelimes@zoom.co.uk

Dir: *500yds from village centre on A424*

Dogs: Bedrooms   Public Areas (except breakfast room)   Garden   Exercise Area (5 mins' walk)

Resident Pets: Casey (Doberman)

Just a short walk from the village centre, this Victorian house provides a comfortable base from which to explore this beautiful area. Bedroom styles vary, with four-poster and ground-floor rooms offered. A warm and genuine welcome is extended, and many guests return on a regular basis. A spacious lounge is available and breakfast is served in the light and airy dining room.

Rooms: 5rms en suite (1 fmly) (1 GF) dble room £48 - £52*

Facilities: TV   STV   TVL   Cen ht   Parking 4

GLOUCESTERSHIRE

STROUD

Hyde Crest ★★★ 67% BB

Cirencester Road GL6 8PE

☎ 01453 731631

email: anthea@hydecrest.demon.co.uk

www.hydecrest.co.uk

Dir: *Off A419, 5m E of Stroud, signed Minchinhampton & Aston Down, house 3rd right opp Ragged Cot pub*

Dogs: Bedrooms (Unattended) Public Areas Garden Exercise Area (in garden and nearby common)

Hyde Crest lies on the edge of the picturesque Cotswold village of Minchinhampton. Bedrooms are located at ground floor level, each with a private patio where welcome refreshments are enjoyed upon arrival (weather permitting). Guests are attentively cared for and scrumptious breakfasts are served in the small lounge-dining room around a communal table.

Rooms: 3rms en suite (3 GF)

Facilities: TV TVL Cen ht Parking 6 Last d order 9.15pm

ALTRINCHAM

Best Western Cresta Court Hotel

★★★ 77% HL

Church Street WA14 4DP

☎ 0161 927 7272 🖹 0161 929 6548

email: rooms@cresta-court.co.uk

www.cresta-court.co.uk

Dogs: Bedrooms (Unattended) Public Areas (except bar & restaurant) Garden Exercise Area (200yds)

This modern hotel enjoys a prime location on the A56, close to the station and town centre shops and amenities. Bedrooms vary in style from spacious four-posters to smaller, traditionally furnished rooms. Public areas include a choice of bars, a small gym, beauty salon and extensive function and conference facilities.

Rooms: 137rms en suite (9 fmly)

dble room £65 - £89*

Facilities: TV STV Modem/Fax Lift Licensed TVL Parking 200 Last d order 8pm

BOLTON

Broomfield House ★★★ 57% GH

33-35 Wigan Road Deanc BL3 5PX

☎ 01204 61570 ▤ 01204 650932

email: chris@broomfield.force9.net

Dir: *M61 junct 5, A58 to 1st lights, onto A676, premises on right*

Dogs: Bedrooms (Unattended) Public Areas
Exercise Area (100yds)

Resident Pets: Max (Labrador)

A friendly relaxed atmosphere prevails at the Broomfield, close to the motorway and west of the town centre. The bedrooms, some suitable for families, have modern facilities, and public areas include a bar and a lounge. Hearty breakfasts are served in the separate dining room.

Rooms: 20rms en suite (2 fmly) (2 GF)
dble room £50*

Facilities: TV Licensed TVL Cen ht
Parking 12

DIGGLE

Sunfield Accommodation

★★ 51% GH

Diglea OL3 5LA

☎ 01457 874030

email: sunfield.accom@lineone.net

www.sunfieldaccommodation.gbr.cc

Dir: *From A670 Oldham to Huddersfield. Turn right towards Diggle Village, right Sam Rd to Diggle Hotel, follow signs for Diggle Ranges.*

Dogs: Bedrooms (Unattended) Exercise Area (own grounds)

This friendly, family run operation is located within easy reach of Manchester and the M62 and affords wonderful views over the Pennines; bedrooms are on the ground floor and pets are made welcome. Breakfast is served at one large table. Good pubs serving food are located at the bottom of the lane.

Rooms: 4rms en suite (1 fmly) (4 GF)
dble room £45 - £50*

Facilities: TV FTV TVL Cen ht Parking 11
Last d order 9.30pm

GREATER MANCHESTER

MANCHESTER

Hotel Ibis Manchester City Centre

⌂ BUD

96 Portland Street M1 4GY

☎ 0161 234 0600 🖷 0161 234 0610

email: H3142@accor-hotels.com

www.accorhotels.com

Dir: *In city centre, between Princess St & Oxford St. 10min walk from Piccadilly*

Dogs: Bedrooms Public Areas

Modern, budget hotel offering comfortable accommodation in bright and practical bedrooms. Breakfast is self-service and dinner is available in the restaurant.

Rooms: 127rms en suite (16 fmly) dble room £56.95 - £66.95*

Facilities: TV STV Modem/Fax Lift Licensed TVL Last d order 9.45pm

OLDHAM

La Pergola ★★★ 70% HL

Rochdale Road Denshaw OL3 5UE

☎ 01457 871040 🖷 01457 873804

email: reception@lapergola.freeserve.co.uk

www.hotel-restaurant-uk.com

Dir: *M62 junct 21, right at rdbt onto A640, under motorway, left at Wagon & Horses public house. Hotel 500yds on left*

Dogs: Bedrooms (Unattended) Public Areas (except food areas) Garden Exercise Area (2 mins)

Situated in open moorland and convenient for the M62, this friendly, family-owned and run hotel offers comfortable and well-equipped bedrooms. There is a good range of food available either in the bar or restaurant, and a comfortable lounge in which to relax. Functions and conferences are well catered for.

Rooms: 26rms en suite (4 fmly)

Facilities: TV Modem/Fax Licensed TVL Parking 75 Last d order 9.45pm

WIGAN

Quality Hotel Wigan ★★★ 71% HL

Riverway WN1 3SS

☎ 01942 826888 🖷 01942 825800

email: enquiries@hotels-wigan.com

www.hotels-wigan.com

Dir: *from A49 take B5238 from rdbt, continue for 1.5m through lights, through 3 more sets of lights, right at 4th set, 1st left*

Dogs: Bedrooms Exercise Area (5 mins' walk)

Close to the centre of the town this modern hotel offers spacious and well-equipped bedrooms. The open plan public areas include a comfortable lounge bar adjacent to the popular restaurant, which serves a good range of dishes. Secure car parking is a bonus.

Rooms: 88rms en suite (16 GF)

dble room £100*

Facilities: TV STV Modem/Fax Lift Licensed TVL Parking 100

BASINGSTOKE

The Hatchings ★★★★ 71% BB

Woods Lane Cliddesden RG25 2JF

☎ 01256 465279

Dir: *2m S of town centre. Off A339 onto B3046 to Cliddesden, pass garage, next right*

Dogs: Bedrooms Public Areas Garden Exercise Area (2 acres for dog walks through garden) Pet Food/Bowls

Resident Pets: Cherry (Greyhound)

This delightful house is in a pretty village convenient for Basingstoke and the M3. The comfortable bedrooms look out onto peaceful gardens and the extra touches are excellent. A hearty full English breakfast is served in the bedrooms, and cereals, bread, jams, fruit and biscuits are freely available.

Rooms: 3rms 1 en suite (3 GF)

dble room £50 - £55*

Facilities: TV Cen ht Parking 10

HAMPSHIRE

FLEET MOTORWAY SERVICE AREA
Days Inn Fleet ⌂ BUD

Fleet Services GU51 1AA

☎ 01252 815587 📄 01252 815587

email: fleethotel@welcomebreak.co.uk

www.welcomebreak.co.uk

Dir: *between junct 4a & 5 southbound on M3*

Dogs: Bedrooms (Unattended) Garden
Exercise Area

This modern building offers accommodation
in smart, spacious and well-equipped
bedrooms, suitable for families and business
travellers, and all with en suite bathrooms.
Continental breakfast is available and other
refreshments may be taken at the nearby
family restaurant.

Rooms: 58rms en suite (46 fmly)
dble room £45 - £65*

Facilities: TV STV TVL Parking 60
Last d order 9.30pm

HURSTBOURNE TARRANT
Esseborne Manor

★★★ 78% ◉◉ HL

Hurstbourne Tarrant Andover SP11 0ER

☎ 01264 736444 📄 01264 736725

email: info@esseborne-manor.co.uk

www.esseborne-manor.co.uk

Dir: *halfway between Andover & Newbury on
A343, just 1m N of Hurstbourne Tarrant*

Dogs: Bedrooms (Unattended) Garden
Exercise Area (100yds)

Set in two acres of well-tended gardens, this
attractive manor house is surrounded by the
open countryside of the North Wessex Downs.
Bedrooms are delightfully individual and are
split between the main house, an adjoining
courtyard and separate garden cottage. A
wonderfully relaxed atmosphere pervades
throughout, with public rooms combining
elegance with comfort.

Rooms: 20rms en suite (2 fmly) (6 GF)
dble room £125 - £180*

Facilities: TV STV Licensed TVL
Parking 50

LYMINGTON

Jevington ★★★★ 62% BB

4/ Waterford Lane SO41 3PT

☎ 01590 672148 📄 01590 672148

email: jevingtonbb@lineone.net

www.caruthers.co.uk

Dir: *From High St at St Thomas's Church onto Church Ln, left fork onto Waterford Ln*

Dogs: Bedrooms Exercise Area (100yds)

Resident Pets: Lady (Terrier cross)

Situated within walking distance of the town centre and marinas, Jevington offers attractive bedrooms furnished to a high standard with coordinated soft furnishings. An appetising breakfast is served at two tables in the dining room, and the friendly proprietors can suggest local places for dinner.

Rooms: 3rms en suite (1 fmly)

dble room £55 - £60*

Facilities: TV FTV Cen ht Parking 3

LYMINGTON

Gorse Meadow Country House Hotel ★★★ 63% GH

Sway Road SO41 8LR

☎ 01590 673354 📄 01590 673336

email:gorse.meadow.guesthouse @wildmushrooms.co.uk

www.wildmushrooms.co.uk

Dir: *Off A337 from Brockenhurst, right onto Sway Rd before Toll House pub, Gorse Meadow 1.5m on right*

Dogs: Bedrooms Sep Accom Garden Exercise Area (in garden under supervision) Pet Food/Bowls **Resident Pets:** Guinevere & Camilla (Great Dane), Otto (Black Labrador)

This imposing Edwardian house is situated in 14 acres of grounds and most bedrooms enjoy views across the gardens and paddocks. An excellent base to enjoy the New Forest. Meals are also available here.

Rooms: 5rms en suite (2 fmly) (2 GF)

dble room £80 - £120*

Facilities: TV Licensed Cen ht Parking 20

Last d order 8pm

HAMPSHIRE

HAMPSHIRE

LYNDHURST

Knightwood Lodge ★★ 64% HL

Southampton Road SO43 7BU

☎ 023 8028 2502 📠 023 8028 3730

email: jackie4r@aol.com

www.knightwoodlodge.co.uk

Dir: *exit M27 junct 1 follow A337 to Lyndhurst. Left at traffic lights in village onto A35 towards Southampton. Hotel 0.25m on left*

Dogs: Bedrooms (Unattended - annexe rooms only) Garden Exercise Area (across road)

This friendly, family-run hotel is situated on the outskirts of Lyndhurst. Comfortable bedrooms are modern and well equipped. The hotel offers an excellent range of facilities including a swimming pool, a jacuzzi and a small gym area. Two separate cottages are available for families or larger groups, and dogs are also welcome as guests in these.

Rooms: 19rms en suite (2 fmly) (5 GF) dble room £80 - £100*

Facilities: TV STV Licensed TVL Parking 15 Last d order 9.30pm 🛥

PORTSMOUTH

Best Western Royal Beach Hotel

★★★ 74% HL

South Parade Southsea PO4 0RN

☎ 023 9273 1281 📠 023 9281 7572

email: enquiries@royalbeachhotel.co.uk

www.royalbeachhotel.co.uk

Dir: *M27 to M275, follow signs to seafront. Hotel on seafront*

Dogs: Bedrooms Public Areas (except restaurant) Exercise Area (100yds)

This former Victorian seafront hotel is a smart and comfortable venue suitable for leisure and business guests alike. Bedrooms and public areas are well presented and generally spacious, and the smart new Coast bar is an ideal venue for a relaxing drink.

Rooms: 124rms en suite (18 fmly) dble room £65 - £125*

Facilities: TV STV Modem/Fax Lift Licensed TVL Parking 50 Last d order 9pm

SOUTHAMPTON
The Woodlands Lodge Hotel
★★★ 70% HL
Bartley Road Woodlands SO40 7GN
☎ 023 8029 2257 ▤ 023 8029 3090
email: reception@woodlands-lodge.co.uk
www.woodlands-lodge.co.uk
Dir: *M27 junct 2, A326 towards Fawley. 2nd rdbt turn right, left after 0.25m by White Horse PH. In 1.5m cross cattle grid, hotel is 70yds on left*
Dogs: Bedrooms (Unattended) Garden Exercise Area (50yds)
Resident Pets: Bentley (Dalmatian), Minty & Rambo (sheep), Christmas (goose), Napolean (cockerel)
This hotel is set in four acres on the edge of the New Forest. Bedrooms come in varying sizes and all bathrooms have a jacuzzi bath. Dining room serves award-winning cuisine.
Rooms: 16rms en suite (1 fmly) (3 GF) dble room £126 - £142
Facilities: TV FTV Licensed Parking 30 Last d order 9pm

SOUTHAMPTON
The Elizabeth House Hotel
★★ 71% HL
42-44 The Avenue SO17 1XP
☎ 023 8022 4327 ▤ 023 8022 4327
email: enquiries@elizabethhousehotel.com
www.elizabethhousehotel.com
Dir: *on A33, left hand side travelling towards city centre, after Southampton Common, before main lights*
Dogs: Bedrooms (Unattended) Garden Exercise Area (300yds)
This hotel is conveniently situated close to the city centre, so provides an ideal base for both business and leisure guests. The bedrooms are well equipped and are attractively furnished with comfort in mind. There is also a cosy and atmospheric bistro in the cellar where evening meals are served.
Rooms: 27rms en suite (9 fmly) (8 GF) dble room £67.50*
Facilities: TV Modem/Fax Licensed TVL Parking 31

HAMPSHIRE

HEREFORDSHIRE

BROMYARD
Little Hegdon Farm House
★★★★ 77% BB

Hegdon Hill Pencombe HR7 4SL

☎ 01885 400263 & 07779 595445

email: howardcolegrave@hotmail.com

www.bedandbreakfastherefordshire.com

Dir: *Between Pencombe & Risbury, at top of Hegdon Hill down farm lane for 500yds*

Dogs: Sep Accom (stable & utility room) Public Areas (except dining area) Garden Exercise Area (adjacent)

Resident Pets: Meg & Snuff (Border Collies), Sam (Patterdale Terrier) , Ebony & Pippa (horses)

Located in a pretty hamlet, this traditional house has been renovated to provide high standards of comfort. Original features include exposed beams and open fires, and the bedrooms are equipped with lots of thoughtful extras and have stunning views of the surrounding countryside.

Rooms: 2rms en suite

Facilities: TV Cen ht Parking 4

HEREFORD
Sink Green Farm ★★★★ 71% FH

Rotherwas HR2 6LE

☎ 01432 870223 🖷 01432 870223

email: enquiries@sinkgreenfarm.co.uk

www.sinkgreenfarm.co.uk

Dir: *On B4399 2m from junction with A49*

Dogs: Bedrooms Public Areas Garden Exercise Area (adjoining)

Resident Pets: Bob & Buzz (dogs)

This charming 16th-century farmhouse stands in attractive countryside and has many original features, including flagstone floors, exposed beams and open fireplaces. Bedrooms are traditionally furnished and one has a four-poster bed. The pleasant garden has a comfortable summer house, hot tub and barbecue. The friendly and relaxed atmosphere leaves a lasting impression.

Rooms: 3rms en suite dble room £54 - £60

Facilities: TV Modem/Fax TVL Cen ht Parking 10 Last d order 9pm

ROSS-ON-WYE

Chasedale Hotel ★★ 67% SHL

Walford Road HR9 5PQ

☎ 01989 562423 & 565801

📄 01989 567900

email: chasedale@supanet.com

www.chasedale.co.uk

Dir: *from Ross-on-Wye town centre, S on B4234, hotel 0.5m on left*

Dogs: Bedrooms (Unattended) Public Areas Garden Exercise Area (200yds)

Resident Pets: Marmite (Chocolate Labrador), Cassis (Black Labrador)

This mid-Victorian property is situated on the south-west outskirts of the town. Privately owned, it provides spacious public areas and extensive grounds. The accommodation is well equipped and includes ground floor and family rooms, whilst the restaurant offers a wide selection of wholesome food.

Rooms: 10rms en suite (2 fmly) (1 GF) dble room £72 - £78

Facilities: TV Licensed Parking 14

Last d order 9pm

ROSS-ON-WYE

Kings Head Hotel ★★ 67% HL

8 High Street HR9 5Hl

☎ 01989 763174 📄 01989 769578

email: enquiries@kingshead.co.uk

www.kingshead.co.uk

Dir: *in town centre, turn right past Royal Hotel*

Dogs: Bedrooms (Unattended) Public Areas (bar only) Garden Exercise Area (200yds) Pet Food/Bowls

The King's Head dates back to the 14th century and has a wealth of charm and character. Bedrooms are well equipped and include both four-poster and family rooms. The restaurant doubles as a coffee shop during the day and is a popular venue with locals. There is also a very pleasant bar and comfortable lounge.

Rooms: 15rms en suite (1 fmly)

Facilities: TV Licensed Parking 13

Last d order 9pm

HEREFORDSHIRE

ROSS-ON-WYE
Wilton Court Hotel
★★★ 77% ◉ ◉ HL
Wilton Lane HR9 6AQ
☎ 01989 562569 📠 01989 768460
email: info@wiltoncourthotel.com
www.wiltoncourthotel.com
Dir: *M50 junct 4 onto A40 towards
Monmouth at 3rd rdbt turn left signed Ross
then take 1st right, hotel on right facing river*
Dogs: Bedrooms (Unattended) Public Areas
(except restaurant) Garden
Dating back to the 16th century, this hotel
has great charm and a wealth of character.
Standing on the banks of the River Wye, a
short walk from the town centre, there is a
genuinely relaxed atmosphere here. Bedrooms
are tastefully furnished and well equipped.
There is a comfortable lounge, bar and
pleasant restaurant. Offers high standards of
food using fresh locally-sourced ingredients.
Rooms: 10rms en suite (1 fmly)
dble room £90 - £130
Facilities: TV Licensed TVL Parking 24

ROSS-ON-WYE
Lumleys ★★★★ 77% BB
Kern Bridge Bishopswood HR9 5QT
☎ 01600 890040 📠 0870 706 2378
email: helen@lumleys.force9.co.uk
www.lumleys.force9.co.uk
Dir: *Off A40 onto B4229 at Goodrich, over
Kern Bridge, right at Inn On The Wye, 400yds
opp picnic ground*
Dogs: Bedrooms (Unattended) Public Areas
(except dining room) Garden Exercise Area
(20yds) Pet Food/Bowls anything required
can be provided
Resident Pets: Megan (Golden Cocker
Spaniel)
This friendly guest house overlooks the River
Wye and has been a hostelry since Victorian
times. It offers the character of a bygone era
with modern facilities. Bedrooms are carefully
furnished and one has a four-poster bed and
its own patio. Choice of sitting rooms.
Rooms: 3rms en suite dble room £60 - £70*
Facilities: TV STV FTV TVL Cen ht
Parking 15 Last d order 9.45pm

BISHOP'S STORTFORD
Down Hall Country House Hotel

★★★★ 75% ❀❀ HL

Hatfield Heath CM22 7AS

☎ 01279 731441 ▤ 01279 730416

email: reservations@downhall.co.uk

www.downhall.co.uk

Dir: *A1060, at Hatfield Heath keep left. Turn right into lane opposite Hunters Meet restaurant & left at end, follow sign*

Dogs: Bedrooms (Unattended) Public Areas (except restaurants) Exercise Area (hotel 110-acre grounds) doggy pack on arrival

Resident Pets: deer, peacocks, rabbits and squirrels in grounds

Imposing Victorian country-house hotel set in 100 acres of mature grounds. Pleasant, spacious bedrooms with modern facilities. There is a choice of restaurants, a cocktail bar, two lounges and leisure facilities.

Rooms: 99rms en suite (20 GF)

dble room £75 - £105*

Facilities: TV STV Modem/Fax Lift Licensed Parking 150 ☁

BISHOP'S STORTFORD
Broadleaf Guest House

★★★ 66% BB

38 Broadleaf Avenue CM23 4JY

☎ 01279 835467

email: b-tcannon@tiscali.co.uk

www.broadleafguesthouse.co.uk

Dir: *1m SW of town centre. Off B1383 onto Whittinton Way & Friedburge Av, Broadleaf Av 6th left*

Dogs: Bedrooms Garden

A delightful detached house situated in a peaceful residential area close to the town centre, and within easy striking distance of the M11 and Stansted Airport. The pleasantly decorated bedrooms are carefully furnished and equipped with many thoughtful touches. Breakfast is served in the smart dining room, which overlooks the pretty garden.

Rooms: 2rms 0 en suite (1 fmly)

dble room £50 - £65*

Facilities: TV Cen ht Parking 2

HERTFORDSHIRE

SOUTH MIMMS

Days Inn South Mimms ⚐ BUD

Bignells Corner EN6 3QQ

☎ 01707 665440 📠 01707 660189

email: southmimmshotel@welcomebreak.co.uk

www.welcomebreak.co.uk

Dir: *M25 junct 23,' at rdbt follow signs*

Dogs: Bedrooms (Unattended) Public Areas (must be kept on lead) Garden Exercise Area (adjacent) welcome snack pack on arrival

This modern building offers accommodation in smart, spacious and well-equipped bedrooms, suitable for families and business travellers, and all with en suite bathrooms. Continental breakfast is available and other refreshments may be taken at the nearby family restaurant.

Rooms: 74rms en suite (55 fmly) dble room £59 - £74*

Facilities: TV STV Lift TVL Parking 100 Last d order 9.30pm

TRING

Pendley Manor ★ ★ ★ ★ 76% ◉ HL

Cow Lane HP23 5QY

☎ 01442 891891 📠 01442 890687

email: info@pendley-manor.co.uk

www.pendley-manor.co.uk

Dir: *M25 junct 20, A41 Tring exit. At rdbt follow Berkhamsted/London signs. 1st left signed Tring Station & Pendley Manor*

Dogs: Bedrooms (Unattended) Public Areas Garden Pet Food/Bowls

This impressive Victorian mansion is set in extensive and mature landscaped grounds where peacocks roam. The spacious bedrooms are situated in the manor house or in the wing and offer a useful range of facilities. Public areas include a cosy bar, a conservatory lounge and an intimate restaurant as well as a leisure centre and spa.

Rooms: 74rms en suite (6 fmly)

Facilities: TV STV Modem/Fax Lift Licensed Parking 250 Last d order 8pm 🐾

CANTERBURY
Cathedral Gate Hotel

★★★ 60% GA

36 Burgate CT1 2HA

☎ 01227 464381 📄 01227 462800

email: cgate@cgate.demon.co.uk

www.cathgate.co.uk

Dir: *In city centre. Next to main gateway into cathedral close*

Dogs: Bedrooms (Unattended) Public Areas (except dining room) Garden Exercise Area (0.5m)

Resident Pets: Dexter, Cody, Britney (cats) Dating from 1438, this hotel has an enviable central location next to the Cathedral. Old beams and winding corridors are part of the character of the property. Bedrooms are traditionally furnished, equipped to modern standards and many have Cathedral views. Luggage can be unloaded at reception before parking in a local car park.

Rooms: 27rms 14 en suite (5 fmly)
dble room £58 - £98

Facilities: TV Licensed Cen ht
Last d order 9.30pm

CANTERBURY
Best Western Abbots Barton Hotel

★★★ 82% HL

New Dover Road CT1 3DU

☎ 01227 760341 📄 01227 785442

email: sales@abbotsbartonhotel.com

www.abbotsbartonhotel.com

Dir: *Turn off A2 onto A2050 at bridge, S of Canterbury. Hotel is 0.75m past Old Gate Inn on left*

Dogs: Bedrooms Public Areas (except food areas) Garden Exercise Area (0.5m) Delightful property with a country-house hotel feel set amid two acres of pretty landscaped gardens close to the city centre and major road networks. The spacious accommodation includes a range of stylish lounges, a smart bar and the Fountain Restaurant, which serves imaginative food. Conference and banqueting facilities are also available.

Rooms: 50rms en suite (2 fmly) (6 GF)
dble room £95 - £180*

Facilities: TV STV Modem/Fax Lift Licensed Parking 80

KENT

KENT

CANTERBURY
Yorke Lodge ★★★★ 84% GA
50 London Road CT2 8LF
☎ 01227 451243 📄 01227 462006
email: enquiries@yorkelodge.com
www.yorkelodge.com
Dir: *750yds NW of city centre. A2 E onto A2050 to city, 1st rdbt left onto London Rd*
Dogs: Bedrooms (Unattended) Exercise Area (200yds)
Resident Pets: Fleur (Dalmatian/Collie cross)
The charming Victorian property stands in a tree-lined road just ten minutes walk from the town centre and railway station. The spacious bedrooms are thoughtfully equipped and carefully decorated; some rooms have four-poster beds. The stylish dining room leads to a conservatory-lounge, which opens onto a superb terrace.
Rooms: 8rms en suite (1 fmly)
dble room £80 - £100
Facilities: TV Modem/Fax Cen ht
Parking 5

CANTERBURY
St Stephens Guest House
★★★ 68% GA
100 St Stephens Road CT2 7JL
☎ 01227 767644 📄 01227 767644
www.come.to/st-stephens
Dir: *A290 from city Westgate & sharp right onto North Ln, 2nd rdbt left onto St Stephen's Rd, right onto Market Way, car park on right*
Dogs: Bedrooms Public Areas (except dining room) Exercise Area (200yds parkland, river walk) owners to supply suitable bedding
A large, privately owned guest house situated close to the university and within easy walking distance of the city centre. The pleasant bedrooms are equipped with a good range of useful extras, and there is a cosy lounge. Breakfast is served at individual tables in the smart dining room.
Rooms: 12rms 11 en suite (2 fmly) (3 GF)
dble room £58 - £60*
Facilities: TV TVL Cen ht Parking 11
Last d order 9.30pm

DARTFORD

Campanile ⌂ BUD

1 Clipper Boulevard West Crossways
Business Park DA2 6QN

☎ 01322 278925 ▤ 01322 278948

email: dartford@campanile-hotels.com

www.campanile.com

Dir: *follow signs for Ferry Terminal from
Dartford Bridge*

Dogs: Bedrooms (Unattended) Public Areas
(except food areas) Garden Exercise Area
(adjacent)

This modern building offers accommodation
in smart, well equipped bedrooms, all with en
suite bathrooms. Refreshments may be taken
at the informal Bistro.

Rooms: 125rms en suite (14 fmly)

Facilities: TV STV Modem/Fax Licensed
Parking 127

DEAL

Sutherland House Hotel

★ ★ ★ ★ ★ 87% GA

186 London Road CT14 9PT

☎ 01304 362853 ▤ 01304 381146

email: info@sutherlandhouse.fsnet.co.uk

www.sutherlandhousehotel.co.uk

Dir: *0.5m W of town centre/seafront on A258*

Dogs: Bedrooms Public Areas (with
consideration for other guests' comfort)
Garden Exercise Area (200yds)

This stylish hotel offers impeccable taste with
its charming, well equipped bedrooms and a
comfortable lounge. Fully stocked bar, books,
magazines, Freeview TV and radio are some
of the many amenities offered. The elegant
dining room is the venue for home-cooked
dinners and breakfasts.

Rooms: 4rms 4 en suite (1 GF)
dble room £55 - £65*

Facilities: TV FTV Modem/Fax Licensed
Cen ht Parking 7 Last d order 9.30pm

KENT

KENT

FOLKESTONE
Quality Hotel Burlington

★★★ 70% HL

Earls Avenue CT20 2HR

☎ 01303 255301 🖹 01303 251301

email: sales@theburlingtonhotel.com

www.theburlingtonhotel.com

Dogs: Bedrooms Public Areas (except restaurant)

Resident Pets: Cherit (Golden Retriever), Monty (Cocker Spaniel), Carlo (King Charles Spaniel), Misty (cat)

Situated close to the beach in a peaceful side road just a short walk from the town centre. The public rooms include a choice of lounges, the Bay Tree restaurant and a large cocktail bar. Bedrooms are pleasantly decorated and equipped with modern facilities; some rooms have superb sea views.

Rooms: 50rms en suite (6 fmly) (5 GF) dble room £79 - £99

Facilities: TV Modem/Fax Lift Licensed Parking 20

MAIDSTONE
Bower Court House ★★★ 70% GA

78 Bower Mount Road ME16 8AT

☎ 01622 752684 🖹 01622 752684

email: mail@bowercourt.co.uk

www.bowercourt.co.uk

Dir: *0.6m W of the town centre. Off A26 Tonbridge Rd onto Oakwood Rd & right onto Bower Mount Rd*

Dogs: Bedrooms Garden Exercise Area (2 mins)

An imposing Edwardian property situated in a quiet side road just a short walk from the town centre and the railway station. The spacious bedrooms are carefully decorated, thoughtfully equipped and have views over the pretty landscaped gardens. Public rooms feature a panelled entrance hall with seating and a smart dining room.

Rooms: 15rms 12 en suite (3 fmly) (4 GF) dble room £55 - £63*

Facilities: TV Cen ht Parking 18

MARGATE

The Greswolde Hotel

★★★ 67% GA

20 Surrey Road Cliftonville CT9 2LA

☎ 01843 223956 📄 01843 223956

email: jbearl@freeuk.com

Dogs: Bedrooms (Unattended) Public Areas
Exercise Area (beach)

Resident Pets: Hatty, Daisy, Teddy, Timmy,
Sam (cats)

An attractive Victorian house set in a peaceful
area close to the seafront. The property has a
lovely period atmosphere with interesting
memorabilia and spacious bedrooms. The
pleasant rooms are comfortably appointed and
equipped. Breakfast is served in the elegant
dining room, and there is a cosy lounge.

Rooms: 5rms en suite (2 fmly)
dble room £45 - £50*

Facilities: TV Licensed Cen ht

MARGATE

Elonville Holidays ★★★★ 71% INN

70-72 Harold Road Cliftonville CT9 2HS

☎ 01843 298635 📄 01843 298635

email: bockings@elonvillehotel.com

www.elonvillehotel.co.uk

Dir: *From Margate clock tower E onto A2051
coast road, Harold Rd 1m on right*

Dogs: Bedrooms (Unattended) Public Areas
(not in dining room (except assist dogs))
Garden Exercise Area (purpose-built dog area
on site)

Expect a warm welcome at this privately
owned establishment, situated just a short
walk from the shops and beach. The pleasant
bedrooms vary in size and style, and all are
thoughtfully equipped. Public rooms include a
lounge bar, and a dining room that overlooks
the garden.

Rooms: 16rms 10 en suite (3 fmly) (1 GF)

Facilities: TV Lift Licensed TVL

Last d order 10pm

KENT

KENT

SITTINGBOURNE
Hempstead House Country Hotel
★★★ 74% ⊛ HL

London Road Bapchild ME9 9PP

☎ 01795 428020 🖹 01795 436362

email: info@hempsteadhouse.co.uk

www.hempsteadhouse.co.uk

Dir: *1.5m from Sittingbourne town centre on A2 towards Canterbury*

Dogs: Bedrooms (Unattended) Public Areas Garden Exercise Area (on site) Pet Food/Bowls

Resident Pets: Jade (Staffordshire Bull Terrier), cats

Expect a warm welcome at this charming Victorian property, situated amidst three acres of mature landscaped gardens. Bedrooms are attractively decorated and furnished, and equipped with thoughtful touches.There are beautifully furnished lounges as well as a superb conservatory dining room.

Rooms: 27rms en suite (7 fmly) (1 GF) dble room £90 - £130*

Facilities: TV STV Modem/Fax Licensed TVL Parking 100 Last d order 9.30pm ☜

TENTERDEN
The White Lion ★★★ 65% INN

The High Street TN30 6BD

☎ 01580 765077 🖹 01580 764157

email: whitelion@celticinnspubs.co.uk

www.celticinns.co.uk

Dir: *In town centre*

Dogs: Bedrooms (Unattended) Public Areas (except restaurant) Garden Exercise Area (0.25m) Pet Food/Bowls

A delightful 15th-century coaching inn situated on the historic high street. Bedrooms are well appointed, thoughtfully equipped, and some have four-poster beds. Public rooms feature a popular bar, a lounge, and an oak-panelled restaurant serving an extensive range of dishes. There is also a small function and meeting room.

Rooms: 15rms en suite (2 fmly)

Facilities: TV Licensed Cen ht Parking 35

BLACKPOOL

Windsor Park Hotel ★★★ 59% GH

96 Queens Promenade FY2 9NS

☎ 01253 357025

email: info@windsorparkhotel.net

Dir: *Queens Promenade, North Shore*

Dogs: Bedrooms (Unattended) Public Areas
Exercise Area (across road & beach)

Resident Pets: Molly (Yorkshire Terrier)

Having stunning views, this family-run guest house on the peaceful North Shore is just a tram ride from the attractions. Home-cooked meals and substantial breakfasts are served in the elegant dining room, and there is a pleasant bar area and a sun lounge. The bedrooms have modern amenities.

Rooms: 9rms en suite (1 fmly)

Facilities: TV Licensed TVL Cen ht
Parking 6 Last d order 9.30pm

BURNLEY

Best Western Higher Trapp Country House Hotel ★★★ 78% HL

Trapp Lane Simonstone BB12 7QW

☎ 01282 227281 📠 01282 227282

email: reception@highertrapphotel.co.uk

www.highertrapphotel.co.uk

Dogs: Bedrooms (Unattended) Garden

Set in beautifully maintained gardens with rolling countryside beyond, accommodation comprises spacious, comfortable bedrooms, some of which are located in the Lodge, a smart annexe building. Public areas include a comfortable lounge, spacious bar and conservatory restaurant where guests will find service friendly and attentive.

Rooms: 29rms en suite (4 GF)

dble room £78 - £89*

Facilities: TV STV Licensed TVL
Parking 100 Last d order 8.50pm

LANCASHIRE

LANCASHIRE

CARNFORTH

Royal Station Hotel ★ ★ 65% HL

Market Street LA5 9BT

☎ 01524 732033 & 733636 📄 01524 720267

email: royalstation@mitchellshotels.co.uk

www.mitchellshotels.co.uk

Dir: *M6 junct 35 onto A6 signed Carnforth. After 1m at x-rds in town centre right into Market St. Hotel opposite railway station*

Dogs: Bedrooms Public Areas (except bar) Exercise Area (5-10 mins' walk)

This commercial hotel enjoys a town centre location close to the railway station. Bedrooms are well equipped and comfortably furnished. A good range of tasty good value meals can be taken in either the bright attractive lounge bar or the restaurant.

Rooms: 13rms en suite (1 fmly)

dble room £44 - £58*

Facilities: TV Licensed Parking 4

Last d order 9.30pm

CHORLEY

Welcome Lodge Charnock Richard

⌂ BUD

Welcome Break Service Area PR7 5LR

☎ 01257 791746 📄 01257 793596

email: charnockhotel@welcomebreak.co.uk

www.welcomebreak.co.uk

Dir: *between junct 27 & 28 of M6 northb'd. 500yds from Camelot Theme Park via Mill Lane*

Dogs: Bedrooms Garden Exercise Area (5yds)

This modern building offers accommodation in smart, spacious and well-equipped bedrooms, suitable for families and business travellers, and all with en suite bathrooms. Continental breakfast is available and other refreshments may be taken at the nearby family restaurant.

Rooms: 100rms en suite (68 fmly)

dble room £35 - £50*

Facilities: TV STV Licensed TVL Parking 100 Last d order 9pm

LANCASTER
The Mill Inn at Conder Green
★★★ 61% HL

Thurnham Mill Lane Conder Green LA2 0BD

☎ 01524 752852 📄 01524 752477

email: thurnham@mitchellshotels.co.uk

www.mitchellshotels.co.uk

Dir: *M6 junct 33 onto A6 towards Galgate, left at lights, 1st left, continue for 2m, hotel on left of bridge.*

Dogs: Bedrooms Public Areas Garden Exercise Area Pet Food/Bowls

This converted cloth mill dates from the 16th century and lies only a few miles from the M6 on the Lancaster Canal. Recently refurbished with spacious bedrooms that include a number of family rooms. Dinner can be enjoyed overlooking the Canal side, or on sunny days on a popular terrace.

Rooms: 15rms en suite (1 fmly)

dble room £70 - £75*

Facilities: TV STV FTV Modem/Fax Lift Licensed Parking 50 Last d order 9pm

MORECAMBE
Clarendon Hotel ★★★ 68% HL

76 Marine Road West West End Promenade LA4 4EP

☎ 01524 410180 📄 01524 421616

email: clarendon@mitchellshotels.co.uk

www.mitchells.co.uk

Dir: *M6 junct 34 follow Morecambe signs. At rdbt with 'The Shrimp' on corner 1st exit to Westgate, follow to seafront. Right at traffic lights, hotel 3rd block along*

Dogs: Bedrooms Exercise Area

This traditional seafront hotel offers modern facilities, and several long serving key staff ensure guests a home-from-home atmosphere. Well maintained throughout, it offers bright, cheerful public areas and ample convenient parking.

Rooms: 29rms en suite (4 fmly)

dble room £70 - £90

Facilities: TV STV Modem/Fax Lift Licensed Parking 22 Last d order 9:30pm

LANCASHIRE

LEICESTERSHIRE

BUCKMINSTER
The Tollemache Arms

★★★★ 71% ◉◉ GA

48 Main Street NG33 5SA

☎ 01476 860007

email: enquiries@thetollemachearms.com

www.thetollemachearms.com

Dir: *Off A1 Colsterworth rdbt onto B676 to Buckminster*

Dogs: Bedrooms Public Areas (except restaurant) Garden Exercise Area (0.25m)
The revamped village inn has a minimalist decor of neutral colours, and strong shades in the pictures, brown leather chairs and crisp white table linen. Its busy restaurant serves high quality food.

Rooms: 5rms en suite (3 fmly)

Facilities: TV Licensed Cen ht Parking 21

LEICESTER FOREST EAST
MOTORWAY SERVICE AREA
Days Inn Leicester Forest East

⌂ BUD

Leicester Forest East Junction 21 M1
LE3 3GB

☎ 0116 239 0534 📠 0116 239 0546

email: leicester.hotel@welcomebreak.co.uk

www.welcomebreak.co.uk

Dir: *on M1 northbound between junct 21 & 21A*

Dogs: Bedrooms (Unattended) Public Areas (dogs only) Exercise Area (within 1m)
This modern building offers accommodation in smart, spacious and well-equipped bedrooms, suitable for families and business travellers, and all with en suite bathrooms. Continental breakfast is available, and other refreshments may be taken at the nearby family restaurant.

Rooms: 92rms en suite (71 fmly)
dble room £45 - £60*

Facilities: TV STV Modem/Fax Lift TVL Parking 100 Last d order 9pm

MELTON MOWBRAY

Sysonby Knoll Hotel ★★★ 75% HL

Asfordby Road LE13 0HP

☎ 01664 563563 📄 01664 410364

email: reception@sysonby.com

www.sysonby.com

Dir: *0.5m from town centre beside A6006*

Dogs: Bedrooms (by arrangement) Public
Areas (except restaurant) Garden Exercise
Area (5 acres on site)

Resident Pets: Stalky (Miniature Dachshund)
This well-established hotel is on the edge of
town and set in attractive gardens. A friendly
and relaxed atmosphere prevails and the
many returning guests have become friends.
Bedrooms, including superior rooms in the
annexe, are generally spacious and
thoughtfully equipped. A choice of lounges,
a cosy bar and a smart a restaurant offer
carefully prepared meals.

Rooms: 30rms en suite (1 fmly) (7 GF)
dble room £75 - £105

Facilities: TV STV Modem/Fax Licensed
Parking 48 Last d order 2pm

CLEETHORPES

Tudor Terrace Guest House

★★★★ 74% GH

11 Bradford Avenue DN35 0BB

☎ 01472 600800 📄 01472 501395

email: tudor.terrace@ntlworld.com

www.tudorterrace.co.uk

Dir: *Off seafront onto Bradford Av*

Dogs: Bedrooms Public Areas (except
dining room) Garden Exercise Area (500yds)
This guest house offers attractive bedrooms
that are thoughtfully designed and furnished
to a high standard. You can relax in the
lounge, or outside on the patio in the well-
maintained garden. Very caring and friendly
service is provided, and the house is non-
smoking except in the garden. Mobility
scooter rental is available.

Rooms: 6rms en suite (1 GF)
dble room £49.50 - £58

Facilities: TV TVL Cen ht Parking 3
Last d order 10pm

LEICESTERSHIRE/LINCOLNSHIRE

LINCOLNSHIRE

GRANTHAM

Best Western Kings Hotel

★★★ 72% HL

North Parade NG31 8AU

☎ 01476 590800 📠 01476 577072

email: kings@bestwestern.co.uk

www.bw-kingshotel.co.uk

Dir: *off A1 at rdbt N end of Grantham onto B1174, follow road for 2m. Hotel on left by bridge*

Dogs: Bedrooms Public Areas (except restaurant) Garden Exercise Area (500yds)
A friendly atmosphere exists within this extended Georgian house. Bedrooms are attractively decorated and furnished. Dining options include the formal Victorian restaurant and the popular Orangery, which also operates as a coffee shop and breakfast room; a lounge bar and a open-plan foyer lounge are also available.

Rooms: 21rms en suite (3 fmly)
dble room £60 - £79*

Facilities: TV STV Modem/Fax Licensed Parking 36 Last d order 8.30pm

LINCOLN

Hillcrest Hotel ★★ 74% HL

15 Lindum Terrace LN2 5RT

☎ 01522 510182 📠 01522 538009

email: reservations@hillcrest-hotel.com

www.hillcrest-hotel.com

Dir: *from A15 Wragby Rd and Lindum Rd, turn into Upper Lindum St at sign. Left at bottom for hotel 200yds on right*

Dogs: Bedrooms Public Areas Garden Exercise Area (100yds) Pet Food/Bowls
The hospitality offered by Jenny Bennett and her team is one of the strengths of this hotel, which sits in a quiet residential location a seven minute walk from the cathedral and shops. Well-equipped bedrooms come in a variety of sizes, and the conservatory/dining room, with views over the park, offers a good range of freshly prepared food. Free wireless internet access for residents.

Rooms: 14rms en suite (6 fmly) (6 GF)
dble room £87 - £97

Facilities: TV Modem/Fax Licensed Parking 8

LINCOLNSHIRE

LINCOLN
Newport Guest House
★★★ 60% GH

26-28 Newport Road LN1 3DF

☎ 01522 528590 🖷 01522 542868

email: info@newportguesthouse.co.uk

www.newportguesthouse.co.uk

Dir: *On A15 400yds N of cathedral*

Dogs: Bedrooms Exercise Area (200yds)
Situated in the quieter upper part of the city
and just a few minutes' walk from the
cathedral, this double fronted terrace house
offers well-equipped and comfortable
bedrooms with Broadband access. The
pleasing public areas include a very
comfortable sitting room and a bright and
attractive breakfast room.

Rooms: 9rms en suite (2 GF)

Facilities: TV Modem/Fax TVL Cen ht
Parking 4

LINCOLN
Jaymar ★★ 52% GA

31 Newland St West LN1 1QQ

☎ 01522 532934 🖷 01522 820182

email: ward.jaymar4@ntlworld.com

www.stayinlincoln.co.uk

Dir: *A46 onto A57 to city, 1st lights left onto
Gresham St, 2nd right, 500yds on left*

Dogs: Bedrooms (Unattended) Public Areas
Garden Exercise Area (50yds) Pet Bowls
food bowl, drinking bowl & mat

Resident Pets: Trixie (Manchester Terrier
cross)

Situated within easy walking distance of the
city, this small, friendly guest house has two
well-equipped bedrooms. A full English
breakfast, with vegetarian options, is served in
the cosy dining room, and an early breakfast
is available on request. Children and pets are
welcome, and you can be collected from the
bus or railway stations if required.

Rooms: 2rms 0 en suite (1 fmly)
dble room £36

Facilities: TV

LINCOLNSHIRE

MARTON
Black Swan Guest House

★★★★ 71% GA

21 High Street Gainsborough DN21 5AH

☎ 01427 718878 📄 01427 718878

email: info@blackswanguesthouse.co.uk

www.blackswanguesthouse.co.uk

Dir: *On A156 in village centre*

Dogs: Bedrooms Garden Exercise Area
(200yds)

Resident Pets: TC & Scooby (cats)
Centrally located in the village, this 18th-
century former coaching inn retains many
original features, and offers good hospitality
and homely bedrooms with modern facilities.
Tasty breakfasts are served in the cosy dining
room and a comfortable lounge with WiFi
internet access is available. Transport to
nearby pubs and restaurants can be provided.

Rooms: 10rms en suite (3 fmly) (4 GF)
dble room £60 - £70*

Facilities: TV Modem/Fax Licensed TVL
Cen ht Parking 10

WOODHALL SPA
Claremont Guest House ★★ 48% GA

9/11 Witham Road LN10 6RW

☎ 01526 352000

www.woodhall-spa-guesthouse-
bedandbreakfast.co.uk

Dir: *On B1191 in centre of Woodhall Spa
close to minirdbt*

Dogs: Bedrooms Public Areas (under
supervision) Garden Exercise Area (50yds)
This large guest house is located close to
the town centre, and has been owned and
run by Mrs Brennan for many years. The
bedrooms are homely, generally quite
spacious, traditionally furnished, and well
equipped. The public areas contain original
features, while breakfast includes home-made
jams.

Rooms: 11rms 5 en suite (5 fmly) (2 GF)

Facilities: TV Parking 5 Last d order 10pm

LONDON NW7

Days Hotel London North

★★★ 68% HL

Welcome Break Service Area NW7 3HU

☎ 020 8906 7000 ▪ 020 8906 7011

email: lgw.hotel@welcomebreak.co.uk

www.welcomebreak.co.uk

Dir: *on M1 between junct 2/4 northbound & southbound*

Dogs: Bedrooms (Unattended) Public Areas (except restaurant or bar area) Garden Exercise Area (adjacent) welcome snack pack on arrival

This modern hotel is the flagship of the Days Inn brand and occupies a prime location on the outskirts of London at London Gateway Services. Bedrooms have a contemporary feel, are spacious and well equipped. Public rooms are airy and include an open plan restaurant, bar/lounge and a range of meeting rooms.

Rooms: 200rms en suite (190 fmly) (80 GF) dble room £49 - £85*

Facilities: TV STV Modem/Fax Lift Licensed TVL Parking 160 Last d order 9pm

LONDON SW3

The Draycott Hotel ★★★★★ 82% TH

26 Cadogan Gardens SW3 2RP

☎ 020 7730 6466 ▪ 020 7730 0236

email: reservations@draycotthotel.com

www.draycotthotel.com

Dir: *From Sloane Sq station towards Peter Jones, keep to left. At Kings Rd. take first right Cadogan Gdns, 2nd right, hotel on left.*

Dogs: Bedrooms (Unattended) Public Areas (except breakfast room) Exercise Area (1m) Pet Food/Bowls.

Enjoying a prime location just yards from Sloane Square, this town house provides an ideal base in one of the most fashionable areas of London. Beautifully appointed bedrooms include a number of very spacious suites. Attractive day rooms, furnished with antique and period pieces, include a choice of lounges, one with access to a lovely garden.

Rooms: 35rms en suite (9 fmly) (2 GF) dble room £180 - £290*

Facilities: TV STV Modem/Fax Lift Licensed

LONDON SW3
The Egerton House Hotel
★★★★★ 85% TH

17 Egerton Terrace Knightsbridge SW3 2BX

☎ 020 7589 2412 📄 020 7584 6540

email: bookings@rchmail.com

www.egertonhousehotel.com

Dir: *Just off Brampton Rd, between Harrods and Victoria & Albert Museum, opposite Brompton Oratory.*

Dogs: Bedrooms Public Areas Pet Food/Bowls

This delightful town house enjoys a prestigious Knightsbridge location, a short walk from Harrods and close to the Victoria & Albert museum. Air-conditioned bedrooms and public rooms of the highest standard, with an exceptional range of facilities include iPods, safes, mini bars and flat screen TVs. Highest levels of personalised service.

Rooms: 29rms en suite (4 fmly) (3 GF) dble room £211.50 - £330*

Facilities: TV STV Modem/Fax Lift Licensed Last d order 10.30pm

LONDON W1
The Chesterfield Mayfair
★★★★ 83% ® HL

35 Charles Street Mayfair W1J 5EB

☎ 020 7491 2622 📄 020 7491 4793

email: bookch@rchmail.com

www.chesterfieldmayfair.com

Dir: *From Hyde Park Corner along Piccadilly, left into Half Moon St. At end left and 1st right into Queens St, then right into Charles St*

Dogs: Bedrooms Garden Exercise Area (3 mins' walk to Berkeley Square) Pet Food/Bowls pet menu available

An atmosphere of exclusivity characterises this stylish Mayfair hotel where attentive service is a highlight. Bedrooms in a variety of contemporary styles, thoughtfully equipped and with marble-clad bathrooms. Bedrooms and public areas are air conditioned.

Rooms: 110rms en suite (7 fmly) dble room £119 - £295*

Facilities: TV STV Modem/Fax Lift Licensed Last d order 11pm

LONDON W1
The Metropolitan

★★★★★ 88% ◉◉◉ HL

Old Park Lane W1K 1LB

☎ 020 7447 1000 🖹 020 7447 1100

email: res.lon@metropolitan.como.bz

www.metropolitan.como.bz

Dir: *on corner of Old Park Ln and Hertford St, within 200yds from Hyde Park corner*

Dogs: Bedrooms (Unattended) Public Areas (restricted) Exercise Area

Overlooking Hyde Park on Park Lane, The Metropolitan is located within easy reach of the fashionable stores of Knightsbridge and Mayfair. The hotel's contemporary style allows freedom and space to relax. Understated luxury is the key here with bedrooms enjoying great natural light. There is also a Shambhala Spa, steam room and fully equipped gym. Nobu offers innovative Japanese cuisine.

Rooms: 150rms en suite (53 fmly) dble room £215 - £3525*

Facilities: TV STV Modem/Fax Lift Licensed Parking 15 Last d order 8pm

KINGSTON UPON THAMES
Chase Lodge Hotel ★★★ 65% GA

10 Park Road Hampton Wick KT1 4AS

☎ 020 8943 1862 🖹 020 8943 9363

email: info@chaselodgehotel.com

www.chaselodgehotel.com

Dir: *A308 onto A310 signed Twickenham, 1st left onto Park Rd*

Dogs: Bedrooms (Unattended) Garden Exercise Area (2 mins' walk) Pet Food/Bowls

Resident Pets: Dibley (Jack Russell)

This delightful guest house is set in a quiet residential area, a short walk from Kingston Bridge. The individually decorated rooms vary in size and are all well-appointed and feature a range of useful extras. An attractive lounge-bar-restaurant is provided where breakfast, snacks and dinner by pre-arrangement are served. On-road parking is available.

Rooms: 11rms en suite (2 fmly) (4 GF) dble room £71 - £145

Facilities: TV STV Modem/Fax Licensed Cen ht

MERSEYSIDE

SOUTHPORT
Whitworth Falls Hotel
★★★★ 73% GA
16 Lathom Road PR9 0JH
☎ 01704 530074
email: whitworthfalls@rapid.co.uk
www.whitworthfallshotel.com
Dir: *A565 N from town centre, over rdbt, 2nd left onto Alexandra Rd, 4th right*
Dogs: Bedrooms Public Areas Exercise Area
Resident Pets: Shelby (King Charles Spaniel), Cleo (Shih Tzu) Sherbert (African Grey parrot), Minnie & Midge (cats)
Located on a mainly residential avenue within easy walking distance of seafront and Lord St shops, this Victorian house provides a range of practical but homely bedrooms. Breakfasts and pre-theatre dinners are served in the attractive dining room. A comfortable sitting room and lounge bar are also available.
Rooms: 12rms en suite (2 fmly) (1 GF) dble room £44 - £56
Facilities: TV Modem/Fax Licensed TVL Cen ht Parking 8

SOUTHPORT
Bay Tree House B & B
★★★★ 77% GA
No1 Irving Street Marine Gate PR9 0HD
☎ 01704 510555 ▤ 01704 510551
email: baytreehouseuk@aol.com
www.baytreehousesouthport.co.uk
Dir: *Off Leicester St*
Dogs: Bedrooms Exercise Area (promenade and park within a few minutes' walk)
Resident Pets: Sam (Jack Russell)
A warm welcome is assured at this immaculately maintained house, located a short walk from promenade and central attractions. Bedrooms are equipped with a wealth of thoughtful extras, and delicious imaginative breakfasts are served in an attractive dining room overlooking the pretty front patio garden.
Rooms: 6rms en suite (2 fmly) dble room £60 - £99
Facilities: TV Cen ht Parking 2

CROMER
Glendale Guest House

★ ★ ★ 61% GH

33 Macdonald Road NR27 9AP

☎ 01263 513278

email: glendalecromer@aol.com

Dir: *A149 coast road from Cromer centre, 4th left*

Dogs: Bedrooms (Unattended) Public Areas (except breakfast room) Garden Exercise Area (2 mins' walk)

Resident Pets: Daisy & Megan (Jack Russells), Jess (Collie/Springer Spaniel)

Victorian property situated in a peaceful side road adjacent to the seafront yet just a short walk from the town centre. Bedrooms are pleasantly decorated, well maintained and equipped with a good range of useful extras. Breakfast is served at individual tables in the smart dining room.

Rooms: 5rms 1 en suite dble room £40 - £58

Facilities: TV Parking 2

CROMER
Cromer House Bed & Breakfast

★ ★ ★ ★ 71% BB

10 Alfred Road NR27 9AN

☎ 01263 510923 📠 01263 510923

email: peterscarbrow@tiscali.co.uk

www.cromerhouse.co.uk

Dogs: Bedrooms Exercise Area (200yds)

Resident Pets: Snoopy (Bearded Collie)

A warm welcome is assured at this friendly guest house situated in a peaceful side road close to the sea front and town centre. Bedrooms are pleasantly decorated and thoughtfully equipped; all rooms either have en suite facilities or private bathrooms. Breakfast is served in the smart dining room and features locally sourced produce.

Rooms: 6rms 3 en suite (1 fmly) dble room £50 - £60*

Facilities: TV Cen ht

NORFOLK

NORFOLK

FAKENHAM

Abbott Farm ★★★ 65% FH

Walsingham Road Binham NR21 0AW

☎ 01328 830519 📄 01328 830519

email: abbot.farm@btinternet.com

www.abbottfarm.co.uk

Dir: *6m NE of Fakenham. From Binham SW onto Walsingham Rd, farm 0.6m on left*

Dogs: Bedrooms Public Areas Garden Exercise Area (10yds) Pet Food/Bowls stainless steel bowls & dried pet food available

Resident Pets: Buster (Retriever/Labrador)

A detached red-brick farmhouse set amidst 150 acres of arable farmland and surrounded by open countryside. The spacious bedrooms are pleasantly decorated and thoughtfully equipped; they include a ground-floor room with a large en suite shower. Breakfast is served in the attractive conservatory, which has superb views of the countryside.

Rooms: 3rms en suite (2 GF)

dble room £48 - £52*

Facilities: TV TVL Cen ht Parking 20

GREAT YARMOUTH

Barnard House ★★★★ 80% BB

2 Barnard Crescent NR30 4DR

☎ 01493 855139 📄 01493 843143

email: enquiries@barnardhouse.com

www.barnardhouse.com

Dir: *0.5m N of town centre. Off A149 onto Barnard Crescent*

Dogs: Bedrooms Public Areas (at other guests' discretion) Garden Exercise Area (20yds) Pet Food/Bowls

Resident Pets: Fergus & Flora (Field Spaniels)

Expect a warm welcome from the caring hosts at this friendly, family-run guest house, set in mature landscaped gardens in a residential area. The smart bedrooms have coordinated fabrics and thoughtful touches. Breakfast is served in the stylish dining room and there is an elegant lounge with plush sofas.

Rooms: 3rms 2 en suite

dble room £50 - £60*

Facilities: TV FTV Modem/Fax TVL Cen ht Parking 3

KING'S LYNN

Maranatha Guest House ★★★ 56%

115/117 Gaywood Road PE30 2PU

☎ 01553 774596 🖷 01553 763747

email: maranathaguesthouse@yahoo.co.uk

www.maranathaguesthouse.tk

Dir: *Signs to College of West Anglia, at junct in front of college onto Gaywood Rd, house opp school*

Dogs: Bedrooms Exercise Area (100yds)

Resident Pets: Goldie (Sheltie), Kim (Border Collie), Speedy (Siamese)

The Victorian house is opposite King Edward School and close to the hospital, and is a short walk from the town centre. The attractively bedrooms are practically equipped, and breakfasts is served in the pleasant lounge-dining room, which also has a pool table.

Rooms: 10rms 6 en suite (2 fmly)

dble room £40 - £60*

Facilities: TV TVL Cen ht Parking 12

Last d order 9.30pm

NORWICH

Stower Grange ★★ 83% ❀ HL

School Road Drayton NR8 6EF

☎ 01603 860210 🖷 01603 860464

email: enquiries@stowergrange.co.uk

www.stowergrange.co.uk

Dir: *Norwich ring road N to Asda supermarket. Take A1067 Fakenham Rd at Drayton village, right at traffic lights along School Rd. Hotel 150yds on right*

Dogs: Bedrooms (Unattended) Public Areas (except restaurant) Garden Exercise Area (800yds) Pet Food/Bowls

Resident Pets: Ellie (Labrador)

Expect a warm welcome at this 17th-century, property situated in a peaceful residential area close to the city centre and airport. The bedrooms are generally spacious, tastefully furnished and equipped with thoughtful touches. Public rooms include a smart open-plan lounge bar and an elegant restaurant.

Rooms: 11rms en suite (1 fmly)

dble room £90 - £150*

Facilities: TV Licensed Parking 40

NORFOLK

NORFOLK

NORWICH

The Larches ★★★ 65% GA

345 Aylsham Road NR3 2RU

☎ 01603 415420 🖹 01603 465340

www.thelarches.com

Dir: *On A140 500yds past ring road, on left adjacent to Lloyds Bank*

Dogs: Bedrooms Garden Exercise Area (50yds)

Modern, detached property situated only a short drive from the city centre and airport. The spacious, well-equipped bedrooms are brightly decorated, pleasantly furnished and have coordinated soft fabrics. Breakfast is served at individual tables in the smart lounge-dining room.

Rooms: 7rms en suite (2 fmly) (1 GF) dble room £45*

Facilities: TV STV TVL Cen ht Parking 10

NORWICH

Edmar Lodge ★★★ 67% GA

64 Earlham Road NR2 3DF

☎ 01603 615599 🖹 01603 495599

email: mail@edmarlodge.co.uk

www.edmarlodge.co.uk

Dir: *Off A47 S bypass onto B1108 Earlham Rd, follow university and hospital signs*

Dogs: Bedrooms Garden Exercise Area (200yds)

Located just a ten minute walk from the city centre, this friendly family-run guest house offers a convenient location and ample private parking. Individually decorated bedrooms are smartly appointed and well equipped. Freshly prepared breakfasts are served within the cosy dining room; a microwave and a refrigerator are also available. Please note that this establishment is strictly non-smoking.

Rooms: 5rms en suite (1 fmly) dble room £40 - £48*

Facilities: TV FTV Modem/Fax Cen ht Parking 6 Last d order 9.30pm

THORNHAM

Lifeboat Inn ★★ 74% ◉ HL

Ship Lane Hunstanton PE36 6LT

☎ 01485 512236 📠 01485 512323

email: reception@lifeboatinn.co.uk

www.lifeboatinn.co.uk

Dir: *follow coast road from Hunstanton A149 for approx 6m and take 1st left after Thornham sign*

Dogs: Bedrooms (Unattended) Public Areas (except restaurant) Garden Exercise Area (100yds) Pet Bowls

This popular 16th-century smugglers' alehouse enjoys superb views across open meadows to Thornham Harbour. The tastefully decorated bedrooms are furnished with pine pieces and have many thoughtful touches. The public rooms have a wealth of character and feature open fireplaces, exposed brickwork and oak beams.

Rooms: 13rms en suite (3 fmly) (1 GF) dble room £96 - £116*

Facilities: TV Licensed Parking 120

WORSTEAD

The Ollands ★★★★ 80%

Swanns Yard North Walsham NR28 9RP

☎ 01692 535150 📠 01692 535150

email: ollands@worstead.freeserve.co.uk

Dir: *Off A149 to village x-rds, off Back St*

Dogs: Bedrooms Public Areas Garden Exercise Area

Resident Pets: Dusty, Mouse, Candy (Lilac Burmese cats), Abbs (Chocolate Burmese cat)

Expect a warm family welcome at this charming detached property in the heart of the picturesque village of Worstead. The well-equipped bedrooms are pleasantly decorated and carefully furnished, and breakfast served in the elegant dining room features local produce.

Rooms: 3rms en suite (1 GF) dble room £52 - £57*

Facilities: TV Cen ht Parking 8

NORFOLK

NORTHAMPTONSHIRE

LAXTON

Spanhoe Lodge ★ ★ ★ ★ 84%

Harringworth Road Near Corby NN17 3AT

☎ 01780 450328 🗎 01780 450328

email: jennie.spanhoe@virgin.net

www.spanhoelodge.co.uk

Dir: *Off A43 to Laxton, through village, Spanhoe Lodge 0.5m on right*

Dogs: Bedrooms Exercise Area (woodlands nearby)

This delightful modern house stands in open countryside and has wonderful gardens. You can expect very caring and friendly service, and well-equipped and pleasantly furnished bedrooms. There is a lovely dining room, lounge, and a fine conservatory. Breakfast is very special here and makes use of fresh local produce.

Rooms: 4rms en suite (3 GF)

dble room £65 - £90*

Facilities: TV Modem/Fax TVL Cen ht

Parking 50 Last d order 9pm

OUNDLE

The Ship Inn ★ ★ ★ 53%

18-20 West Street PE8 4EF

☎ 01832 273918 🗎 01832 270232

email: enquiries@theshipinn-oundle.co.uk

www.theship-oundle.co.uk

Dir: *In town centre*

Dogs: Bedrooms (Unattended) Public Areas (some restrictions apply) Garden Exercise Area (100yds)

Resident Pets: Midnight (cat)

This traditional-style inn is situated in the centre of this historic town. The pleasantly appointed bedrooms are split between three converted buildings to the rear of the property; some of the newer rooms have pine furniture and bright coordinated fabrics. Public rooms include a busy taproom, a lounge bar and a separate dining room.

Rooms: 14rms 11 en suite (1 fmly) (8 GF)

dble room £50 - £60*

Facilities: TV Licensed TVL Cen ht

Parking 70 Last d order 9.30pm

WELLINGBOROUGH

Hotel Ibis Wellingborough ⭧ BUD

Enstone Court NN8 2DR

☎ 01933 228333 📄 01933 228444

email: H3164@accor-hotels.com

www.ibishotel.com

Dir: *at junct of A45 & A509 towards Kettering, SW outskirts of Wellingborough*

Dogs: Bedrooms Public Areas Exercise Area
Modern, budget hotel offering comfortable accommodation in bright and practical bedrooms. Breakfast is self-service and dinner is available in the restaurant.

Rooms: 78rms en suite (20 fmly) (2 GF)

Facilities: TV STV Modem/Fax Lift Licensed TVL Parking 74 Last d order 8.30pm

BAMBURGH

Waren House Hotel ★ ★ ★ 78% CHH

Waren Mill NE70 7EE

☎ 01668 214581 📄 01668 214484

email: enquiries@warenhousehotel.co.uk

www.warenhousehotel.co.uk

Dir: *2m E of A1 turn onto B1342 to Waren Mill, at T-junct turn right, hotel 100yds on right*

Dogs: Bedrooms Garden
Exercise Area (on site)
This delightful Georgian mansion is set in six acres of woodland and offers a welcoming atmosphere and views of the coastline. The individually themed bedrooms and suites include many with large bathrooms. Good, home-cooked food is served in the elegant dining room. A comfortable lounge and library are also available.

Rooms: 13rms en suite (1 GF)
dble room £103 - £137

Facilities: TV Modem/Fax Licensed
Parking 20

NORTHAMPTONSHIRE/NORTHUMBERLAND

NORTHUMBERLAND

BELFORD

Market Cross Guest House

★★★★ 80%

1 Church Street NE70 7LS

☎ 01668 213013

email: details@marketcross.net

www.marketcross.net

Dir: *Off A into village, opp church*

Dogs: Bedrooms Public Areas Exercise Area (200yds)

Resident Pets: Ellie & Sophie (Dalmatians), Sylvie (cat)

Lying in the heart of the village, this Grade II listed building offers delightful, individually styled and thoughtfully equipped bedrooms. Breakfast is a real treat, an extensive and impressive range of delicious cooked dishes using local produce.

Rooms: 3rms en suite (1 fmly)

dble room £65 - £75*

Facilities: TV FTV TVL Cen ht Parking 3

Last d order 8.45pm

CORNHILL-ON-TWEED

Tillmouth Park Country House Hotel ★★★ 83% ◉◉ HL

Berwick-upon-Tweed TD12 4UU

☎ 01890 882255 📄 01890 882540

email: reception@tillmouthpark.force9.co.uk

www.tillmouthpark.com

Dir: *off A1M at East Ord rdbt at Berwick-upon-Tweed. Take A698 to Cornhill and Coldstream. Hotel 9m on left*

Dogs: Bedrooms (Unattended) Public Areas (in bar only) Garden Exercise Area (on site) Pet Food/Bowls on request

Resident Pets: Carter & Teal (Black Labradors)

An imposing mansion with gracious public rooms, including a stunning galleried lounge with a drawing room adjacent. The elegant dining room overlooks the gardens; lunches and early dinners are available in the bistro.

Rooms: 14rms en suite (1 fmly)

dble room £90 - £180

Facilities: TV FTV Modem/Fax Licensed TVL Parking 50 Last d order 9pm

EMBLETON
Dunstanburgh Castle Hotel

★★ 74% HL

Alnwick NE66 3UN

☎ 01665 576111 🖹 01665 576203

email: stay@dunstanburghcastlehotel.co.uk

www.dunstanburghcastlehotel.co.uk

Dir: *from A1, take B1340 to Denwick past*
Rennington & Masons Arms. Take next right
signed Embleton, and into village

Dogs: Bedrooms (Unattended) Garden
Exercise Area (10yds)

Resident Pets: Uncle Bob (dog)

The focal point of the village, this friendly
family-run hotel has a dining room and grill
room offering different menus, plus a cosy bar
and two lounges. In addition to the main
bedrooms, a small courtyard conversion
houses three stunning suites, each with a
lounge and gallery bedroom above.

Rooms: 20rms en suite (4 fmly)
dble room £71 - £107

Facilities: TV Licensed TVL Parking 16

FARNSFIELD
Grange Cottage ◆◆◆ 69%

Main Street Newark-on-Trent NG22 8EA

☎ 01623 882259

email:
bedandbreakfast@grange-cottage.co.uk

www.grange-cottage.co.uk

Dir: *In village opp Plough Inn car park*

Dogs: Bedrooms Public Areas Garden
Exercise Area (1-acre wooded garden) Pet
Food/Bowls dried dog food available

Resident Pets: Ellie (Pointer), Major
(Belgian Shepherd)

Grange Cottage is a charming 18th-century
Georgian building set in 2 acres of delightful
gardens and grounds behind security gates.
The bedrooms are comfortable and homely,
each individually furnished with lots of family
touches. A freshly-cooked breakfast is served
at one large table in the elegant dining room.

Rooms: 5rms 2 en suite (1 GF)

Facilities: TV Cen ht Parking 6

NOTTINGHAMSHIRE

HOLME PIERREPONT

Holme Grange Cottage ★★★ 66% GA

Adbolton Lane Nottingham NG12 2LU

☎ 0115 981 0413 📠 0115 981 0174

email: jean.colinwightman@talk21.com

Dir: *Off A52 SE of Nottingham, opp National Water Sports Centre*

Dogs: Bedrooms Public Areas Garden Exercise Area (adjacent)

Resident Pets: Peggy (Cavalier King Charles Spaniel)

A stone's throw from the National Water Sports Centre, this establishment with its own all-weather tennis court is ideal for the active guest. Indeed, when not providing warm hospitality and freshly cooked breakfasts, the proprietor is usually on the golf course.

Rooms: 3rms 1 en suite (1 fmly) dble room £45 - £60*

Facilities: TV TVL Cen ht Parking 6 Last d order 8pm

MANSFIELD

Portland Hall Hotel ★★ 67% HL

Carr Bank Park Windmill Lane NG18 2AL

☎ 01623 452525 📠 01623 452550

email: enquiries@portlandhallhotel.co.uk

www.portlandhallhotel.co.uk

Dir: *from town centre take A60 to Worksop for 100yds then right at pelican crossing into Nursery St 50yds, left over railway bridge onto Windmill Ln*

Dogs: Bedrooms Public Areas (except restaurant) Garden Exercise Area (50yds)

Resident Pets: Rusty & Molly (Labradors)

A former Georgian mansion, overlooking 15 acres of renovated parklands, the house retains some fine features, with original plasterwork and friezes in the cosy lounge bar and around the domed skylight over the spiral stairs. The popular attractive restaurant offers a flexible choice of carvery or menu options; service is skilled and attentive.

Rooms: 10rms en suite (1 fmly)

Facilities: TV Modem/Fax Licensed TVL Parking 80 Last d order 9pm

NEWARK-ON-TRENT

Willow Tree Inn ★★★ 58% INN

Front Street Barnby-in-the-Willows NG24 2SA

☎ 01636 626613 📠 01636 626060

www.willowtreeinn.co.uk

Dir: *Off A1/A17 3.5m to Newark Golf Course, 300yds to Barnby sign, turn right & inn 1m*

Dogs: Bedrooms (Unattended) Public Areas (bar only) Garden Exercise Area (100yds)

Resident Pets: Lillie (Golden Labrador), Basil (cat)

The Grade II listed Willow Tree dates from the 17th century. Bedrooms of varying styles are in the main building and an adjacent annexe; each room is well equipped. The public areas include an attractive lounge bar where real ales and bar food are served. Alternatively, freshly prepared and imaginative meals are offered in the cosy restaurant.

Rooms: 7rms en suite (4 fmly) (5 GF)

Facilities: TV Licensed Cen ht Parking 50
Last d order 9.45pm

NOTTINGHAM

The Strathdon ★★ 65% HL

Derby Road City Centre NG1 5FT

☎ 0115 941 8501 📠 0115 948 3725

email:
info@strathdon-hotel-nottingham.com

www.strathdon-hotel-nottingham.com

Dir: *follow city centre signs. Enter one-way system into Wollaton Street, keep right and next right to hotel*

Dogs: Bedrooms Public Areas (except dining room & bar)

This city-centre hotel has modern facilities and is very convenient for all city attractions. A popular themed bar includes large-screen TV and serves an extensive range of popular fresh food, while more formal dining is available in Bobbins Restaurant on certain evenings.

Rooms: 68rms en suite (4 fmly)
dble room £69 - £105*

Facilities: TV STV Modem/Fax Lift
Licensed Last d order 10.45pm

NOTTINGHAM

The Nottingham Gateway Hotel

★★★ 68% HL

Nuthall Road Cinderhill NG8 6AZ

☎ 0115 979 4949 📄 0115 979 4744

email: sales@nottinghamgatewayhotel.co.uk

www.nottinghamgatewayhotel.co.uk

Dir: *M1 junct 26, A610, hotel on*
3rd rdbt on left

Dogs: Bedrooms (Unattended) Exercise Area
(100yds)

Located approximately three miles from the
city centre, with easy access to the M1. This
modern hotel provides spacious public areas,
with popular restaurant and lounge bar, and
the contemporary accommodation is suitably
well equipped. Ample car parking is a bonus.

Rooms: 108rms en suite (18 fmly)

dble room £50 - £90*

Facilities: TV Lift Licensed TVL
Parking 250 Last d order 9.15pm

BANBURY

**Best Western Wroxton House
Hotel** ★★★ 70% HL

Wroxton St Mary OX15 6QB

☎ 01295 730777 📄 01295 730800

email:
reservations@wroxtonhousehotel.com

www.wroxtonhousehotel.com

Dir: *A422 from Banbury, 2.5m to Wroxton,*
hotel on right entering village

Dogs: Bedrooms (Unattended) Public Areas
(except restaurant) Garden Exercise Area
(20yds)

Dating in parts from 1647, this partially
thatched hotel is set just off the main road.
Comfortable, well equipped bedrooms have
either been created out of converted cottages
or are situated in a more modern wing. There
is an open plan reception lounge and bar; the
restaurant has a peaceful atmosphere.

Rooms: 32rms en suite (1 fmly) (7 GF)

dble room £85 - £150

Facilities: TV STV Modem/Fax Licensed
TVL Parking 50 Last d order 9.30pm

BURFORD

The Lamb ★★★ 78% ◎◎ HL

Sheep St OX18 4LR

☎ 01993 823155 📠 01993 822228

email: info@lambinn-burford.co.uk

www.cotswold-inns-hotels.co.uk

Dir: *Turn off A40 into Burford, downhill, take 1st left into Sheep St, hotel last on right*

Dogs: Bedrooms (Unattended - 3 ground floor rooms only) Public Areas (except restaurant) Exercise Area (adjacent)

This enchanting old inn is just a short walk from the centre of a delightful Cotswold village. An abundance of character and charm is found inside with a cosy lounge and log fire, and in intimate bar with flagged floors. An elegant restaurant is on offer where locally sourced produce is carefully prepared. Bedrooms, some with original features are comfortable and well appointed.

Rooms: 15rms en suite (1 fmly) (3 GF) dble room £145 - £235*

Facilities: TV Licensed Last d order 9pm

KINGHAM

The Mill House Hotel & Restaurant

★★★ 79% ◎◎ HL

OX7 6UH

☎ 01608 658188 📠 01608 658492

email: stay@millhousehotel.co.uk

www.millhousehotel.co.uk

Dir: *off A44 onto B4450. Hotel indicated by tourist sign*

Dogs: Bedrooms (Unattended) Garden Exercise Area (10-acre grounds) Pet Food/Bowls

Resident Pets: Ben (Labrador)

This Cotswold-stone, former mill house has been carefully converted into a comfortable and attractive hotel. It is set in well-kept grounds bordered by its own trout stream. Bedrooms are comfortable and well equipped. There is a peaceful lounge and bar, plus a restaurant - the imaginative dishes are a highlight of any stay.

Rooms: 23rms en suite (1 fmly) (7 GF) dble room £180 - £200

Facilities: TV STV Licensed Parking 62 Last d order 9pm / 9.30pm Fri/Sat

OXFORDSHIRE

KINGHAM
The Tollgate Inn & Restaurant

★★★★ 77% INN

Church Street OX7 6YA

☎ 01608 658389

email: info@thetollgate.com

www.thetollgate.com

Dogs: Bedrooms (Unattended) Garden
Exercise Area (5 mins' walk)

Resident Pets: Guinness (Labrador)

Situated in the idyllic Cotswold village of
Kingham this Grade II listed Georgian
building has been lovingly restored to provide
a complete home-from-home among some of
the most beautiful and historic countryside in
Britain. It provides comfortable, well equipped
accommodation in pleasant surroundings. A
good choice of menu for lunch and dinner is
available with good use made of fresh and
local produce. A hearty breakfast is provided
in the modern, well equipped dining room.

Rooms: 9rms en suite (1 fmly) (4 GF)
dble room £80 - £100*

Facilities: TV Licensed Cen ht Parking 12

OXFORD
Days Inn Oxford ⬆ BUD

M40 junction 8A Waterstock OX33 1LJ

☎ 01865 877000 📠 01865 877016

email: oxford.hotel@welcomebreak.co.uk

www.welcomebreak.co.uk

Dir: *M40 junct 8a, Welcome Break service
area.*

Dogs: Bedrooms (Unattended) Public Areas
(must be kept on lead) Garden Exercise Area
(adjacent) welcome snack pack on arrival

This modern building offers accommodation
in smart, spacious and well-equipped
bedrooms, suitable for families and business
travellers, and all with en suite bathrooms.
Continental breakfast is available and other
refreshments may be taken at the nearby
family restaurant.

Rooms: 59rms en suite (56 fmly)
dble room £54 - £60*

Facilities: TV STV Parking 100

Last d order 9.30pm

UPPINGHAM

Falcon Hotel ★ ★ ★ 66% HL

The Market Place LE15 9PY

☎ 01572 823535 📄 01572 821620

email: sales@thefalconhotel.com

www.thefalconhotel.com

Dir: *A47 onto A6003, left at lights, hotel on right*

Dogs: Bedrooms (Unattended) Public Areas (dogs must be on leads) Garden Exercise Area Pet Food/Bowls bowls available, food on request

An attractive, 16th-century coaching inn situated in the heart of this bustling market town. Public areas feature an open-plan lounge bar, with a relaxing atmosphere and comfortable sofas. The brasserie area offers a cosmopolitan-style snack menu, while more formal meals are provided in the Garden Terrace Restaurant.

Rooms: 25rms en suite (4 fmly) (3 GF) dble room £95 - £130

Facilities: TV FTV Modem/Fax Licensed TVL Parking 33

BRIDGNORTH

Oldfield Cottage ★ ★ ★ 76% BB

Oldfield WV16 6AQ

☎ 01746 789257 📄 01746 789257

email: oldfieldcottage@aol.com

www.stmem.com/oldfieldcottage

Dir: *B4364 from Bridgnorth, after 3m pass Down Inn, 2nd left signed Oldfield, 0.25m on right*

Dogs: Bedrooms Public Areas (must be under restraint) Garden Exercise Area (100yds, good walks)

Resident Pets: Pem & Dinah (Springer Spaniels)

Located in the hamlet of Oldfield and set in mature gardens, this traditional cottage provides homely bedrooms in converted outbuildings. Memorable breakfasts, using quality local or home-made produce, are served in the conservatory.

Rooms: 2rms en suite (2 GF) dble room £55*

Facilities: TV TVL Cen ht Parking 3 Last d order 9pm

RUTLAND/SHROPSHIRE

SHROPSHIRE

CHURCH STRETTON

Stretton Hall Hotel ★ ★ ★ 70% ● HL

All Stretton SY6 6HG

☎ 01694 723224 & 0845 1668404

🖹 01694 724365

email: aa@strettonhall.co.uk

www.strettonhall.co.uk

Dir: *from Shrewsbury, on A49, right onto B4370 signed All Stretton. Hotel 1m on left opposite The Yew Tree pub*

Dogs: Bedrooms (Unattended) Public Areas (except restaurant) Garden Exercise Area
This fine 18th-century country house stands in spacious gardens. Original oak panelling features throughout the lounge bar, lounge and halls. Bedrooms are traditionally furnished and have modern facilities. Family and four-poster rooms are available and the restaurant has been tastefully refurbished.

Rooms: 12rms en suite (1 fmly)

dble room £85 - £130

Facilities: TV Modem/Fax Licensed Parking 70

CLEOBURY MORTIMER

The Old Bake House ★ ★ ★ ★ 76%

46-47 High Street Kidderminster DY14 8DQ

☎ 01299 270193

Dir: *On A4117 in village 100yds from church*

Dogs: Bedrooms Public Areas (with advance warning) Garden Exercise Area (250yds) Pet Food/Bowls

Resident Pets: Holly (Bearded Collie cross)
A conversion of two 18th-century houses, a village inn and a bakery has resulted in a homely and carefully furnished guest house providing bedrooms filled with a wealth of thoughtful extras. Spacious ground-floor areas include comfortable sitting rooms and a dining section, the setting for memorable breakfasts.

Rooms: 3rms 2 en suite

dble room £50 - £56* .

Facilities: TVL Cen ht Parking 2

KNOCKIN

Top Farm House ★ ★ ★ 76% GH

SY10 8HN

☎ 01691 682582 🖹 01691 682070

email: p.a.m@knockin.freeserve.co.uk

www.topfarmknockin.co.uk

Dir: *In Knockin, past Bradford Arms & shop, past turning for Kinnerley*

Dogs: Bedrooms Public Areas (except dining room) Garden

This impressive half-timbered Tudor house, set amid pretty gardens, retains many original features including a wealth of exposed beams and open fires. Bedrooms are equipped with many thoughtful extras, and the open-plan ground-floor area includes a comfortable sitting room and elegant dining section, where imaginative comprehensive breakfasts are served.

Rooms: 3rms en suite (1 fmly)

dble room £60 - £70*

Facilities: TV Modem/Fax TVL Cen ht

Parking 6 Last d order 9pm

LUDLOW

The Church Inn ★ ★ ★ 71% INN

The Buttercross SY8 1AW

☎ 01584 872174 🖹 01584 877146

www.thechurchinn.com

Dir: *In town centre at top of Broad St*

Dogs: Bedrooms (Unattended) Public Areas

Set right in the heart of the historic town, this Grade II listed inn has been renovated to provide quality accommodation with smart modern bathrooms, some with spa baths. Other areas include a small lounge, a well-equipped meeting room, and cosy bar areas where imaginative food and real ales are served.

Rooms: 9rms en suite (3 fmly)

dble room £60 - £80*

Facilities: TV Licensed TVL Cen ht

SHROPSHIRE

SHROPSHIRE

LUDLOW
Bromley Court B & B

★ ★ ★ ★ ★ 88% BB

73 Lower Broad Street SY8 1PH

☎ 01584 876996 & 0854 065 6192

email: phil@ludlowhotels.com

www.ludlowhotels.com

Dir: *Off B4361 at bridge into town centre*

Dogs: Bedrooms Garden Exercise Area
(200yds to common & river) Pet Food/Bowls

Resident Pets: Indie (Chocolate Labrador)

Located close to the river and attractions of this historic town, this award-winning renovation of Georgian cottages provides split-level suites. All have comfortable sitting areas and kitchenettes, and the carefully furnished bedrooms are filled with thoughtful extras. A peaceful patio garden is available, and wholesome breakfasts are served in a cottage-style dining room in a separate house.

Rooms: 3rms en suite dble room £95 - £120

Facilities: TV Modem/Fax TVL Cen ht

MUCH WENLOCK
Yew Tree Farm ★ ★ ★ ★ 74% FH

Longville In The Dale TF13 6EB

☎ 01694 771866 📠 01694 771867

email: hilbery@tiscali.co.uk

www.ytfarm.co.uk

Dir: *N off B4371 at Longville, left at pub, right at x-rds, farm 1.2m on right*

Dogs: Bedrooms Garden Exercise Area
(surrounding countryside) Pet Food/Bowls

Resident Pets: Inyanga, Saffie & Tuli (Norfolk Terriers), sheep, chickens

Peacefully located between Much Wenlock and Church Stretton on ten acres of unspoiled countryside, where rare breed pigs, sheep and chickens are reared and own produce is a feature on the comprehensive breakfast menu. Bedrooms are equipped with thoughtful extras and a warm welcome is assured.

Rooms: 2rms 1 en suite dble room £50 - £60*

Facilities: TV TVL Cen ht Parking 4

Last d order 8.30pm

OSWESTRY
Best Western Wynnstay Hotel
★★★ 85% ◉◉ HL
Church Street SY11 2SZ
☎ 01691 655261 📄 01691 670606
email: info@wynnstayhotel.com
www.wynnstayhotel.com
Dir: *B4083 to town, fork left at Honda Garage and right at traffic lights. Hotel opposite church*
Dogs: Bedrooms (Unattended) Public Areas (assist dogs only) Garden Exercise Area (30yds)
This Georgian property, once a coaching inn and posting house, surrounds a 200-year-old Crown Bowling Green. There is a health, leisure and beauty centre. Well-equipped bedrooms include several suites, four-poster rooms and a self-catering apartment. The restaurant has a well-deserved reputation, and there is a less formal bar meal operation.
Rooms: 29 en suite (4 fmly)
dble room £100 - £135
Facilities: TV STV Modem/Fax Licensed Parking 70 Last d 9.30pm ☜

OSWESTRY
Pen-y-Dyffryn Hotel
★★★ 77% ◉◉ HL
Rhydycroesau SY10 7JD
☎ 01691 653700 📄 01978 211004
email: stay@peny.co.uk
www.peny.co.uk
Dir: *from A5 into Oswestry town centre. Follow signs to Llansilin on B4580, hotel 3m W of Oswestry before Rhydycroesau village*
Dogs: Bedrooms (Unattended) Public Areas (not after 6pm) Garden Exercise Area (on site) Pet Food/Bowls excellent dog walks
Peacefully situated in five acres of grounds, this charming old former rectory dates back to around 1840. Public rooms have real fires in cold weather, and the accommodation includes several mini-cottages, each with its own patio. This hotel attracts many guests for its food and attentive, friendly service.
Rooms: 12rms en suite (1 fmly) (1 GF)
dble room £114 - £152*
Facilities: TV STV FTV Modem/Fax Licensed Parking 18

SHROPSHIRE

SHROPSHIRE/SOMERSET

TELFORD

Days Inn Telford ⌂ BUD

Telford Services Priorslee Road TF11 8TG

☎ 01952 238400 🖹 01952 238410

email: telford.hotel@welcomebreak.co.uk

www.welcomebreak.co.uk

Dir: *M54 junct 4*

Dogs: Bedrooms Public Areas (must be kept on lead) Garden Exercise Area (adjacent)

This modern building offers accommodation in smart, spacious and well-equipped bedrooms, suitable for families and business travellers, and all with en suite bathrooms. Continental breakfast is available, and other refreshments may be taken at the nearby family restaurant.

Rooms: 48rms en suite (45 fmly) (21 GF) dble room £39 - £60*

Facilities: TV STV Modem/Fax Parking 50

CREWKERNE

Manor Farm ★★★★ 69% GA

Wayford TA18 8QL

☎ 01460 78865 & 0776 7620031

🖹 01460 78865

www.manorfarm.biz

Dir: *B3165 from Crewkerne to Lyme Regis, 3m in Clapton right onto Dunsham Ln, Manor Farm 0.5m up hill on right*

Dogs: Sep Accom (kennels) Public Areas Garden Exercise Area (in grounds) Pet Food/Bowls

Resident Pets: Charlie & Ginger (cats)

Located off the beaten track, this fine Victorian country house has extensive views over Clapton towards the Axe Valley. The comfortably furnished bedrooms are well equipped; front-facing rooms enjoy splendid views. Breakfast is served at separate tables in the dining room, and a spacious lounge is also provided.

Rooms: 5rms 5 en suite dble room £60 - £70

Facilities: TV STV TVL Cen ht Parking 14

Last d order 9pm

DULVERTON

Lion Hotel ★ ★ 64% HL

Bank Square TA22 9BU

☎ 01398 323444 🖷 01398 323980

email: jeffeveritt@tiscali.co.uk

Dir: *from A361 at Tiverton rdbt onto A396. Left at Exbridge onto B3223. Over bridge in Dulverton, hotel in Bank Square*

Dogs: Bedrooms (Unattended) Public Areas (except dining room) Exercise Area (walks nearby)

Resident Pets: George (Black Labrador) Old-fashioned hospitality is always evident at this charming, traditional inn in the centre of Dulverton, an ideal base from which to explore Exmoor National Park. The bar is popular with locals and visitors alike, offering a variety of local real ales and quality meals. A pleasant dining room provides a quieter, non-smoking option.

Rooms: 13rms en suite (2 fmly)

dble room £74 - £78*

Facilities: TV Licensed TVL Parking 6

DULVERTON

Threadneedle ★ ★ ★ ★ 75% GA

Tiverton EX16 9JH

☎ 01398 341598

email: info@threadneedlecottage.co.uk

www.threadneedlecottage.co.uk

Dir: *On Devon/Somerset border just off B3227 between Oldways End & East Anstey*

Dogs: Bedrooms Sep Accom (kennel) Public Areas (must be on lead, by arrangement) Garden Exercise Area (50yds. Walks/rides on Exmoor)

Resident Pets: Scamp & Charlie (Shetland Sheepdogs), Jack & Jester (horses) Situated on the edge of Exmoor near Dulverton, Threadneedle is built in the style of a Devon longhouse. The well-appointed family home offers comfortable, en suite accommodation. Traditional West Country dishes are served, by arrangement.

Rooms: 2rms en suite (1 fmly)

dble room £64 - £69

Facilities: TV Cen ht Parking 12

Last d order 8.45pm

SOMERSET

SOMERSET

HIGHBRIDGE

Sundowner Hotel ★★ 68% HL

74 Main Road West Huntspill TA9 3QU

☎ 01278 784766 📄 01278 794133

email: runnalls@msn.com

www.smoothhound.co.uk/hotels/sundowner

Dir: *from M5 junct 23, 3m N on A38*

Dogs: Bedrooms Public Areas (except
restaurant) Garden Exercise Area (bridle path
at end of car park)

Friendly service and an informal atmosphere
are just two of the highlights of this small
hotel. The open-plan lounge/bar is a
comfortable, homely area in which to relax
after a busy day exploring the area or working
in the locality. An extensive menu, featuring
freshly cooked, imaginative dishes, is offered
in the popular restaurant.

Rooms: 8rms en suite (1 fmly)

Facilities: TV Licensed TVL Parking 18
Last d order 9.30pm

ILMINSTER

Best Western Shrubbery Hotel

★★★ 77% HL

TA19 9AR

☎ 01460 52108 📄 01460 53660

email: stuart@shrubberyhotel.com

www.shrubberyhotel.com

Dir: *0.5m from A303 towards Ilminster.*

Dogs: Bedrooms (Unattended) Public Areas
(except restaurant) Garden Exercise Area
Pet Food/Bowls food by prior arrangement -
chargeable

Set in attractive terraced gardens, the
Shrubbery is a well established hotel.
Bedrooms are well equipped and bright, they
include three ground-floor rooms and new
executive rooms. Bar meals or full meals are
available in the bar, lounges and restaurant.
There is a range of function rooms.

Rooms: 21rms en suite (3 fmly)

dble room £120 - £130*

Facilities: TV STV FTV Modem/Fax
Licensed TVL Parking 100

NETHER STOWEY
Castle Comfort Country House

★ ★ ★ ★ ★ 85% GA

Bridgwater TA5 1LE

☎ 01278 741264 📄 01278 741144

email: reception@castle-of-comfort.co.uk

www.castle-of-comfort.co.uk

Dir: *On A39 1.3m W of Nether Stowey on left*

Dogs: Bedrooms (Unattended) Sep Accom
(kennel) Public Areas (except lounge &
restaurant) Garden Exercise Area (on site)

Resident Pets: Humbug & Treacle (cats)

Dating in part from the 16th century, this
former inn is set on the northern slopes of the
Quantock Hills in an Area of Outstanding
Natural Beauty. Bedrooms and bathrooms are
well equipped; public rooms are smart and
comfortable. Delightful gardens and a heated
swimming pool are available in summer. An
imaginative choice of dishes at dinner.

Rooms: 6rms en suite (1 fmly) (1 GF)
dble room £95 - £129*

Facilities: TV Licensed Cen ht Parking 10

PORLOCK
Andrews on the Weir

★ ★ ★ ★ 77% ◉◉◉ RR

Porlock Weir TA24 8PB

☎ 01643 863300 📄 01643 863311

email: information@andrewsontheweir.co.uk

www.andrewsontheweir.co.uk

Dir: *A39 from Minehead to Porlock, through
village, 1st right signed Harbour Porlock Weir
1.5m*

Dogs: Bedrooms (Unattended) Exercise Area
(100 yards)

Resident Pets: Narla (black Labrador)

Enjoying a delightful elevated position
overlooking Porlock Bay, Andrews on the Weir
is furnished in country house style. Bedrooms
are spacious,and one has a four-poster bed.
The sitting room/bar is elegant. A highlight
is the choice of imaginative and innovative
dishes available in the restaurant.

Rooms: 5rms en suite
dble room £100 - £180*

Facilities: TV Licensed Parking 6
Last d order 9.30pm

SOMERSET

SOMERSET

RUDGE
The Full Moon Inn

★ ★ ★ ★ 69% INN

BA11 2QF

☎ 01373 830936 📠 01373 831366

email: info@thefullmoon.co.uk

web: ww.thefullmoon.co.uk

Dir: *Off A36 into village centre*

Dogs: Bedrooms (Unattended) Garden
Exercise Area (0.5m)

Resident Pets: Jazz (dog)

This quaint village inn is very popular for its
extensive range of food. Most of the modern,
well-equipped accommodation is on the
ground and first floors of two purpose-built
annexes, each having its own lounge for guest
use; two rooms have easier access. Other
rooms are located in the main house.
Facilities include a swimming pool, a function
room and skittle alley.

Rooms: 16rms en suite (2 fmly) (4 GF)
dble room £74.50*

Facilities: TV STV Licensed TVL Cen ht
Parking 50 🏊

SEDGEMOOR MOTORWAY SERVICE AREA
Days Inn Sedgemoor ⌂ BUD

M5 Northbound J22-21 Sedgemoor BS24 0JL

☎ 01934 750831 📠 01934 750808

email:
sedgemoor.hotel@welcomebreak.co.uk

www.welcomebreak.co.uk

Dir: *M5 junct 21/22*

Dogs: Bedrooms Public Areas Garden
Exercise Area (adjacent)

This modern building offers accommodation
in smart, spacious and well-equipped
bedrooms, suitable for families and business
travellers, and all with en suite bathrooms.
Continental breakfast is available and other
refreshments may be taken at the nearby
family restaurant.

Rooms: 40rms en suite (39 fmly) (19 GF)
dble room £45 - £55*

Facilities: TV STV Parking 40

SOMERTON

Stowford House ★★★★ 70% BB

Charlton Adam TA11 7AT

☎ 01458 223717 ▤ 01458 223940

email: harperr@totalise.co.uk

Dir: *Off A37 into Charlton Adam, house in village centre*

Dogs: Bedrooms Public Areas Garden Exercise Area (500yds)

Stowford House is a delightful conversion of a Victorian Methodist chapel and the village school. Centrally situated in peaceful Charlton Adam, it offers charming accommodation and a friendly atmosphere. Bedrooms are cosy and equipped with modern facilities, and the public rooms retain many stunning original features.

Rooms: 2rms en suite (1 GF)

Facilities: TV Cen ht Parking 2

STANTON DREW

Greenlands ★★★★ 68% FH

Bristol BS39 4ES

☎ 01275 333487 ▤ 01275 331211

Dir: *A37 onto B3130, on right before Stanton Drew Garage*

Dogs: Bedrooms (Unattended) Public Areas Garden Exercise Area (in adjoining field)

Resident Pets: Spoof (Labrador)

Situated near the ancient village of Stanton Drew in the heart of the Chew Valley, Greenlands is convenient for Bristol Airport and Bath, Bristol and Wells. There are comfortable, well-equipped bedrooms and a downstairs lounge, though breakfast is the highlight of any stay here.

Rooms: 4rms en suite

Facilities: TV STV TVL Cen ht Parking 8

SOMERSET

SOMERSET

TAUNTON

Blorenge House ★★★ 67% GA

57 Staple Grove Road TA1 1DG

☎ 01823 283005 📄 01823 283005

email: enquiries@blorengehouse.co.uk

www.blorengehouse.co.uk

Dir: *M5 junct 25, towards cricket ground &
Morrisons on left, left at lights, right at 2nd
lights, house 150yds on left*

Dogs: Bedrooms Public Areas (except
dining rooms) Garden Exercise Area
(150yds) Pet Food/Bowls

This fine Victorian property offers spacious
accommodation within walking distance of the
town centre. The bedrooms (some at ground
floor level and some with four- poster beds)
are individually furnished and vary in size.
A lounge is available and the garden and
outdoor swimming pool are open to guests
during daytime hours most days of the week.

Rooms: 25rms 20 en suite (4 fmly) (3 GF)
dble room £58*

Facilities: TV TVL Cen ht Parking 25
Last d order 8.30pm ☜

TAUNTON

The Hatch Inn ★★★★ 71% INN

Village Road Hatch Beauchamp TA3 6SG

☎ 01823 480245 📄 01823 481104

email: bagleyjag@aol.com

Dir: *6m SE of Taunton. Off A358 into Hatch
Beauchamp*

Dogs: Bedrooms Public Areas Garden
Exercise Area

This village inn caters well for locals and
leisure or business guests. The majority of
bedrooms are particularly spacious and come
with a number of useful extras. Relaxed and
friendly service continues through dinner and
breakfast, which use a good selection of
carefully prepared ingredients.

Rooms: 7rms en suite (1 fmly)
dble room £65 - £80*

Facilities: TV Licensed Cen ht Parking 15
Last d order 9pm

WELLINGTON

Bindon Country House Hotel & Restaurant ★★★ 85% ⚜⚜ CHH

Langford Budville TA21 0RU

☎ 01823 400070 📄 01823 400071

email: stay@bindon.com

www.bindon.com

Dir: *from Wellington B3187 to Langford Budville, through village, right towards Wiveliscombe, right at junct, pass Bindon Farm, right after 450yds*

Dogs: Bedrooms (Unattended) Garden Exercise Area (5 mins' walk to 220-acre nature reserve) Pet Food/Bowls Dog mobile bath hire possible

Resident Pets: Ziggy & Indie (Schnauzers) This tranquil country-house hotel, which is mentioned in the Domesday Book, is set in woodland gardens. Sumptuous bedrooms, stylish public rooms and impressive cuisine.

Rooms: 12rms en suite (2 fmly) (1 GF) dble room £115 - £215*

Facilities: TV FTV Licensed TVL Parking 30 Last d order 9.30pm ♨

WELLS

The Crown at Wells ★★ 75% HL

Market Place Somerset BA5 2RP

☎ 01749 673457 📄 01749 679792

email: stay@crownatwells.co.uk

www.crownatwells.co.uk

Dir: *on entering Wells follow signs for Hotels/Deliveries. Hotel in Market Place*

Dogs: Bedrooms

Exercise Area (5 mins' walk)

Retaining its original features and period charm, this historic old inn is situated in the heart of the city, just a short stroll from the cathedral. The building's frontage has even been used for film sets. Bedrooms, all with modern facilities, vary in size and style. Public areas focus around Anton's, the popular bistro, which offers a relaxed atmosphere. The Penn Bar offers an alternative eating option and real ales.

Rooms: 15rms en suite (2 fmly) dble room £70 - £110*

Facilities: TV Licensed Parking 15 Last d order 10pm

SOMERSET

SOMERSET

WELLS

Ancient Gate House Hotel

★★ 67% HL

20 Sadler Street BA5 2SE

☎ 01749 672029 ▤ 01749 670319

email: info@ancientgatehouse.co.uk

www.ancientgatehouse.co.uk

Dir: *1st hotel on left on Cathedral Green*

Dogs: Bedrooms Public Areas (except restaurant) Garden Exercise Area (10yds)
Guests are treated to good old-fashioned hospitality in a friendly informal atmosphere at this charming hotel. Bedrooms, many of which boast unrivalled cathedral views and four-poster beds, are well equipped and furnished in keeping with the age and character of the building. The hotel's Rugantino Restaurant remains popular, offering typically Italian specialities and traditional English dishes.

Rooms: 8rms en suite dble room £91*

Facilities: TV Modem/Fax Licensed
Last d order 9.30pm

WELLS

White Hart Hotel ★★ 76% HL

Sadler Street BA5 2EH

☎ 01749 672056 ▤ 01749 671074

email: info@whitehart-wells.co.uk

www.whitchart-wells.co.uk

Dir: *Sadler St at start of one-way system. Hotel opposite cathedral*

Dogs: Bedrooms (Unattended) Exercise Area (fields nearby)
A former coaching inn dating back to the 15th century, this hotel offers comfortable, modern accommodation. Some bedrooms are in an adjoining former stable block and some are at ground floor level. Public areas include a guest lounge, a popular restaurant and bar. The restaurant serves a good choice of fish, meat, vegetarian dishes and daily specials.

Rooms: 15rms en suite (3 fmly) (2 GF)
dble room £99 - £110*

Facilities: TV Modem/Fax Licensed
Parking 17

WELLS

Infield House ★★★★ 71% BB

36 Portway BA5 2BN

☎ 01749 670989 🖷 01749 679093

email: infield@talk21.com

www.infieldhouse.co.uk

Dir: *500yds W of city centre on A371 Portway*

Dogs: Bedrooms Garden Exercise Area (0.5m) Pet Food/Bowls food with prior notice

Resident Pets: Pepper (Pembroke Corgi)

This charming Victorian house offers comfortable, spacious rooms of elegance and style. The friendly hosts are very welcoming and provide a relaxing home from home. Guests may bring their pets, by arrangement. Dinners, also by arrangement, are served in the pleasant dining room where good home cooking ensures an enjoyable and varied range of options.

Rooms: 3rms en suite dble room £52 - £56

Facilities: TV TVL Cen ht Parking 3

Last d order 9.30pm

WELLS

Coxley Vineyard Hotel ★★ 72% HL

Coxley BA5 1RQ

☎ 01749 670285 🖷 01749 679708

email: max@orofino.freeserve.co.uk

www.coxleyvineyard.com

Dir: *A39 from Wells signed Coxley. Village halfway between Wells & Glastonbury. Hotel off main road at end of village.*

Dogs: Bedrooms Public Areas (bar but not restaurant) Garden Exercise Area (surrounding countryside) Pet Food/Bowls

This privately owned hotel was built on the site of an old cider farm. It was later part of a commercial vineyard and some of the vines are still in evidence. It provides modern, well equipped bedrooms; most are situated on the ground floor. There is a comfortable bar and a spacious restaurant with an impressive lantern ceiling. The hotel is a popular venue for conferences and other functions.

Rooms: 9rms en suite (5 fmly) (8 GF) dble room £75 - £89.50

Facilities: TV Licensed Parking 50 ☜

SOMERSET

SOMERSET

WELLS

Birdwood House ★★★ 56% GA

Birdwood Bath Road BA5 3EW

☎ 01749 679250

email: info@birdwood-bandb.co.uk

www.birdwood-bandb.co.uk

Dir: *From town centre follow signs on one-way system to the Horringtons, onto B3139, last house 1.5m on left near double-bend sign*

Dogs: Bedrooms Sep Accom (kennel) Public Areas (must be on a lead) Garden Exercise Area Pet Food/Bowls

Resident Pets: Florrie (Springer Spaniel), Daisy (cat), cows, peahen

Set in extensive grounds and gardens just a short drive from the town centre, this imposing house dates from the 1850s. The bedrooms are comfortable and equipped with a number of extra facilities. Breakfast is served around a communal table in the pleasant dining room or conservatory, which is available for guest use throughout the day.

Rooms: 4rms 2 en suite (1 fmly)

Facilities: TV TVL Cen ht Parking 12

WESTON-SUPER-MARE

Camellia Lodge ★★★★ 71% BB

76 Walliscote Road BS23 1ED

☎ 01934 613534 📠 01934 613534

email: dachefscamellia@aol.com

www.camellialodge.co.uk

Dir: *200yds from seafront*

Dogs: Bedrooms (Unattended) Public Areas (except food areas) Exercise Area (200yds)

Resident Pets: Jack (dog), Rosie & Riley (cats)

Guests return regularly for the warm welcome they receive at this immaculate Victorian family home, which is just off the seafront and within walking distance of the town centre. Bedrooms have a range of thoughtful touches, and carefully prepared breakfasts are served in the relaxing dining room. Home cooked dinners are also available by prior arrangement.

Rooms: 5rms en suite (2 fmly) dble room £55 - £60

Facilities: TV Cen ht Last d order 9pm

WESTON-SUPER-MARE

Rookery Manor ★★★★ 73% GA

Edingworth Road Edingworth
WESTON-SUPER-MARE BS24 0JB

☎ 01934 750200 🗎 01934 750014

email: enquiries@rookery-manor.co.uk

www.rookery-manor.co.uk

Dir: *M5 junct 22, A370 towards Weston, 2m right to Rookery Manor*

Dogs: Bedrooms Public Areas Garden
Exercise Area Pet Food/Bowls request in
advance

Situated in its own delightful gardens and
grounds within easy reach of Junction 22 of
the M5, this 16th century manor house is
best known for its wedding and conference
facilities. Bedrooms, each with its own access
from the garden, are modern and bright. A
range of a la carte dishes is offered in the
restaurant and there is a hard tennis court.

Rooms: 22rms en suite (2 fmly) (10 GF)
dble room £85 - £105*

Facilities: TV Modem/Fax Licensed TVL
Cen ht Parking 460 Last d order 10pm

BURTON UPON TRENT

Riverside Hotel ★★ 72% HL

Riverside Drive Branston DE14 3EP

☎ 01283 511234 🗎 01283 511441

email: riverside.branston@oldenglishinns.co.uk

www.oldenglish.co.uk

Dir: *on A5121 follow signs for Branston over
small humped-backed bridge and turn right
into Warren Lane. 2nd left into Riverside
Drive*

Dogs: Bedrooms (Unattended) Garden
Exercise Area (adjacent)

With its quiet residential location and well-
kept terraced garden stretching down to the
River Trent, this hotel has all the ingredients
for a relaxing stay. Many of the tables in the
Garden Room restaurant have views over the
garden. Bedrooms are tastefully furnished and
decorated and provide a good range of extras.

Rooms: 22rms en suite (10 GF) dble room
£80 - £90*

Facilities: TV STV Licensed Parking 200

SOMERSET/STAFFORDSHIRE

STAFFORDSHIRE/SUFFOLK

UTTOXETER
Oldroyd Guest House & Motel
★★★ 63% GH
18-22 Bridge Street ST14 8AP
☎ 01889 562763 ▤ 01889 568916
email: enquiries@oldroyd-guesthouse.com
www.oldroyd-guesthouse.com
Dir: On A518 near racecourse
Dogs: Bedrooms Garden Exercise Area
(500yds) Pet Food/Bowls
Resident Pets: Romy (Labrador), Billy
(canary)
This privately owned and personally run guest
house is close to the town centre and 8 miles
from Alton Towers. Bedrooms have modern
facilities, and some family and ground-floor
rooms are available. Breakfast is served at
separate tables in the bright and pleasant
breakfast room.
Rooms: 15rms 13 en suite (7 fmly) (5 GF)
dble room £45 - £59*
Facilities: TV TVL Cen ht Parking 20

BARNINGHAM
College House Farm ★★★★ 71%
Bardwell Road Barningham Suffolk IP31 1DF
☎ 01359 221512 ▤ 01359 221512
email: jackie.brightwell@talk21.com
Dir: Off B1111 to village x-rds & onto
Bardwell Rd
Dogs: Bedrooms Garden Exercise Area (3m)
Pet Food/Bowls
Resident Pets: Luther, Bliss, Lenny, Jude &
Seamus (cats), Ocre, Cat, Ryan & Dillon
(horses)
Expect a warm welcome at this charming
Grade II listed Jacobean property, which
stands in a peaceful location close to Bury St
Edmunds. Its abundant original character is
complemented by fine period furnishings.
Bedrooms are generally quite spacious and
thoughtfully equipped. Public rooms include
an elegant dining room and a cosy lounge.
Rooms: 6rms 3 en suite (4 fmly)
Facilities: TV Cen ht Parking 8
Last d order 9.30pm

BURY ST EDMUNDS
Ravenwood Hall Hotel

★ ★ ★ 86% ◉◉ HL

Rougham IP30 9JA

☎ 01359 270345 📠 01359 270788

email: enquiries@ravenwoodhall.co.uk

www.ravenwoodhall.co.uk

Dir: *3m E off A14, junct 45. Hotel on left*

Dogs: Bedrooms Public Areas (except restaurant) Garden Exercise Area (directly outside rooms) Pet Food/Bowls food by prior request - special dog area and pet loo

Resident Pets: Mackerson (Black Labrador), pygmy goats, geese

Delightful 15th-century property set in seven acres of woodland and landscaped gardens. The building has many original features. The spacious, attractive bedrooms are tastefully furnished and well equipped. There is an elegant restaurant and a smart lounge bar.

Rooms: 14rms en suite (5 GF)

dble room £110 - £165

Facilities: TV Licensed Parking 150

Last d order 6pm 🐾

ELMSWELL
Kiln Farm Guest House

★ ★ ★ 69% GH

Kiln Lane Bury St Edmunds IP30 9QR

☎ 01359 240442

email: davejankilnfarm@btinternet.com

Dir: *Exit A14 junct 47, just off A1088*

Dogs: Bedrooms Public Areas Garden Exercise Area (adjacent)

Please note that this establishment has recently changed hands. Delightful Victorian farmhouse set in a peaceful rural location amid 3 acres of landscaped grounds with lovely views. Bedrooms are housed in a converted barn; each is pleasantly decorated and furnished in country style. Breakfast is served in the bar-dining room and there is a cosy lounge.

Rooms: 8rms en suite (2 fmly) (6 GF)

dble room £70 - £100*

Facilities: TV Licensed TVL Cen ht Parking 20 Last d order 7.30pm

SUFFOLK

SUFFOLK

FRAMLINGHAM

Church Farm ★★★ 64% GA

Church Road Kettleburgh IP13 7LF

☎ 01728 723532

email: jbater@suffolkonline.net

Dir: *Off A12 to Wickham Market, signs to Easton Farm Park & Kettleburgh 1.25m, house behind church*

Dogs: Bedrooms Public Areas (if other guests approve) Garden Exercise Area (adjacent)

Resident Pets: Minnie (Jack Russell), Jessie (Labrador), Boots (Border/Jack Russell)

A charming 300-year-old farmhouse close to the village church amid superb grounds with a duck pond, shrubs and lawns. The property retains exposed beams and open fireplaces. Bedrooms are pleasantly decorated, and a ground-floor bedroom is available.

Rooms: 3rms 1 en suite (1 GF)

dble room £52 - £56

Facilities: TVL Cen ht Parking 10

Last d order 9.30pm

LAVENHAM

Lavenham Great House Hotel

★★★★★ 87% ⍟⍟ RR

Market Place CO10 9QZ

☎ 01787 247431 ▤ 01787 248007

email: greathouse@clara.co.uk

www.greathouse.co.uk

Dir: *Off A1141 onto Market Ln, behind cross on Market Place*

Dogs: Bedrooms Garden Exercise Area (100yds)

The 18th-century front on Market Place conceals a 15th-century timber-framed building that houses a restaurant with rooms. The restaurant is a pocket of France and offers high-quality rural cuisine served by French staff. The spacious bedrooms are individually decorated and thoughtfully equipped with many useful extras; some rooms have a separate lounge area.

Rooms: 5rms en suite (2 fmly)

dble room £96 - £150*

Facilities: TV FTV Modem/Fax Licensed Cen ht Last d order 9.30pm

LONG MELFORD
The Black Lion Hotel
★ ★ ★ 80% ❀ HL

Church Walk The Green CO10 9DN

☎ 01787 312356 📠 01787 374557

email: enquiries@blacklionhotel.net

www.blacklionhotel.net

Dir: *at junct of A134 & A1092*

Dogs: Bedrooms Public Areas (except restaurant) Garden Exercise Area (adjacent) Pet Food/Bowls food by prior request (chargeable)

Resident Pets: Mackerson (Black Labrador) This charming 15th-century hotel is situated on the edge of this bustling town overlooking the green. Bedrooms are generally spacious, attractively decorated, tastefully furnished and equipped with useful extras. An interesting range of dishes is served in the lounge bar or in the more formal restaurant.

Rooms: 10rms en suite (1 fmly) dble room £120 - £165

Facilities: TV Modem/Fax Licensed Parking 10

LOWESTOFT
Somerton House ★ ★ ★ ★ 72% GA

7 Kirkley Cliff NR33 0BY

☎ 01502 565665 📠 01502 501176

email: somerton@screaming.net

www.hotelssuffolk.uk.com

Dir: *On A12 S on seafront, 100yds from Claremont Pier*

Dogs: Bedrooms Public Areas (except dining room) Exercise Area (seafront nearby) Grade II Victorian terrace situated in a peaceful area of town overlooking the sea. Bedrooms are smartly furnished in a period style and have many thoughtful touches; some rooms have four poster or half-tester beds. Breakfast is served in the smart dining room and guests have the use of a cosy lounge.

Rooms: 7rms 5 en suite (1 fmly) (1 GF)

Facilities: TV STV Modem/Fax Licensed TVL Cen ht Last d order 9.45pm

SUFFOLK

SUFFOLK

NEWMARKET

Best Western Heath Court Hotel

★★★ 75% HL

Moulton Road CB8 8DY

☎ 01638 667171 📠 01638 666533

email: quality@heathcourthotel.com

www.heathcourthotel.com

Dir: *leave A14 at Newmarket & Ely exit onto A142. Follow town centre signs over mini rdbt. At clocktower left into Moulton Rd*

Dogs: Bedrooms (Unattended) Exercise Area (100yds) Pet Food/Bowls

This establishment has recently changed hands. Modern red-brick hotel situated close to Newmarket Heath and perfectly placed for the town centre. Informal meals can be taken in the lounge bar or a modern carte menu is offered in the restaurant. The smartly presented bedrooms are mostly spacious and some have air conditioning.

Rooms: 41rms en suite (2 fmly)
dble room £110 - £130

Facilities: TV STV Modem/Fax Lift Licensed TVL Parking 60

SAXMUNDHAM

Sandpit Farm ★★★★ 76% BB

Bruisyard IP17 2EB

☎ 01728 663445

email: susannemarshall@suffolkonline.net

www.aldevalleybreaks.co.uk

Dir: *4m W of Saxmundham. A1120 onto B1120, 1st left for Bruisyard, house 1.5m on left*

Dogs: Sep Accom (outbuildings & stables) Garden Exercise Area (garden & field)

Resident Pets: Twiggy & Inca (Black Labradors), chickens, guinea fowl

A warm welcome awaits you at this delightful Grade II listed farmhouse set in 20 acres of grounds. Bedrooms have many thoughtful touches and lovely country views, and there are two cosy lounges to enjoy. Breakfast features quality local produce and freshly laid free-range eggs.

Rooms: 2rms en suite dble room £60 - £70*

Facilities: TVL Cen ht Parking 4

CHOBHAM

Pembroke House ♦♦♦♦ 86%

Valley End Road GU24 8TB

☎ 01276 857654 📠 01276 858445

email: pembroke_house@btinternet.com

Dir: *A30 onto B383 signed Chobham, 3m right onto Valley End Rd, B&B 1m on left*

Dogs: Bedrooms Public Areas Garden
Exercise Area (large garden & fields)
Pet Food/Bowls

Resident Pets: Puzzle, Carrie, Pandora
(Jack Russells)

Proprietor Julia Holland takes obvious pleasure in treating you as a friend at her beautifully appointed and spacious home. The elegantly proportioned public areas include an imposing entrance hall and dining room with views over the surrounding countryside. Bedrooms are restful and filled with thoughtful extras.

Rooms: 5rms 2 en suite (1 fmly)
dble room £80 - £120*

Facilities: TV STV Cen ht Parking 10

HORLEY

The Lawn Guest House

★ ★ ★ ★ 74% GH

30 Massetts Road RH6 7DF

☎ 01293 775751 📠 01293 821803

email: info@lawnguesthouse.co.uk

www.lawnguesthouse.co.uk

Dir: *M23 junct 9, signs to A23 Redhill, 3rd exit at rdbt by Esso station, 300yds right at lights*

Dogs: Bedrooms Garden Exercise Area
(0.5m)

Convenient for Gatwick Airport, this fine detached Victorian house offers comfortable bedrooms, equipped with many thoughtful extras. The atmosphere is relaxed, the welcome friendly, and an Internet facility is available. A choice of breakfast is served in an attractive dining room. Holiday parking and airport transfer is a real bonus.

Rooms: 12rms en suite (4 fmly)
dble room £58 - £60*

Facilities: TV Modem/Fax Cen ht Parking
15 Last d order 9.30pm

SURREY

SURREY/EAST SUSSEX

PEASLAKE
Hurtwood Inn Hotel

★★★ 73% ◉ HL

Walking Bottom Guildford GU5 9RR

☎ 01306 730851 📄 01306 731390

email: sales@hurtwoodinnhotel.com

www.hurtwoodinnhotel.com

Dir: *off A25 at Gomshall opposite Jet Filling Station towards Peaslake. After 2.5m turn right at village shop, hotel in village centre*

Dogs: Bedrooms (Unattended) Public Areas (except restaurant) Garden Exercise Area (surrounding woods)

With its tranquil location this hotel makes an ideal base for exploring the attractions of the area. The brightly decorated bedrooms are well appointed, and some have views over the gardens. Public areas include the restaurant, a private dining room and a bar/bistro where drinks by the fire can be enjoyed. 'Oscars' is the setting to enjoy award-winning meals.

Rooms: 21rms en suite (6 fmly) (6 GF) dble room £50 - £100

Facilities: TV Modem/Fax Licensed Parking 22 Last d order 9pm

BATTLE
Powder Mills Hotel

★★★ 75% ◉ HL

Powdermill Lane TN33 0SP

☎ 01424 775511 📄 01424 774540

email: powdc@aol.com

www.powdcrmillshotel.com

Dir: *pass Abbey on A2100. 1st right, hotel 1m on right*

Dogs: Bedrooms (Unattended) Public Areas (except restaurant) Garden Exercise Area

Resident Pets: Jessica, Holly & Jenny (Springer Spaniels)

A delightful 18th-century country house hotel set amidst 150 acres of landscaped grounds with lakes and woodland. The bedrooms are tastefully furnished and thoughtfully equipped, some rooms have sun terraces with lovely views over the lake. Public rooms include a cosy lounge bar, music room, drawing room, library, restaurant and conservatory.

Rooms: 40rms en suite (3 GF) dble room £130 - £160

Facilities: TV STV Modem/Fax Licensed TVL Parking 101 ⬥

BATTLE

Fox Hole Farm ★★★★ 80% FH

Kane Hythe Road TN33 9QU

☎ 01424 772053 📠 01424 772053

email: foxholefarm@amserve.com

Dir: *Off A271 onto B2096 farm 0.75m from junct on right*

Dogs: Bedrooms Public Areas (except dining room) Garden Exercise Area (20yds)

Resident Pets: Foxy (Border Terrier)

A delightful 18th-century woodcutter's cottage set in forty acres of grounds a short drive from historic Battle. The spacious bedrooms are individually decorated and thoughtfully equipped. Breakfast includes home-baked bread and is served in the charming dining room. The cosy sitting room has exposed beams and an inglenook fireplace.

Rooms: 3rms en suite (1 GF)

dble room £55 - £65

Facilities: TV Cen ht Parking 6

Last d order 10pm

BRIGHTON

Granville Hotel ★★★ 72% HL

124 King's Road BN1 2FA

☎ 01273 326302 📠 01273 728294

email: granville@brighton.co.uk

www.granvillehotel.co.uk

Dir: *opposite West Pier*

Dogs: Bedrooms (Unattended) Public Areas (reception and bar only) Garden Exercise Area (20yds to beach) Pet Food/Bowls

Resident Pets: Mai-Mai (Jack Russell), Nan-Nan (West Highland Terrier)

This stylish hotel is located on Brighton's busy seafront. Bedrooms are carefully furnished and decorated with great style. A trendy cocktail bar and restaurant is located in the cellar with street access and a cosy terrace for warmer months. Tasty traditional breakfasts are also available.

Rooms: 24rms en suite (2 fmly) (1 GF)

dble room £85 - £185*

Facilities: TV Modem/Fax Lift Licensed TVL Parking 3

EAST SUSSEX

EAST SUSSEX

BRIGHTON

Ambassador Hotel ★★★★ 74% GA

22-23 New Steine Marine Parade BN2 1PD

☎ 01273 676869 ▤ 01273 689988

email: info@ambassadorbrighton.co.uk

www.ambassadorbrighton.co.uk

Dir: *A23 to Brighton Pier, left onto A259, 9th left, onto Garden Sq, 1st left*

Dogs: Bedrooms Public Areas
Exercise Area (adjacent)

At the heart of bustling Kemp Town, overlooking the attractive garden square next to the seaside, this well established property has a friendly and relaxing atmosphere. Bedrooms are well equipped and vary in size with the largest having the best views. A small lounge with a separate bar is available.

Rooms: 24rms en suite (9 fmly) (3 GF)
dble room £55 - £115*

Facilities: TV Modem/Fax Licensed Cen ht

EASTBOURNE

Gladwyn Hotel ★★★★ 72% GA

16 Blackwater Road BN21 4JD

☎ 01323 733142

email: gladwynhotel@aol.com

www.gladwynhotel.com

Dir: *A259 into town centre, off South St onto Hardwick Rd & Blackwater Rd. Hotel overlooks Devonshire Park*

Dogs: Bedrooms (Unattended) Public Areas (except breakfast room) Garden
Pet Food/Bowls

Resident Pets: Saffe (Staffordshire cross), Billy (Staffordshire Bull Terrier)

A warm welcome is guaranteed at this delightful guest house located opposite the famous tennis courts. Bedrooms each feature an individual theme and character. Breakfasts are served in the dining room overlooking the garden, which is available during the summer.

Rooms: 10rms en suite (1 fmly) (2 GF)
dble room £60 - £64*

Facilities: TV Modem/Fax Licensed TVL
Last d order 9.30pm

HASTINGS & ST LEONARDS
Beauport Park Hotel ★★★ 72% HL

Battle Road TN38 8EA

☎ 01424 851222 📠 01424 852465

email: reservations@beauportparkhotel.co.uk

www.beauportparkhotel.co.uk

Dir: *3m N off A2100*

Dogs: Bedrooms (Unattended) Public Areas
(except dining areas) Garden Exercise Area
(50yds) Pet Food/Bowls

Elegant Georgian manor house set in 40
acres of mature gardens on the outskirts
of Hastings. The individually decorated
bedrooms are tastefully furnished and
thoughtfully equipped with modern facilities.
Public rooms convey much original character
and feature a large conservatory, a lounge bar,
a restaurant and a further lounge, as well as
conference and banqueting rooms.

Rooms: 25rms en suite (2 fmly)
dble room £130*

Facilities: TV STV Modem/Fax Licensed
Parking 60 Last d order 9.30pm 🕾 🍽

NEWICK
Newick Park Hotel & Country Estate ★★★ 85% ◉◉ HL

BN8 4SB

☎ 01825 723633 📠 01825 723969

email: bookings@newickpark.co.uk

www.newickpark.co.uk

Dir: *S off A272 in Newick between Haywards
Heath and Uckfield. Pass church, left at junct
and hotel 0.25m on right*

Dogs: Bedrooms (certain rooms only)
Garden Exercise Area (surrounding 250 acres)

Resident Pets: Ellie & Maddy (Black
Labradors)

Delightful Grade II listed Georgian country
house set amid 250 acres of Sussex parkland
and landscaped gardens. The spacious
bedrooms are well equipped and have superb
garden views. There is a study, a sitting room,
lounge bar and an elegant restaurant.

Rooms: 16rms en suite (5 fmly) (1 GF)
dble room £165 - £285*

Facilities: TV STV Modem/Fax Licensed
TVL Parking 52 🍽

EAST SUSSEX

EAST SUSSEX/WEST SUSSEX

SEAFORD

The Silverdale ★★★★ 73%

21 Sutton Park Road BN25 1RH

☎ 01323 491849 📠 01323 890854

email: silverdale@mistral.co.uk

www.silverdale.mistral.co.uk

Dir: *On A259 in the centre of Seaford, close to memorial*

Dogs: Bedrooms Public Areas (unless other guests object) Exercise Area (2 mins' walk) Pet Food/Bowls local map of dog walks & pubs that accept dogs; towel, bowls, treats

Resident Pets: Bertie & Bessie (American Cocker Spaniels)

This family-run establishment is well situated for the town centre and the seafront. The pleasant bedrooms have many useful extras, and breakfast and dinner are served in the dining room. The cosy well-stocked lounge bar specialises in English wines and malt whiskies.

Rooms: 7rms en suite (2 fmly) (1 GF)

dble room £60 - £75

Facilities: TV Modem/Fax Licensed Cen ht Parking 5

HENFIELD

Frylands ★★★★ 71%

Wineham BN5 9BP

☎ 01403 710214 📠 01403 711449

email: b&b@frylands.co.uk

www.frylands.co.uk

Dir: *2m NE ot Henfield. Off B2116 towards Wineham, 1.5m left onto Fryland Ln, Frylands 0.3m on left*

Dogs: Sep Accom (outbuilding) Garden Exercise Area (25yds)

Resident Pets: Polly (Springer Spaniel)

The friendly hosts offer comfortable accommodation at this delightful 16th-century farmhouse, set in peaceful countryside. Day rooms and bedrooms are full of character and the well-appointed dining room is the setting for freshly cooked breakfasts. There is ample off-road parking and free car storage for travellers using Gatwick Airport is available.

Rooms: 3rms 0 en suite (1 fmly)

dble room £50 - £55*

Facilities: TV Modem/Fax Cen ht Parking 6

PULBOROUGH

Arun House ★★★ 57% BB

Bury RH20 1NT

☎ 01798 831736

email: arunway@hotmail.com

www.arunhousesussex.co.uk

Dir: *5m S of Pulborough. On A29, signed near Carringdales & Turners garages*

Dogs: Sep Accom (outbuildings) Public Areas (by prior arrangement) Exercise Area (on doorstep)

Resident Pets: Amber & Charlie (Labradors)

Located on the A29 and convenient for Arundel, Amberley Castle and the South Downs Way, this friendly family home is popular with ramblers and cyclists and offers comfortable accommodation. Guests may sit on the terrace and enjoy the views across the garden, with its pond, ducks and free-range chickens. The adjoining café is most welcoming.

Rooms: 3rms 0 en suite (1 fmly)

Facilities: TV Licensed Cen ht Parking 6

SELSEY

St Andrews Lodge Hotel

★★★★ 70% GA

Chichester Road PO20 0LX

☎ 01243 606899 📠 01243 607826

email: info@standrewslodge.co.uk

www.standrewslodge.co.uk

Dir: *B2145 into Selsey, on right just before the church*

Dogs: Bedrooms (Unattended) Public Areas Garden Exercise Area (200yds)

Resident Pets: Pepper & Poppy (cats)

This friendly hotel is just half a mile from the seafront. The refurbished bedrooms are bright and spacious, and have a range of useful extras. Five ground-floor rooms, one with easier access, overlook the large south-facing garden, which is perfect for a drink on a summer evening.

Rooms: 10rms en suite (3 fmly) (5 GF)

Facilities: TV Modem/Fax Licensed TVL Cen ht Parking 14 Last d order 9.30pm

WEST SUSSEX

SLINFOLD
The Red Lyon ★★★ 60% INN

The Street RH13 0RR

☎ 01403 790339 📄 01403 791863

email: enquiries@theredlyon.co.uk

www.theredlyon.co.uk

Dir: *Off A29*

Dogs: Public Areas (except restaurant)
Garden Exercise Area (20yds)
Pet Food/Bowls

Located in the village centre, this delightful 18th-century inn, with parts dating from the 14th century, has a wealth of beams. Tasty meals at lunch and dinner are offered in the timber-panelled dining room. The bedrooms and bathrooms are bright, spacious and well equipped. A pleasant beer garden and ample parking are also available.

Rooms: 4rms en suite (1 fmly)
dble room £45 - £60*

Facilities: TV Licensed TVL Cen ht
Parking 30 Last d order 8.45pm

WORTHING
Cavendish Hotel ★★ 62% HL

115 Marine Parade BN11 3QG

☎ 01903 236767 📄 01903 823840

email: reservations@cavendishworthing.co.uk

www.cavendishworthing.co.uk

Dir: *on seafront, 600yds W of pier*

Dogs: Bedrooms (Unattended) Public Areas (except restaurant) Exercise Area (20yds)

This popular, family-run hotel enjoys a prominent seafront location. Bedrooms are well equipped and soundly decorated. Guests have an extensive choice of meal options, with a varied bar menu, and carte and daily menus offered in the restaurant. Limited parking is available at the rear of the hotel.

Rooms: 17rms en suite (4 fmly)
dble room £69 - £85*

Facilities: TV STV Licensed TVL
Parking 5

WORTHING

Manor Guest House ★ ★ ★ ★ 73%
GH

100 Broadwater Road BN14 8AN

☎ 01903 236028 & 07713 633168

email: stay@manorworthing.com

www.manorworthing.com

Dir: *A27 onto A24 to town centre. House
175yds on left after St Marys Church*

Dogs: Bedrooms (Unattended) Public Areas
(except in dining room) Garden Exercise
Area (1 min walk)

Resident Pets: Jack (Westie)

This guest house just a half mile from the
town centre is operated by eager to please
hosts, Sandy and Steve. Bedrooms are neatly
presented with many thoughtful extras.
Freshly cooked breakfasts and dinners served
in the well appointed dining room. There is
limited off road parking.

Rooms: 6rms 3 en suite (2 fmly) (1 GF)
dble room £80 - £100*

Facilities: TV FTV Licensed Cen ht
Parking 6

NEWCASTLE UPON TYNE

**Newcastle Marriott Hotel Gosforth
Park** ★ ★ ★ ★ 77% ◉ ◉ HL

High Gosforth Park Gosforth NE3 5HN

☎ 00191 236 4111 📄 0191 236 8192

www.newcastlemarriottgosforthpark.co.uk

Dir: *onto A1056 to Killingworth & Wideopen.
3rd exit to Gosforth Park, hotel ahead*

Dogs: Bedrooms (Unattended) Garden
Exercise Area

Set within its own grounds, this modern hotel
offers extensive conference and banqueting
facilities, along with indoor and outdoor
leisure and a choice of formal and informal
dining. Many of the air-conditioned bedrooms
have views over the park; executive rooms
feature extras such as CD players. The hotel is
conveniently located for the by-pass, airport
and racecourse.

Rooms: 178rms en suite (30 fmly)
dble room £89 - £119

Facilities: TV STV Modem/Fax Lift
Licensed TVL Parking 340
Last d order 9.45pm 🏊

TYNE & WEAR

SUNDERLAND
Quality Hotel Sunderland

★★★ 74% HL

Witney Way Boldon NE35 9PE

☎ 0191 519 1999 📄 0191 519 0655

email: enquiries@hotels-sunderland.com

www.hotels-sunderland.com

Dir: *From Tyne Tunnel A19, 2.5m S take 1st exit to rdbt with A184*

Dogs: Bedrooms (Unattended) Public Areas (except restaurant) Garden Exercise Area (hotel grounds)

This modern, purpose-built hotel is within easy reach of major business and tourism amenities and is well suited to the needs of both business and leisure travellers. The bedrooms are spacious and well equipped. Public areas include a leisure centre, a variety of meeting rooms and a spacious bar and restaurant.

Rooms: 82rms en suite (10 fmly) (41 GF) dble room £60 - £120*

Facilities: TV Modem/Fax Licensed TVL Parking 150 Last d order 9.45pm 🍵

WHICKHAM
Gibside Hotel ★★★ 74% HL

Front Street NE16 4JG

☎ 0191 488 9292 📄 0191 488 8000

email: reception@gibside-hotel.co.uk

www gibside-hotel.co.uk

Dir: *off A1M towards Whickham on B6317, onto Front St, 2m on right*

Dogs: Bedrooms (Unattended) Garden Exercise Area (100yds) Pet Food/Bowls

Conveniently located in the village centre, this hotel is close to the Newcastle by-pass and its elevated position affords views over the Tyne Valley. Bedrooms come in two styles, classical and contemporary. Public rooms include the Egyptian-themed Sphinx bar and a more formal restaurant. Secure garage parking is available.

Rooms: 45rms en suite (2 fmly) (13 GF)

Facilities: TV STV Lift Licensed Parking 28 Last d order 7.30pm

ROYAL LEAMINGTON SPA

Bubbenhall House ★★★★ 78% GA

Paget's Lane CV8 3BJ

☎ 024 7630 2409 & 07746 282541

🖹 024 7630 2409

email:

wharrison@bubbenhallhouse.freeserve.co.uk

www.bubbenhallhouse.com

Dir: *5m NE of Leamington. Off A445 at Bubbenhall S onto Pagets Ln, 1m on single-track lane over 4 speed humps*

Dogs: Bedrooms Public Areas (except dining room) Garden Exercise Area (5-acre grounds adjoining country park) Pet Food/Bowls

Resident Pets: Zippy (Black Labrador), Kitty (cat)

Located in extensive mature grounds with an abundance of wildlife, this impressive late Edwardian house was once the home of Alexander Issigonis, designer of the Mini. There are interesting features including anJacobean-style staircase, an elegant dining room and choice of sumptuous lounges.

Rooms: 3rms en suite dble room £65 - £75*

Facilities: TV TVL Cen ht Parking 12

STRATFORD-UPON-AVON

Avon Lodge ♦♦♦ 60%

Ryon Hill Warwick Road CV37 0NZ

☎ 01789 295196

Dogs: Bedrooms Exercise Area (fenced paddock on site)

Resident Pets: Jacko & Rollie (German Shephards), Ollie (cat)

Located in immaculate mature gardens on the outskirts of town, this former Victorian cottage has been carefully modernised and extended to provide cosy bedrooms. Imaginative breakfasts are served in the attractive cottage-style dining room.

Rooms: 6rms en suite (1 fmly)

Facilities: TV TVL Cen ht Parking 7

Last d order 9.30pm

WARWICKSHIRE

WARWICKSHIRE

WARWICK

The Hare on the Hill ★★★★ 80%

37 Coventry Road CV34 5HN

☎ 01926 491366

email: prue@thehareonthehill.co.uk

www.thehareonthehill.co.uk

Dir: *On A429 Coventry Rd near Warwick station*

Dogs: Bedrooms (Unattended) Public Areas (unless resident dog objects!) Garden Exercise Area (150yds) Pet Food/Bowls

Resident Pets: Ed (Scottie dog)

This well-furnished Victorian house is very convenient for the town and provides well-equipped and characterful bedrooms and a delightful lounge. The use of organic produce is of great importance here and excellent breakfasts are served around a large table in the hall, which retains its original mosaic floor. Friendly and attentive service.

Rooms: 7rms en suite (1 fmly) (1 GF) dble room £80 - £95*

Facilities: TV Modem/Fax TVL Cen ht Parking 12

WARWICK MOTORWAY SERVICE AREA

Days Inn Stratford-upon-Avon

⌂ BUD

Warwick Services M40 Northbound junction 12-13 Banbury Road CV35 0AA

☎ 01926 651681 ▤ 01926 651634

email: warwick.north.hotel@welcomebreak.co.uk

www.welcomebreak.co.uk

Dir: *M40 northbound between junct 12 & 13*

Dogs: Bedrooms Public Areas Garden Exercise Area (adjacent)

This modern building offers accommodation in smart, spacious and well-equipped bedrooms, suitable for families and business travellers, and all with en suite bathrooms. Continental breakfast is available and other refreshments may be taken at the nearby family restaurant.

Rooms: 54rms en suite (45 fmly) dble room £49 - £65*

Facilities: TV STV TVL Parking 100

WARWICK MOTORWAY SERVICE AREA

Days Inn Warwick South ⇧ BUD

Warwick Services M40 Southbound Banbury Road CV35 0AA

☎ 01926 650168 📠 01926 651601

www.welcomebreak.co.uk

Dir: *M40 southbound between junct 14 & 12*

Dogs: Bedrooms Public Areas Garden Exercise Area (adjacent)

This modern building offers accommodation in smart, spacious and well-equipped bedrooms, suitable for families and business travellers, and all with en suite bathrooms. Continental breakfast is available and other refreshments may be taken at the nearby family restaurant.

Rooms: 40rms en suite (38 fmly)

dble room £45 - £55*

Facilities: TV STV Parking 500

Last d order 8.30pm

BIRMINGHAM

Rollason Wood Hotel ★★ 50% GA

130 Wood End Road Erdington B24 8BJ

☎ 0121 373 1230 📠 0121 382 2578

email: rollwood@globalnet.co.uk

www.rollasonwoodhotel.co.uk

Dir: *M6 junct 6, A5127 to Erdington, right onto A4040, 0.25m on left*

Dogs: Bedrooms Garden Exercise Area (200yds to park)

Well situated for routes and the city centre, this owner-managed establishment is popular with contractors. The choice of three different bedroom styles suits most budgets, and rates include full English breakfasts. Ground-floor areas include a popular bar, cosy television lounge and a dining room.

Rooms: 35rms 11 en suite (5 fmly)

dble room £36 - £49.50*

Facilities: TV Licensed TVL Cen ht Parking 35 Last d order 8.00pm

WARWICKSHIRE/WEST MIDLANDS

WEST MIDLANDS/ISLE OF WIGHT

BIRMINGHAM

Fountain Court Hotel ★ ★ 68% HL

339-343 Hagley Road Birmingham B17 8NH

☎ 0121 429 1754 📠 0121 429 1209

email: info@fountain-court.co.uk

www.fountain-court.co.uk

Dir: *on A456, towards Birmingham, 3m from M5 junct 3*

Dogs: Bedrooms Garden Exercise Area (approx 200yds)

Resident Pets: Lucky & Pebbles (Jack Russells), Tiger (cat)

This family-owned hotel is on the A456, near to the M5 and a short drive from the city centre. A warm welcome is assured and day rooms include comfortable lounges and a cottage-style dining room, the setting for home-cooked dinners and comprehensive breakfasts.

Rooms: 23rms en suite (4 fmly) (3 GF) dble room £60 - £70

Facilities: TV Licensed TVL Parking 20 Last d order 9.30pm

COWES

Best Western New Holmwood Hotel ★ ★ ★ 72% HL

Queens Road Egypt Point PO31 8BW

☎ 01983 292508 📠 01983 295020

email: nholmwdh@aol.com

www.newholmwoodhotel.co.uk

Dir: *from A3020 at Northwood Garage lights, left & follow road to rdbt. 1st left then sharp right into Baring Rd, 4th left into Egypt Hill. At bottom turn right, hotel on right*

Dogs: Bedrooms (Unattended) Public Areas (except restaurant) Garden

Exercise Area (2 mins' walk to beach)

Just by the Esplanade, this hotel has an enviable outlook. Bedrooms are comfortable and very well equipped. The glass-fronted restaurant looks out to sea and serves a range of interesting meals. For summer there is a sun terrace and a small pool area.

Rooms: 26rms en suite (1 fmly) (9 GF) dble room £96 - £125*

Facilities: TV STV Modem/Fax Licensed Parking 20 ⚓

COWES

Windward House ★ ★ ★ 67% GA

69 Mill Hill Road PO31 7EQ

☎ 01983 280940 & 07771 573580

🖹 01983 280940

email: sueogston1@tiscali.co.uk

Dir: *A320 Cowes-Newport, halfway up Mill Hill Rd on right from floating bridge from E Cowes Red Funnel Ferries*

Dogs: Bedrooms Public Areas (except dining room) Garden Exercise Area (0.25m) Pet Food/Bowls

Resident Pets: Gem (German Shepherd)

A friendly atmosphere prevails at this comfortable Victorian house, located close to the centre of Cowes. Bedrooms are bright and neat, and downstairs there is a spacious lounge equipped with satellite television, video and music systems. Breakfast is served in a separate dining room around a shared table.

Rooms: 6rms 3 en suite (2 fmly) (1 GF) dble room £40 - £60*

Facilities: TV TVL Cen ht Parking 4 🐾

COWES

1 Lammas Close ★ ★ ★ ★ 70% BB

PO31 8DT

☎ 01983 282541 🖹 01983 282541

Dir: *0.5m W of town centre. Off The Parade onto Castle Hill & Baring Rd. 3rd right onto Lammas Cl, 1st house on left*

Dogs: Bedrooms Public Areas Garden Exercise Area (350yds) Pet Food/Bowls

Resident Pets: Weasley (cat), Classy (Golden Retriever)

Looking across the Solent and situated one mile from central Cowes. Yachts-people will find kindred spirits in the very friendly Mr and Mrs Rising. A hearty and enjoyable breakfast in the elegant dining room completes the picture. Guest can be met on arrival in Cowes and also taken in daily if required, free of charge.

Rooms: 1rm 0 en suite dble room £60 - £80*

Facilities: TV FTV Modem/Fax Cen ht Parking 2

ISLE OF WIGHT

ISLE OF WIGHT

SANDOWN
Riviera Hotel ★★ 68% HL

2 Royal Street PO36 8LP

☎ 01983 402518 🖹 01983 402518

email: enquiries@rivierahotel.org.uk

www.rivierahotel.org.uk

Dir: *Top of Sandown High St, turning past main Post Office.*

Dogs: Bedrooms (Unattended) Public Areas (except dining room) Garden Exercise Area (100yds)

Please note that this establishment has recently changed hands. Regular guests return year after year to this friendly and welcoming family-run hotel. It is located near to the High Street and just a short stroll from the beach, pier and shops. Bedrooms, including several at ground floor level, are very well furnished and comfortably equipped. Enjoyable home-cooked meals are served in the spacious dining room.

Rooms: 43rms en suite (6 fmly) (11 GF)

Facilities: TV Licensed Parking 30 Last d order 8pm

SANDOWN
The Wight Montrene Hotel

★★ 69% HL

11 Avenue Road PO36 8BN

☎ 01983 403722 🖹 01983 405553

email: enquiries@montrene.co.uk

www.montrene.co.uk

Dir: *100yds after mini rdbt between High St and Avenue Rd*

Dogs: Bedrooms (Unattended) Public Areas (except restaurant, pool, gym & games room) Garden Exercise Area (150yds)

Resident Pets: Magnum (Great Pyrenian Mountain Dog)

A family hotel set in secluded grounds, a short walk from Sandowns beach and shops. Bedrooms are either on the ground or first floor. Guests can use the heated swimming pool or enjoy evening entertainment in the bar. The dinner menu changes nightly.

Rooms: 41rms en suite (19 fmly) (19 GF) dble room £76 - £94*

Facilities: TV Modem/Fax Licensed TVL Parking 40 Last d order 9.30pm 🍃

SEAVIEW
Seaview Hotel & Restaurant
★★★ 77% ◉◉ HL
High Street PO34 5EX
☎ 01983 612711 📄 01983 613729
email: reception@seaviewhotel.co.uk
www.seaviewhotel.co.uk
Dir: *from B3330 Ryde-Seaview road, turn left via Puckpool along seafront*

Dogs: Bedrooms (Unattended) Public Areas Garden Exercise Area (25yds) Pet Food/Bowls
This charming hotel enjoys a quiet location just a short stroll from the seafront. Guests are offered a choice of tastefully and nautically themed dining and bar venues and can relax in the homely lounge and well-appointed bedrooms. There is also a useful car park to the rear of the property.
Rooms: 17rms en suite (3 fmly) (3 GF)
dble room £74 - £177
Facilities: TV Licensed Parking 10

VENTNOR
Hillside Hotel ★★ 68% SHL
Mitchell Avenue PO38 1DR
☎ 01983 852271 📄 01983 852271
email: aa@hillside-hotel.co.uk
www.hillside-hotel.co.uk
Dir: *off A3055 onto B3327. Hotel 0.5m on right behind tennis courts*

Dogs: Bedrooms (Unattended) Public Areas (except dining room & lounge) Garden
Resident Pets: Jack (Jack Russell), Ellie (Doberman), Fudge (Cocker Spaniel), Hamish (cat)
Hillside Hotel dates back to the 19th century and enjoys a superb location overlooking Ventnor and the sea beyond. Public areas consist of a traditional lounge, a cosy bar area with an adjoining conservatory and a light, airy dining room. A welcoming and homely atmosphere is assured.
Rooms: 12rms en suite (1 fmly) (1 GF)
Facilities: TV Licensed Parking 12
Last d order 9.15pm

ISLE OF WIGHT

WILTSHIRE

CALNE
**Best Western Lansdowne Strand
Hotel** ★★★ 72% HL
The Strand SN11 0EH
☎ 01249 812488 🖹 01249 815323
email: reservations@lansdownestrand.co.uk
www.lansdownestrand.co.uk
Dir: *From Chippenham join A4 signed Calne.
Straight over at both rdbts, hotel is in town
centre*

Dogs: Bedrooms (Unattended) Exercise Area
Pet Food/Bowls provided with one day's notice
Please note that this establishment has
recently changed hands. In the centre of the
market town, this 16th-century, former
coaching inn still retains many period
features. Individually decorated bedrooms
vary in size. There are two friendly bars; one
offers a wide selection of ales and a cosy fire.
An interesting menu is available in the
brasserie-style restaurant.
Rooms: 26rms en suite (2 fmly)
Facilities: TV STV Licensed TVL
Parking 14 Last d order 9.30pm

LOWER CHICKSGROVE
Compasses Inn ★★★ 67% ❀ INN
Tisbury SP3 6NB
☎ 01722 714318 🖹 01722 714318
email: thecompasses@aol.com
www.thecompassesinn.com
Dir: *Off A30 signed Lower Chicksgrove, 1st
left onto Lagpond Ln, single-track lane to
village*

Dogs: Bedrooms (Unattended) Public Areas
Garden Exercise Area (adjacent) Pet Bowls
This charming 17th-century inn, within easy
reach of Bath, Salisbury, Glastonbury and the
Dorset coast, offers comfortable
accommodation in a peaceful setting.
Carefully prepared dinners are enjoyed in the
warm atmosphere of the bar-restaurant, while
breakfast is served in a separate dining room.
Rooms: 4rms en suite (1 fmly)
dble room £75 - £05
Facilities: TV Licensed Cen ht Parking 40
Last d order 9pm

MELKSHAM

Shaw Country Hotel ★★ 74% HL

Bath Road Shaw SN12 8EF

☎ 01225 702836 & 790321 📠 01225 790275

email: info@shawcountryhotel.co.uk

www.shawcountryhotel.co.uk

Dir: *1m from Melksham, 9m from Bath on A365*

Dogs: Bedrooms Garden Exercise Area

Located within easy reach of both Bath and the M4, this relaxed and friendly hotel sits in its own gardens, and has a patio area ideal for enjoying a cool drink during warm summer months. The house boasts some very well-appointed bedrooms, a comfortable lounge and bar and the Mulberry Restaurant, where a wide selection of innovative dishes make up both carte and set menus. A spacious function room is a useful addition.

Rooms: 13rms en suite (2 fmly)

Facilities: TV Licensed TVL Parking 30

Last d order 8.30pm

NETTLETON

Fosse Farmhouse Chambre d'Hote

♦♦♦♦ 75%

Nettleton Shrub Chippenham SN14 7NJ

☎ 01249 782286 📠 01249 783066

email: caroncooper@compuserve.com

www.fossefarmhouse.com

Dir: *1.5m N from Castle Combe on B4039, left at Gib, farm 1m on right*

Dogs: Bedrooms Garden Exercise Area (adjacent) Pet Food/Bowls

Set in quiet Wiltshire countryside close to Castle Combe, the guest house has well-equipped bedrooms decorated in keeping with its 18th-century origins. Excellent dinners are served in the farmhouse, and cream teas can be enjoyed in the old stables or the delightful garden.

Rooms: 3rms en suite (1 fmly)

dble room £85 - £135

Facilities: TV Licensed Cen ht Parking 12

Last d order 9.30pm

WILTSHIRE

WILTSHIRE

PURTON
The Pear Tree at Purton

★★★ 80% ◉◉ HL

Church End SN5 4ED

☎ 01793 772100 📠 01793 772369

email: stay@peartreepurton.co.uk

www.peartreepurton.co.uk

Dir: *M4 junct 16 follow signs to Purton, at Spar shop turn right. Hotel 0.25m on left*

Dogs: Bedrooms Public Areas Garden Exercise Area (surrounding fields) Pet Food/Bowls welcome pack - bowl & chews

Resident Pets: Jake (Springer Spaniel)

Charming 15th-century, former vicarage set amidst fully landscaped gardens in a peaceful location. The resident proprietors and staff provide efficient, dedicated service and friendly hospitality. The spacious bedrooms are individually decorated and have a good range of thoughtful extras. Fresh ingredients feature on the lunch and dinner menus.

Rooms: 17rms en suite (2 fmly) (6 GF) dble room £110 - £170*

Facilities: TV STV Licensed Parking 60

SALISBURY
Byways Guest House

★★★ 60% GA

31 Fowlers Road SP1 2QP

☎ 01722 328364 📠 01722 322146

email: info@bywayshouse.co.uk

www.bywayshouse.co.uk

Dir: *A30 onto A36 signed Southampton, follow Youth Hostel signs to hostel, Fowlers Rd opp*

Dogs: Bedrooms Exercise Area (next door)

Located in a quiet street with off-road parking, Byways is within walking distance of the town centre. Several bedrooms have been decorated in a Victorian style and another two have four-poster beds. All rooms offer good levels of comfort, with one adapted for easier access.

Rooms: 23rms 38 en suite (6 fmly) (13 GF) dble room £50 - £75*

Facilities: TV Licensed Cen ht Parking 15

SWINDON

Portquin Guest House

★★★ 65% GA

Broadbush Broad Blunsdon SN26 7DH

☎ 01793 721261

email: portquin@msn.com

www.portquinguesthouse.com

Dir: *A419 onto B4019 at Blunsdon signed Highworth, continue 0.5m*

Dogs: Bedrooms Public Areas (except dining room) Garden Exercise Area (adjacent) Pet Food/Bowls

Resident Pets: Basil & Diva (horses)

This friendly guest house near Swindon provides a warm welcome and views of the Lambourn Downs. The rooms vary in shape and size, with six in the main house and three in an adjacent annexe. Full English breakfasts are served at two large tables in the kitchen-dining area.

Rooms: 9rms en suite (2 fmly) (4 GF) dble room £50 - £70*

Facilities: TV Modem/Fax Cen ht Parking 12 Last d order 9pm

SWINDON

The Check Inn ★★★ 58% INN

Woodland View North Wroughton SN4 9AA

☎ 01793 845584 ▤ 01793 814640

email: information@checkinn.co.uk

www.checkinn.co.uk

Dir: *A361 Swindon to Devizes, after dual carriageway bridge over M4 take the 1st right onto Woodland View*

Dogs: Bedrooms (Unattended) Public Areas (must be on lead) Garden Exercise Area (100yds) Pet Food/Bowls

Resident Pets: Emma (Collie/Retriever cross)

Located close to the M4, The Check Inn combines a traditional freehouse inn offering real ales with more modern, well-decorated and furnished bedrooms and bathrooms. A large car park is provided at the rear. A good selection of generously portioned, home-cooked meals is available.

Rooms: 3rms en suite (1 fmly) dble room £42.50*

Facilities: TV Licensed Cen ht Parking 48

WILTSHIRE

WILTSHIRE/WORCESTERSHIRE

WINTERBOURNE STOKE
Scotland Lodge Farm ◆◆◆◆
SP3 4TF

☎ 01980 621199 📄 01980 621188
email: william.lockwood@bigwig.net
www.smoothhound.co.uk/hotels/scotandl
Dir: *0.25m W of village on A303, near B3083 junct & Scotland Lodge*

Dogs: Bedrooms (Downstairs only) Public Areas Garden Exercise Area Pet Food/Bowls
Resident Pets: 2 West Highland Terriers
Set in 46 acres of paddocks and grassland, this farm provides comfortable, well-appointed rooms featuring numerous thoughtful extra touches. Full English breakfasts are served at the large farmhouse table in the conservatory/lounge overlooking the paddocks. The proprietors are keen equestrians and are happy to offer stabling. Dogs are welcome by arrangement.
Rooms: 3rms en suite (1 fmly) (2 GF)
Facilities: TV Cen ht Parking 5
Last d order 9.30pm

BEWDLEY
Ramada Hotel & Resort
Kidderminster ★★★ 77% HL
Habberley Road Nr Kidderminster DY12 1LJ
☎ 01299 406400 📄 01299 400921
email: sales.kidderminster@ramadajarvis.co.uk
www.ramadajarvis.co.uk
Dir: *A456 towards Kidderminster to ring road, follow signs to Bewdley. Pass Safari Park then exit A456/Town Centre, take sharp right after 200yds onto B4190, hotel 400yds on right*

Dogs: Bedrooms (by prior arrangement) Garden Exercise Area
Located within sixteen acres of landscaped grounds, this former Victorian house has been renovated and extended to provide good standards of comfort and facilities. A range of well equipped bedrooms include family and executive rooms. An on-site Sebastian Coe Health Club is available to resident guests.
Rooms: 44rms en suite (3 fmly) (18 GF)
Facilities: TV STV Modem/Fax Licensed Parking 150 Last d order 9.30pm 🏊

EVESHAM

The Evesham Hotel

★★★ 79% ☻ HL

Coopers Lane Off Waterside WR11 1DA

☎ 01386 765566 & 0800 716969 (Res)

🖹 01386 765443

email: reception@eveshamhotel.com

www.eveshamhotel.com

Dir: *Coopers Lane is off road by River Avon*

Dogs: Bedrooms (Unattended) Garden
Exercise Area

Dating from 1540 and set in extensive grounds, this delightful hotel has well-equipped accommodation that includes a selection of quirkily themed rooms - Alice in Wonderland, Egyptian, and Aquarium (which has a tropical fish tank in the bathroom). A reputation for food is well deserved, with a particularly strong choice for vegetarians. Children are welcome and toys are always available.

Rooms: 40rms en suite (3 fmly) (11 GF)
dble room £128*

Facilities: TV Licensed Parking 50

Last d order 9pm 🕭

EVESHAM

Best Western Northwick Hotel

★★★ 74% HL

Waterside WR11 1BT

☎ 01386 40322 🖹 01386 41070

email: enquiries@northwickhotel.co.uk

www.northwickhotel.co.uk

Dir: *off A46 onto A44 over traffic lights and right at next set onto B4035. Past hospital, hotel on right opposite river*

Dogs: Bedrooms (Unattended) Public Areas
(except restaurant & bar)
Exercise Area (1 min walk)

Located close to the centre of the town, the hotel overlooks the River Avon and its adjacent park. Bedrooms are traditional in style and feature broadband internet access; one room has been adapted for disabled access. Public areas offer a choice of drinking options, meeting rooms and a restaurant.

Rooms: 29rms en suite (4 fmly) (1 GF)
dble room £107.50*

Facilities: TV STV Modem/Fax Licensed
Parking 85

WORCESTERSHIRE

WORCESTERSHIRE

MALVERN

Four Hedges ★ ★ ★ 61% BB

The Rhydd Hanley Castle WR8 0AD

☎ 01684 310405

email: fredgies@aol.com

Dir: *4m E from Malvern at junct of B4211 & B4424*

Dogs: Bedrooms (Unattended) Public Areas Garden Exercise Area (adjoining 7 acres)

Resident Pets: Juno (Border Collie), Machu & Pichu (cats)

Situated in a rural location, this detached house stands in mature grounds with wild birds in abundance. The bedrooms are equipped with thoughtful extras. Tasty English breakfasts, using free-range eggs, are served in a cosy dining room at a table made from a 300-year-old elm tree.

Rooms: 4rms 2 en suite

Facilities: TV TVL Cen ht Parking 5

Last d order 9.30pm

MARTLEY

Admiral Rodney Inn ◆◆◆◆ 81%

Berrow Green WR6 6PL

☎ 01886 821375 📠 01886 822048

email: rodney@admiral.fslife.co.uk

www.admiral-rodney.co.uk

Dir: *A44 onto B4197 at Knightwick, 2m on left*

Dogs: Bedrooms (Unattended) Public Areas (except restaurant) Garden Exercise Area (adjacent)

Resident Pets: Sally (Collie cross)

Located in the pretty village of Berrow Green, this 16th-century inn has been renovated to provide high standards of comfort and facilities. Spacious, carefully furnished bedrooms are complemented by luxurious modern bathrooms. Ground floor areas include quality bars with log fires and a unique tiered and beamed restaurant, where imaginative dishes are served.

Rooms: 3rms en suite dble room £55 - £65*

Facilities: TV Licensed Cen ht Parking 40

Last d order 9.45pm

REDDITCH

Quality Hotel Redditch

★★★ 66% HL

Pool Bank Southcrest B97 4JS

☎ 01527 541511 🖹 01527 402600

email: enquiries@hotels-redditch.com

www.hotels-redditch.com

Dir: *Into Redditch, follow signs for all other Redditch Districts to Southcrest signed, then follow hotel signs*

Dogs: Bedrooms Garden
Exercise Area (on site)

Originally a manor house, this hotel enjoys a peaceful location in extensive wooded grounds. Bedrooms vary in size and style, but all are well appointed and equipped. Both the restaurant and bar/conservatory overlook the attractive, sloping gardens, with views stretching across to the Vale of Evesham.

Rooms: 73rms en suite (20 fmly) (22 GF)
dble room £60 - £105*

Facilities: TV STV Modem/Fax Licensed
Parking 100 Last d order 9.15pm

UPTON UPON SEVERN

White Lion Hotel ★★★ 74% ◉ HL

21 High Street WR8 0HJ

☎ 01684 592551 🖹 01684 593333

email: reservations@whitelionhotel.biz

www.whitelionhotel.biz

Dir: *A422, A38 towards Tewkesbury. In 8m take B4104, after 1m cross bridge, turn left to hotel, past bend on left*

Dogs: Bedrooms (Unattended) Public Areas
Garden Exercise Area (approx 500yds)

Resident Pets: Oscar (Giant Schnauzer)

Famed for being the inn depicted in Henry Fielding's novel 'Tom Jones', this 16th-century hotel is a reminder of old England. The quality furnishing and decor schemes throughout the public areas all enhance its character. The hotel has a well-deserved reputation for its good food, which is complemented by friendly, attentive service.

Rooms: 13rms en suite (2 fmly) (2 GF)
dble room £99 - £125

Facilities: TV FTV Modem/Fax Licensed
Parking 18 Last d order 9.15pm

EAST RIDING OF YORKSHIRE

BEVERLEY

The Manor House ★★ 76% ◉ ◉ HL

Northlands Walkington HU17 8RT

☎ 01482 881645 📄 01482 866501

email: info@walkingtonmanorhouse.co.uk

www.walkingtonmanorhouse.co.uk

Dir: *from M62 junct 38 follow 'Walkington' signs. 4m SW off B1230. Through Walkington, left at lights. Left at 1st x-roads. Approx 400yds hotel on left*

Dogs: Bedrooms Garden

Resident Pets: Arthur (Great Dane)

This delightful country-house hotel is set in open country amid well-tended gardens. The spacious bedrooms have been attractively decorated and thoughtfully equipped. Public rooms include a conservatory restaurant and a very inviting lounge. A good range of dishes is available from two menus, with an emphasis on fresh, local produce.

Rooms: 7rms en suite (1 fmly) (1 GF)

dble room £120 - £140

Facilities: TV Licensed Parking 40

Last d order 9.30pm

KINGSTON UPON HULL

Stop Inn Hull ★★ 60% HL

11 Anlaby Road HU1 2PJ

☎ 01482 323299 📄 01482 214730

email: hull@stop-inns.com

www.stop-inns.com/hull

Dir: *M62 to A63, over flyover, left at lights, hotel 500yds on left*

Dogs: Bedrooms

An unpretentious hotel situated in the centre of the city with well-equipped and generally spacious bedrooms. Staff are friendly, and whilst there is no formal restaurant a limited range of dishes is served in the lounge bar during the evening. Free parking is also available and complimentary use of an adjacent leisure centre.

Rooms: 59rms en suite (5 fmly)

dble room £52*

Facilities: TV Lift Licensed TVL

Parking 15 Last d order 9.30pm

KINGSTON UPON HULL

Quality Hotel Royal Hull

★★★ 72% HL

170 Ferensway HU1 3UF

☎ 01482 325087 ▤ 01482 323172

email: enquiries@hotel-hull.com

www.hotels-hull.com

Dir: *From M62 take A63 to Hull. Over flyover, left at 2nd lights signed Railway Station. Hotel on left at 2nd lights*

Dogs: Bedrooms (Unattended) Exercise Area (1m)

A former Victorian railway hotel modernised in recent years. Bedrooms are well equipped, most with air conditioning, and a number of premier rooms. A spacious lounge provides an ideal setting for light meals, drinks and relaxation. There are extensive banqueting and conference facilities, as well as an adjacent leisure club.

Rooms: 155rms en suite (6 fmly)

dble room £48 - £114*

Facilities: TV Modem/Fax Lift Licensed TVL Parking 130 Last d order 9.30pm ☕

BOLTON ABBEY

The Devonshire Arms Country House Hotel & Spa

★★★★ 88% ◉◉◉◉ HL

BD23 6AJ

☎ 01756 710441 & 718111 ▤ 01756 710564

email: reservations@thedevonshirearms.co.uk

www.devonshirehotels.co.uk

Dir: *on B6160, 250yds N of junct with A59*

Dogs: Bedrooms (Unattended - designated rooms only) Public Areas (except restaurants & club) Garden Exercise Area (adjacent) Pet Food/Bowls food on request

Resident Pets: Emma (Spaniel), Sasha and Poppy (Labradors), Pip (Lurcher)

This hotel, owned by the Duke and Duchess of Devonshire, dates back to the 17th century. Bedrooms are elegant and the service is friendly. The restaurant offers award-winning cuisine; the brasserie lighter alternatives.

Rooms: 40rms en suite (1 fmly) (17 GF)

dble room £195 - £380

Facilities: TV STV Modem/Fax Licensed Parking 150 ☕

NORTH YORKSHIRE

BURNSALL

Burnsall Manor House ★★★ 66% GH

Main St Skipton BD23 6BW

☎ 01756 720231 🖹 01756 720231

email: joe@manorhouseuk.co.uk

www.manorhouseuk.co.uk

Dir: *On B6160 in village centre*

Dogs: Bedrooms Public Areas (except restaurant) Garden Exercise Area (adjacent)

Resident Pets: Charlie (Welsh Spaniel), Brynn (Golden Retriever)

A warm welcome awaits you at this 19th-century house, situated on the River Wharfe. Bedrooms are traditionally furnished and have delightful views. Freshly prepared meals can be enjoyed in the spacious dining room. There is also a cosy bar, television lounge, and in the warmer months, the large garden provides a peaceful setting in which to relax.

Rooms: 8rms 7 en suite dble room £53 - £61

Facilities: Licensed TVL Cen ht Parking 11

HARROGATE

Alexa House & Stable Cottages

★★★★ 78% GH

26 Ripon Road HG1 2JJ

☎ 01423 501988 🖹 01423 504086

email: enquiries@alexa-house.co.uk

www.alexa-house.co.uk

Dir: *Off A61, 0.5m from junct with A59*

Dogs: Bedrooms (Unattended) Garden Exercise Area (400yds)

This popular establishment has stylish, well-equipped bedrooms split between the main house and cottage rooms. All rooms come with homely extras. Light meals are available and dinners are available for groups by arrangement. The opulent day rooms include an elegant lounge with honesty bar, and a bright dining room. The hands-on proprietors ensure high levels of customer care.

Rooms: 13rms en suite (2 fmly) (4 GF) dble room £80 - £90

Facilities: TV Modem/Fax Licensed Cen ht Parking 10

HARROGATE
Shelbourne Guest House

★★★ 67% GA

78 Kings Road HG1 5JX

☎ 01423 504390 📠 01423 504390

email: sue@shelbourne house.co.uk

www.shelbournehouse.co.uk

Dir: *Signs to International Centre, over lights by Moat House Hotel, premises on right*

Dogs: Bedrooms Exercise Area (100yds)

Resident Pets: Jack & Keith (cats)

Situated opposite the conference centre and near to the town centre, this elegant Victorian house extends a warm welcome to all guests. Bedrooms are tastefully decorated and well equipped. There is a guest's lounge and an attractive breakfast room where hearty breakfasts are served at the individual tables.

Rooms: 8rms en suite (2 fmly)

dble room £65 - £75*

Facilities: TV Modem/Fax Licensed TVL Cen ht Parking 1

HAWNBY
Laskill Grange ★★★★ 77% GA

Hawnby YO62 5NB

☎ 01439 798268 📠 01439 798498

email: suesmith@laskillfarm.fsnet.co.uk

www.laskillgrange.co.uk

Dir: *6m N of Helmsley on B1257*

Dogs: Bedrooms Public Areas (except dining room & lounge) Garden Exercise Area (adjacent fields & lanes)

Country lovers will enjoy this charming 19th-century farmhouse. Guests can take a walk in the surrounding countryside, fish the River Seph which runs through the grounds, or visit nearby Rievaulx Abbey. Comfortable bedrooms are in the main house and are well furnished and supplied with many thoughtful extras.

Rooms: 4rms en suite (4 GF)

dble room £60 - £70*

Facilities: TV Licensed TVL Cen ht Parking 20 Last d order 8pm

NORTH YORKSHIRE

NORTH YORKSHIRE

HELMSLEY
Pheasant Hotel ★★★ 78% SHL

Harome YO62 5JG

☎ 01439 771241 📄 01439 771744

Dir: *2.5m SE, leave A170 after 0.25m. Right signed Harome for further 2m*

Dogs: Bedrooms Garden Exercise Area (country lanes nearby)

Guests can expect a family welcome at this hotel, which has spacious, comfortable bedrooms and enjoys a dclightful setting next to the village pond. The beamed, flagstoned bar leads into the charming lounge and conservatory dining room, where very enjoyable English food is served. A separate building contains the swimming pool. The hotel offers dinner-inclusive tariffs, and has many regulars.

Rooms: 14rms en suite (1 GF)

dble room £151 - £165

Facilities: TV STV FTV Licensed

Parking 20 ⌒

KNARESBOROUGH
Gallon House ◆◆◆◆ 84%

47 Kirkgate HG5 8BZ

☎ 01423 862102

email: gallon-house@ntlworld.com

www.gallon-house.co.uk

Dir: *Next to railway station*

Dogs: Bedrooms Public Areas Garden Exercise Area (100yds) Pet Food/Bowls dog welcome pack inc water bowl, towel, dog biscuits

Resident Pets: Lucy (Springer Spaniel)

This delightful Tudor-style building has spectacular views over the River Nidd, and offers very stylish accommodation and a homely atmosphere. The bedrooms are all individual with many homely extras. Rick's culinary delights are not too be missed: dinner (by arrangement) features quality local and home-made produce.

Rooms: 3rms en suite

Facilities: TV Licensed Cen ht

Last d order 8.30pm

LEYBURN

Golden Lion Hotel ★ 65% HL

Market Place DL8 5AS

☎ 01969 622161 📄 01969 623836

email: annegoldenlion@aol.com

www.thegoldenlion.co.uk

Dir: *on A684 in market square*

Dogs: Bedrooms (Unattended) Public Areas
Exercise Area (100yds)

Dating back to 1765, this traditional inn
overlooks the cobbled market square where
weekly markets still take place. Bedrooms,
including some family rooms, offer
appropriate levels of comfort. The restaurant,
with murals depicting scenes of the Dales,
offers a good range of meals. Food can also
be enjoyed in the cosy bar which is a popular
meeting place for local people.

Rooms: 15rms 14 en suite (5 fmly) dble
room £56 - £72*

Facilities: TV Lift Licensed

Last d order 9.30pm

LUMBY

Quality Hotel Leeds Selby Fork

★★★ 72% HL

Leeds LS25 5LF

☎ 01977 682761 📄 01977 685462

email: info@qualityhotelleeds.co.uk

www.choicehotelseurope.co.uk

Dir: *A1M junct 42/A63 signposted Selby,
hotel on A63 on left*

Dogs: Bedrooms Public Areas (except
restaurant) Garden Exercise Area (14-acre
grounds)

A modern hotel situated in extensive grounds
near the A1/A63 junction. Attractive day
rooms include the Seasons Restaurant and
the Spa Leisure Club is a popular feature.
Service, provided by friendly staff, includes
an all-day lounge menu and 24-hour room
service.

Rooms: 97rms en suite (18 fmly) (56 GF)
dble room £95*

Facilities: TV Licensed TVL Parking 230
🏊

NORTH YORKSHIRE

NORTH YORKSHIRE

MALHAM

Beck Hall ★★★ 57% GH

Cove Road BD23 4DJ

☎ 01729 830332

email: alice@beckhallmalham.com

www.beckhallmalham.com

Dir: *A65 to Gargrave, turn right to Malham. B&B 100yds on right after minirdbt*

Dogs: Bedrooms (Unattended) Public Areas (with other guests' permission) Garden Exercise Area (on doorstep) Pet Food/Bowls

Resident Pets: Harvey (cat)

A small stone bridge over Malham Beck leads to this delightful property. Dating from 1710, the house has true character, with bedrooms carefully furnished with four-poster beds. Delicious afternoon teas are available in the colourful garden in warmer months, while roaring log fires welcome you in the winter.

Rooms: 11rms 10 en suite (1 fmly) dble room £50 - £64*

Facilities: TV STV Modem/Fax Licensed Cen ht Parking 40 Last d order 8.45pm

RIPON

Best Western Ripon Spa Hotel

★★★ 79% HL

Park Street HG4 2BU

☎ 01765 602172 ⊟ 01765 690770

email: spahotel@bronco.co.uk

www.bw-riponspa.com

Dir: *From A61 follow signs for B6265 towards Fountains Abbey. Hotel on left after hospital*

Dogs: Bedrooms (Unattended) Public Areas (except food areas) Garden Exercise Area

This privately owned hotel is set in extensive and attractive gardens just a short walk from the city centre. The bedrooms are well equipped to meet the needs of leisure and business travellers alike, while the comfortable lounges are complemented by the convivial atmosphere of the Turf Bar.

Rooms: 40rms en suite (5 fmly) (4 GF) dble room £108 - £123*

Facilities: TV STV Modem/Fax Lift Licensed Parking 60 Last d order 9.30pm

ROSEDALE ABBEY
Blacksmith's Country Inn
★★★ 71% HL

Hartoft End Pickering YO18 8EN

☎ 01751 417331 ▤ 01751 417167

email: info@hartoft-bci.co.uk

www.hartoft-bci.co.uk

Dir: *off A170 in village of Wrelton, N to Hartoft*

Dogs: Bedrooms (Unattended) Public Areas (bar only) Garden Exercise Area (fields all around)

Resident Pets: Tico (Alsatian), Heidi (cat)

Set amongst the wooded valleys and hillsides of the Yorkshire Moors, this charming hotel offers a choice of popular bars and intimate, cosy lounges, and retains the atmosphere of a country inn. Food is available either in the bars or the spacious restaurant. Bedrooms are equipped to comfortable modern standards.

Rooms: 19rms en suite (2 fmly) (4 GF)
dble room £80 - £110*

Facilities: TV Licensed TVL Parking 100
Last d order 9pm

THIRSK
Golden Fleece Hotel ★★ 76% HL

42 Market Place YO7 1LL

☎ 01845 523108 ▤ 01845 523996

email: reservations@goldenfleecehotel.com

www.goldenfleecehotel.com

Dir: *off A19 to Thirsk*

Dogs: Bedrooms (Unattended) Public Areas (except restaurant) Exercise Area (100yds)

This delightful hotel began life as a coaching inn, and enjoys a central location in the market square. Bedrooms are comfortably furnished, extremely well equipped and individually styled with beautiful soft furnishings. Guests can eat in the attractive bar, or choose more formal dining in the smart restaurant where there is guaranteed friendly, attentive service.

Rooms: 23rms en suite (3 fmly)
dble room £70 - £90*

Facilities: TV STV Modem/Fax Licensed
Parking 35 Last d order 8pm

NORTH YORKSHIRE

NORTH YORKSHIRE

YORK

Clifton Bridge Hotel ★★ 72% HL

Water End YO30 6LL

☎ 01904 610510 📄 01904 640208

email: enq@cliftonbridgehotel.co.uk

Dir: *turn off A1237 onto A19 towards city centre. Right at lights by church, hotel 50yds on left*

Dogs: Bedrooms Public Areas Garden Exercise Area (10yds) Pet Food/Bowls
Standing between Clifton Green and the River Ouse, and within walking distance of the city, this hotel offers good hospitality and attentive service. The house is well furnished and features oak panelling in the public rooms. Bedrooms are attractively decorated and thoughtfully equipped. Good home cooking is served in the cosy dining room.

Rooms: 15rms en suite (1 fmly) (3 GF)

Facilities: TV Licensed TVL Parking 10

YORK

Ascot House ★★★★ 77% GH

80 East Parade YO31 7YH

☎ 01904 426826 📄 01904 431077

email: admin@ascothouseyork.com

www.ascothouseyork.com

Dir: *0.5m NE of city centre. Off A1036 Heworth Green onto Mill Ln, 2nd left*

Dogs: Bedrooms (Unattended) Public Areas (except dining room) Garden Exercise Area (5 mins' walk)

Resident Pets: Gemma & Millie (Black Labradors)
June and Keith Wood provide friendly service at the 1869 Ascot House, a 15-minute walk from the town centre. Bedrooms are thoughtfully equipped, many with four-poster or canopy beds and other period furniture. Reception rooms include a cosy lounge that also retains its original features.

Rooms: 15rms 12 en suite (3 fmly) (2 GF) dble room £60 - £75*

Facilities: TV Licensed TVL Cen ht Parking 14 Last d order 6pm

YORK

Greenside ★ ★ ★ 58% GH

124 Clifton YO30 6BQ

☎ 01904 623631 🖹 01904 623631

email: greenside@amserve.com

www.greensideguesthouse.co.uk

Dir: *A19 N towards city centre, over lights for Greenside, on left opp Clifton Green*

Dogs: Bedrooms (Unattended) Sep Accom (entrance halls) Garden Exercise Area (25yds)

Overlooking Clifton Green, this detached house is just within walking distance of the city centre. Accommodation consists of simply furnished bedrooms and there is a cosy lounge and a dining room, where dinners by arrangement and traditional breakfasts are served. It is a family home, and other families are welcome.

Rooms: 6rms 3 en suite (2 fmly) (3 GF) dble room £46*

Facilities: TV TVL Cen ht Parking 6

YORK

The Priory Hotel ★ ★ ★ 63% GA

126-128 Fulford Road YO10 4BE

☎ 01904 625280 🖹 01904 637330

email: reservations@priory-hotelyork.co.uk

www.priory-hotelyork.co.uk

Dir: *500yds S of city centre on A19*

Dogs: Bedrooms (Unattended) Public Areas (except dining rooms) Garden Exercise Area

Resident Pets: Elsa & Boo (dogs), TC & Guinness (cats)

The same family has run this comfortable establishment for three generations. Reception rooms include a comfortable foyer, lounge and cosy bar, all decorated in keeping with the large Victorian house, and a modern breakfast room. Bedrooms are modern in style and provide a high standard of comfort. Gothic arches lead to the landscaped gardens.

Rooms: 16rms en suite (5 fmly) (1 GF) dble room £60 - £85*

Facilities: TV FTV Modem/Fax Licensed TVL Cen ht Parking 25

Last d order 10.30pm

NORTH YORKSHIRE

NORTH YORKSHIRE

YORK
The Grange Hotel
★ ★ ★ 82% ◉ ◉ HL
1 Clifton YO30 6AA
☎ 01904 644744 ▤ 01904 612453
email: info@grangehotel.co.uk
www.grangehotel.co.uk
Dir: *on A19 York/Thirsk road, approx 500yds from city centre*
Dogs: Bedrooms (Unattended) Exercise Area (1m)
This bustling Regency town house is just a few minutes' walk from the centre of York. A professional service is efficiently delivered in a friendly manner. Public rooms have been stylishly furnished; these include three dining options, the informal cellar brasserie, the seafood bar and The Ivy, which offers fine dining in a lavishly decorated environment. The bedrooms are comfortably appointed and have been thoughtfully equipped.
Rooms: 30rms en suite (6 GF)
dble room £125 - £260
Facilities: TV STV Modem/Fax Licensed Parking 26

YORK
St Georges ★ ★ ★ 62% GA
6 St Georges Place Tadcaster Road YO24 1DR
☎ 01904 625056 ▤ 01904 625009
email: sixstgeorg@aol.com
www.members.aol.com/sixstgeorg
Dir: *A64 onto A1036 N to city centre, as racecourse ends, St Georges Place on left*
Dogs: Bedrooms Public Areas (except dining areas) Garden Exercise Area (50yds)
Resident Pets: George, Ebony, Bob & Coral (dogs) & Kitson (cat)
Located near the racecourse, this family-run establishment is within walking distance of the city. The attractive bedrooms are equipped with modern facilities, and some rooms have four-poster beds and others can accommodate families. A cosy lounge is available and hearty breakfasts are served in the delightful dining room.
Rooms: 10rms en suite (5 fmly) (1 GF)
dble room £55 - £65
Facilities: TV Cen ht Parking 7
Last d order 9.45pm

YORK

The Royal York Hotel & Events Centre ★★★★ 73% HL

Station Rd YO24 2AA

☎ 01904 653681 ▤ 01904 623503

email: sales.york@principal-hotels.com

www.principal-hotels.com

Dir: *adjacent to railway station*

Dogs: Bedrooms Public Areas Garden
Situated in three acres of landscaped grounds in the very heart of the city, this newly refurbished Victorian railway hotel has views over the city and York Minster. Contemporary bedrooms are divided between those in the main hotel and the air-conditioned garden mews. There is also a leisure complex and state-of-the-art conference centre.

Rooms: 167rms en suite (8 fmly)

Facilities: TV STV Modem/Fax Lift
Licensed Parking 80 Last d order 9.30pm

DONCASTER

Danum Hotel ★★★ 70% HL

High Street DN1 1DN

☎ 01302 342261 ▤ 01302 329034

email: info@danumhotel.com

www.danumhotel.co.uk

Dir: *M18 junct 3, A6182 to Doncaster. Over rdbt, right at next. Right at 'give way' sign, left at mini rdbt, hotel ahead*

Dogs: Bedrooms (Unattended) Public Areas (except restaurant)
Situated in the centre of the town, this Edwardian hotel offers spacious public rooms together with soundly equipped accommodation. A pleasant restaurant on the first floor serves quality dinners, and especially negotiated rates at a local leisure centre are offered.

Rooms: 64rms en suite (5 fmly)
dble room £80 - £105*

Facilities: TV STV Modem/Fax Lift
Licensed TVL Parking 36
Last d order 9.45pm

SOUTH YORKSHIRE

DONCASTER

Regent Hotel ★★★ 74% HL

Regent Square DN1 2DS

☎ 01302 364180 📄 01302 322331

email: reservations@theregenthotel.co.uk

www.theregenthotel.co.uk

Dir: *on corner of A630 & A638, 1m from racecourse*

Dogs: Bedrooms Exercise Area (10yds)
This town centre hotel overlooks a delightful
small square. Public rooms include the
modern bar and delightful restaurant, where
an interesting range of dishes is offered.
Service is friendly and attentive. Modern
bedrooms have been furnished in a
contemporary style and offer high levels
of comfort.

Rooms: 52rms en suite (6 fmly) (8 GF)
dble room £75 - £110

Facilities: TV STV Modem/Fax Lift
Licensed TVL Parking 20
Last d order 9.30pm

ROTHERHAM

Best Western Elton Hotel

★★★ 77% HL

Main Street Bramley S66 2SF

☎ 01709 545681 📄 01709 549100

email: bestwestern.eltonhotel@btinternet.com

www.bw-eltonhotel.co.uk

Dir: *M18 junct 1 follow A631 Rotherham,
turn right to Ravenfield, hotel at end of
Bramley village, follow brown signs*

Dogs: Bedrooms (Unattended) Garden
Exercise Area (0.25m) Pet Food/Bowls
Within easy reach of the M18, this
welcoming, stone-built hotel is set in well-
tended gardens. The Elton offers good modern
accommodation, with larger rooms in the
extension that are particularly comfortable and
well equipped. A civil licence is held for
wedding ceremonies and conference rooms
are available.

Rooms: 29rms en suite (4 fmly) (11 GF)
dble room £76 - £96

Facilities: TV STV Modem/Fax Licensed
Parking 48 Last d order 9.15pm

SHEFFIELD

Cutlers Hotel ★ ★ 66% HL

Theatreland George Street S1 2PF

☎ 0114 273 9939 ▤ 0114 276 8332

email: enquiries@cutlershotel.co.uk

www.cutlershotel.co.uk

Dir: *In retail, commerce & academic centre,*
50yds from Crucible Theatre. Follow theatre
signs

Dogs: Bedrooms (Unattended) Public Areas
(except restaurant & lounge bar) Exercise
Area (50yds)

Situated close to the Crucible Theatre in
the city centre, this small hotel offers
accommodation in well-equipped bedrooms
with extras including hairdryers, trouser
presses and business facilities. Public areas
include a lower ground floor bistro, and room
service is an option. Small meeting rooms are
also available. Discounted overnight parking
is provided in the nearby public car park.

Rooms: 45rms en suite (4 fmly)

Facilities: TV STV Modem/Fax Lift
Licensed TVL

WOODALL

Days Inn Sheffield ⇧ BUD

Woodall Service Area S26 7XR

☎ 0114 248 7992 ▤ 0114 248 5634

email: woodall.hotel@welcomebreak.co.uk

www.welcomebreak.co.uk

Dir: *M1 southbound, at Woodall Services,*
between juncts 30/31

Dogs: Bedrooms (Unattended) Public Areas
(must be kept on lead) Garden Exercise Area
(adjacent) welcome snack pack on arrival

This modern building offers accommodation
in smart, spacious and well-equipped
bedrooms, suitable for families and business
travellers, and all with en suite bathrooms.
Continental breakfast is available and other
refreshments may be taken at the nearby
family restaurant.

Rooms: 38rms en suite (32 fmly)

dble room £45 - £55*

Facilities: TV STV TVL Parking 40

Last d order 9pm

BRADFORD
Best Western Guide Post Hotel

★★★ 73% HL

Common Road Low Moor BD12 0ST

☎ 01274 607866 ▤ 01274 671085

email: sales@guideposthotel.net

www.guideposthotel.net

Dir: *take M606, then signed*

Dogs: Bedrooms (Unattended) Public Areas
Exercise Area (2 mins)

Resident Pets: William (Springer Spaniel)
Situated south of the city, this hotel offers
attractively styled, modern, comfortable
bedrooms. The restaurant offers an extensive
range of food using fresh, local produce;
lighter snack meals are served in the bar.
There is also a choice of well-equipped
meeting and function rooms.

Rooms: 43rms en suite (3 fmly) (14 GF)
dble room £29.50 - £90*

Facilities: TV STV Modem/Fax Licensed
Parking 100

HARTSHEAD MOOR SERVICE AREA
Days Inn Bradford ⌂ BUD

Hartshead Moor Service Area Clifton HD6 4JX

☎ 01274 851706 ▤ 01274 855169

email: hartsheadmoor.hotel@welcomebreak.co.uk

www.welcomebreak.co.uk

Dir: *M62 between junct 25 and 26*

Dogs: Bedrooms (Unattended) Public Areas
(must be kept on lead) Garden Exercise Area
(adjacent) welcome snack pack on arrival
This modern building offers accommodation
in smart, spacious and well-equipped
bedrooms, suitable for families and business
travellers, and all with en suite bathrooms.
Continental breakfast is available and other
refreshments may be taken at the nearby
family restaurant.

Rooms: 38rms en suite (33 fmly)
dble room £45 - £55*

Facilities: TV STV TVL Parking 100
Last d order 10pm

HUDDERSFIELD

Cedar Court Hotel ★★★★ 68% HL

Ainley Top HD3 3RH

☎ 01422 375431 🖹 01422 314050

email: huddersfield@cedarcourthotels.co.uk

www.cedarcourthotels.co.uk

Dir: *500yds from M62 junct 24*

Dogs: Bedrooms (Unattended) Garden
Exercise Area

Sitting adjacent to the M62, this hotel is an ideal location for business travellers or for those touring West Yorkshire. Bedrooms are spacious and comfortable and there is a busy lounge with snacks available all day, as well as a modern restaurant and a fully equipped leisure centre. There are extensive meeting and banqueting facilities.

Rooms: 114rms en suite (6 fmly) (10 GF)
dble room £75 - £159

Facilities: TV STV Modem/Fax Lift
Licensed Parking 250 Last d order 9pm 🕿

KEIGHLEY

Dalesgate Hotel ★★ 67% HL

406 Skipton Road Utley BD20 6HP

☎ 01535 664930 🖹 01535 611253

email: stephen.e.atha@btinternet.com

www.dalesgate.co.uk

Dir: *In town centre follow A629 over rdbt.
Right after 0.75m into St. John's Rd. 1st right
into hotel car park*

Dogs: Bedrooms (Unattended) Public Areas
(except in bar & restaurant) Exercise Area
(500yds)

Resident Pets: Max (German Shepherd
cross)

Originally the residence of a local chapel minister, this modern, well-established hotel provides well-equipped, comfortable bedrooms. It also boasts a cosy bar and pleasant restaurant, serving an imaginative range of dishes. A large car park is provided.

Rooms: 20rms en suite (2 fmly) (3 GF)
dble room £55 - £65*

Facilities: TV Licensed Parking 25
Last d order 10pm

WEST YORKSHIRE

WEST YORKSHIRE

LEEDS

The Merrion Hotel ★★★ 72% HL

Merrion Centre LS2 8NH

☎ 0113 243 9191 📠 0113 242 3527

email: themerrion@brook-hotels.co.uk

www.themerrion@brook-hotels.co.uk

Dir: *from M1, M62 and A61 onto city loop road to junct 7*

Dogs: Bedrooms (Unattended) Public Areas (except food service areas)

This smart, modern hotel benefits from a city centre location. Bedrooms are smartly appointed and thoughtfully equipped for both business and leisure guests. Public areas include a comfortable lounge and a pleasing restaurant with an adjacent bar. There is direct access to a car park via a walkway.

Rooms: 109rms en suite

dble room £55 - £115*

Facilities: TV STV Modem/Fax Lift Licensed TVL Last d order 9.45pm

LEEDS

Golden Lion Hotel ★★★ 72% HL

2 Lower Briggate LS1 4AE

☎ 0113 243 6454 📠 0113 243 4241

email: info@goldenlion-hotel-leeds.com

www.thegoldenlion-leeds.co.uk

Dir: *M621 junct 3. Keep in right lane. Follow until road splits into 4 lanes. Keep right and right at lights. Asda House on left. Left at lights. Over bridge, turn left, hotel opposite. Parking 150yds further on*

Dogs: Bedrooms (Unattended)

This smartly presented hotel is set in a Victorian building on the south side of the city. The well-equipped bedrooms offer a choice of standard or executive grades. Staff are friendly and helpful, ensuring a warm and welcoming atmosphere. Free overnight parking is provided in a 24-hour car park close-by the hotel.

Rooms: 89rms en suite (5 fmly)

dble room £112 - £120*

Facilities: TV STV Modem/Fax Lift Licensed TVL Last d order 10pm

WAKEFIELD

Cedar Court Hotel ★★★★ 71% HL

Denby Dale Road WF4 3QZ

☎ 01924 276310 ▤ 01924 280221

email: sales@cedarcourthotels.co.uk

www.cedarcourthotels.co.uk

Dir: *adjacent to M1 junct 39*

Dogs: Bedrooms Public Areas (except food service areas) Garden Exercise Area (on site)

This hotel enjoys a convenient location just off the M1. Traditionally styled bedrooms offer a good range of facilities while open-plan public areas include a busy bar and restaurant operation. Conferences and functions are extremely well catered for and a modern leisure club completes the picture.

Rooms: 150rms en suite (2 fmly) (74 GF)

Facilities: TV STV Modem/Fax Lift Licensed TVL Parking 350 Last d order 8pm

WAKEFIELD

Stanley View Guest House ♦♦♦ 61%

226-230 Stanley Road WF1 4AE

☎ 01924 376803 ▤ 01924 369123

email: enquiries@stanleyviewguesthouse.co.uk

www.stanleyviewguesthouse.co.uk

Dir: *M62 junct 30, on A642 N of city centre*

Dogs: Bedrooms Public Areas

Part of an attractive terrace, this well-established guest house is just 0.5m from the city centre and has private parking at the rear. The well-equipped bedrooms are brightly decorated, and there is a licensed bar and comfortable lounge. Hearty home-cooked meals are served in the attractive dining room.

Rooms: 17rms 12 en suite (6 fmly)

Facilities: TV STV Licensed TVL Cen ht Parking 10

WEST YORKSHIRE

WEST YORKSHIRE/JERSEY

WETHERBY

Prospect House ★ ★ 48% GA

8 Caxton Street LS22 6RU

☎ 01937 582428

Dir: *In town centre off A661 West Gate*

Dogs: Bedrooms (Unattended) Public Areas
(except at meal times) Garden
Exercise Area (100yds)

Resident Pets: Rusty (Poodle), Pinky
(Chocolate Torti cat), Perky (Oriental Blue cat)

A friendly welcome awaits at this centrally
located guest house. Comfortable bedrooms
are provided and a traditional breakfast
served. Mrs Watkin's hand worked tapestries
are quite a talking point in the dining room.

Rooms: 6rms 4 en suite dble room £54 - £56*

Facilities: TVL Cen ht Parking 6
Last d order 8.45pm

GROUVILLE

The Beausite Hotel ★ ★ ★ 71% HL

Les Rue des Pres Grouville Bay JE3 9DJ

☎ 01534 857577 📠 01534 857211

email: beausite@jerseymail.co.uk

www.southernhotels.com

Dogs: Bedrooms Exercise Area (200yds)

Within 300 metres of the Royal Jersey Golf
Club, this hotel is situated on the south-east
side of the island; a short distance from the
picturesque harbour at Gorey. With parts
dating back to 1636, the public rooms retain
original character and charm; bedrooms are
generally spacious and modern in design. The
indoor swimming pool, fitness room, saunas
and spa bath are an added bonus.

Rooms: 75rms en suite (5 fmly) (18 GF)
dble room £70 - £108.50*

Facilities: TV STV Licensed TVL Parking
60 Last d order 7.45pm ≋

ST BRELADE

Hotel Miramar ★★ 72% HL

Mont Gras D'Eau JE3 8ED

☎ 01534 743831 📄 01534 745009

email: miramarjsy@localdial.com

www.miramarjersey.com

Dir: *From airport take B36 at lights, turn left onto A13, take 1st turning on right down Mont Gras D'Eau*

Dogs: Bedrooms (Unattended)
Exercise Area (0.25m)

A friendly welcome awaits at this family run hotel set within its own delightful sheltered gardens, overlooking the beautiful Bay of St Brelade. There are comfortable well-appointed bedrooms, some situated on the ground floor, and two on the lower ground floor with their own terrace overlooking the pool. There is an outdoor heated swimming pool and Jacuzzi. The dining room offers a varied menu.

Rooms: 38rms en suite (2 fmly) (14 GF)
dble room £56 - £76*

Facilities: TV Licensed Parking 30
Last d order 9pm 🍽

PORT ERIN

Falcon's Nest ★★ 69% HL

The Promenade Isle of Man IM9 6AF

☎ 01624 834077 📄 01624 835370

email: falconsnest@enterprise.net

www.falconsnesthotel.co.uk

Dir: *follow coastal road, S from airport or ferry. Hotel on seafront, immediately after steam railway station*

Dogs: Bedrooms (Unattended) Public Areas (except in food areas) Exercise Area (50yds to beach/park)

Situated overlooking the bay and harbour, this Victorian hotel offers generally spacious bedrooms. There is a choice of bars, one of which attracts many locals. Meals can be taken in the lounge bar, the conservatory or in the attractively decorated main restaurant.

Rooms: 35rms en suite (9 fmly)
dble room £70 - £85*

Facilities: TV STV Modem/Fax Licensed
Parking 40 Last d order 8.30pm

JERSEY/ISLE OF MAN

ARGYLL & BUTE

CAIRNDOW
Cairndow Stagecoach Inn
★★ 66% HL

PA26 8BN

☎ 01499 600286 & 600252 📄 01499 600220

email: cairndowinn@aol.com

www.cairndowinn.com

Dir: *from North, either A82 to Tarbet, then A83 to Cairndown or A85 to Palmally, A819 to Inveraray and A83 to Cairndown.*

Dogs: Bedrooms (Unattended) Garden Exercise Area (50yds)

A relaxed, friendly atmosphere prevails at this 18th-century inn, overlooking the beautiful Loch Fyne. Bedrooms offer individual décor and thoughtful extras. Traditional public areas include a comfortable beamed lounge, a well-stocked bar where food is served throughout the day, and a spacious restaurant with conservatory extension.

Rooms: 13rms en suite (2 fmly)
dble room £60 - £80*

Facilities: TV Modem/Fax Licensed Parking 32 Last d order 7.30pm

CLACHAN-SEIL
Willowburn Hotel ★★ 85% ◉ ◉ SHL

By Oban PA34 4TJ

☎ 01852 300276

email: willowburn.hotel@virgin.net

www.willowburn.co.uk

Dir: *0.5m from Atlantic Bridge, on left*

Dogs: Bedrooms (Unattended) Public Areas (bar only) Garden Exercise Area (0.5m, open spaces)

Resident Pets: Sisko (Black Labrador), Laren (Border Collie), Odo (cat), Tussock (Hovawort)

This welcoming small hotel enjoys a peaceful setting, with grounds stretching down to the shores of Clachan Sound. Friendly unassuming service, a relaxed atmosphere and fine food are keys to its success. Bedrooms are bright, cheerful and thoughtfully equipped. Guests can watch the wildlife from the dining room, lounge or cosy bar.

Rooms: 7rms en suite (1 GF)

Facilities: TV Licensed Parking 20 Last d order 9pm

CONNEL

Falls of Lora Hotel ★ ★ ★ 75% HL

PA37 1PB

☎ 01631 710483 📄 01631 710694

email: enquiries@fallsoflora.com

www.fallsoflora.com

Dir: *hotel set back from A85 from Glasgow, 0.5m past Connel sign*

Dogs: Bedrooms Public Areas (except dining Areas or lounge) Garden Exercise Area (100yds)

Personally run and welcoming, this long-established and thriving holiday hotel enjoys inspiring views over Loch Etive. The spacious ground floor takes in a comfortable, traditional lounge and a well-stocked bar. Guests can eat in the popular, informal bistro. Bedrooms come in a variety of styles, ranging from the cosy standard rooms to high quality luxury rooms.

Rooms: 30rms en suite (4 fmly) (4 GF) dble room £49 - £119

Facilities: TV Licensed Parking 40 Last d order 9pm

ERISKA

Isle of Eriska

★ ★ ★ ★ ★ 83% @@@ CHH

Eriska Ledaig PA37 1SD

☎ 01631 720371 📄 01631 720531

email: office@eriska-hotel.co.uk

www.eriska-hotel.co.uk

Dir: *leave A85 at Connel, onto A828, follow for 4m, then follow signs from N of Benderloch*

Dogs: Bedrooms Sep Accom (kennel) Garden Exercise Area (300-acre grounds) Pet Food/Bowls

Situated on a private island with delightful beaches and walking trails, this hotel offers a tranquil setting for relaxation. Bedrooms are comfortable. Local seafood, meats and game feature on the award-winning menu. Facilities include an indoor swimming pool, gym, spa treatment rooms and golf course.

Rooms: 17rms en suite (2 GF) dble room £275 - £380*

Facilities: TV Modem/Fax Licensed Parking 40 Last d order 9pm 🌊

ARGYLL & BUTE

ARGYLL & BUTE

INVERARAY
Loch Fyne Hotel & Leisure Club
★★★ 81% HL

PA32 8XT

☎ 0870 950 6270 ≣ 01499 302348

email: lochfyne@crerarhotels.com

www.crerarhotels.com

Dir: *from A83 Loch Lomond, through town centre on A80 to Lochgilphead. Hotel in 0.5m*

Dogs: Bedrooms (Unattended) Garden Exercise Area (0.5m) Pet Food/Bowls

This popular holiday hotel overlooks Loch Fyne. Bedrooms are mainly spacious and offer comfortable modern appointments. Guests can relax in the well-stocked bar and enjoy views over the Loch, or enjoy a meal in the delightful restaurant. There is also a well-equipped leisure centre.

Rooms: 74rms en suite

dble room £110 - £160

Facilities: TV Lift Licensed Parking 50

Last d order 8.45pm ☕

PORT ASKAIG
Port Askaig Hotel ★★ 64% SHL

Islay PA46 7RD

☎ 01496 840245 ≣ 01496 840295

email: hotel@portaskaig.co.uk

www.portaskaig.co.uk

Dir: *at Ferry Terminal*

Dogs: Bedrooms (Unattended) Public Areas Garden Exercise Area Pet Food/Bowls

Resident Pets: Tam (West Highland Terrier)

This endearing family-run hotel, set in an 18th-century building, offers comfortable bedrooms. The lounge provides fine views over the Sound of Islay to Jura and there is a choice of bars that are popular with locals. Traditional dinners are served in the bright restaurant and a full range of bar snacks and meals is also available.

Rooms: 8rms 6 en suite (1 fmly)

Facilities: TV Licensed TVL Parking 21

Last d order 9pm

TOBERMORY
Tobermory Hotel ★★ 74% ◉ HL

53 Main Street Isle of MULL PA75 6NT

☎ 01688 302091 ▤ 01688 302254

email: tobhotel@tinyworld.co.uk

www.thetobermoryhotel.com

Dir: *on waterfront, overlooking Tobermory Bay*

Dogs: Bedrooms Exercise Area (300yds)
This friendly hotel, with its pretty pink frontage, sits on the seafront amid other brightly coloured, picture-postcard buildings. There is a comfortable and relaxing lounge where drinks are served (there is no bar) prior to dining in the stylish restaurant. Bedrooms come in a variety of sizes; all are bright and vibrant with the superior rooms having video TVs.

Rooms: 16rms 15 en suite (3 fmly) (2 GF) dble room £76 - £114*

Facilities: TV Licensed TVL
Last d order 9pm

TOBERMORY
Highland Cottage

★★★ 85% ◉◉ SHL

Breadalbane Street Isle of Mull PA75 6PD

☎ 01688 302030

email: davidandjo@highlandcottage.co.uk

www.highlandcottage.co.uk

Dir: *A848 Craignure/Fishnish ferry terminal, pass Tobermory signs, straight on at mini rdbt across narrow bridge, turn right. Hotel on right opposite fire station*

Dogs: Bedrooms Garden Exercise Area (park 5 mins' walk)
Providing the highest level of natural and unassuming hospitality, this delightful little gem lies high above the island's capital. It is an Aladdin's Cave of treasures.There are two lounges, one with an honesty bar. The cosy dining room offers memorable dinners . Bedrooms are all equipped with video TVs and music centres; some have four-posters.

Rooms: 6rms en suite (1 GF) dble room £130 - £165*

Facilities: TV STV FTV Licensed
Parking 6 Last d order 10pm

ARGYLL & BUTE

ABERDEEN
Marcliffe Hotel & Spa

★ ★ ★ ★ 86% ❀ HL

North Deeside Road AB15 9YA

☎ 01224 861000 📄 01224 868860

email: enquiries@marcliffe.com

www.marcliffe.com

Dir: *A90 onto A93 signed Braemar. 1m on
right after turn at lights*

Dogs: Bedrooms (Unattended) Public Areas
(only guide dogs) Garden Exercise Area
(100yds) Pet Food/Bowls Selection of beds,
dishes, pet menu

Set in attractive grounds south-west of the
city, this impressive hotel gives a caring
service. The Conservatory restaurant, terraces
and courtyards all give a sense of the
Mediterranean, while the elegant cocktail
lounge is more classic in style. Bedrooms are
comfortable. There is an elegant new Spa.

Rooms: 42rms en suite (4 fmly) (12 GF)
dble room £140 - £295*

Facilities: TV STV Modem/Fax Lift
Licensed Parking 222

ABERDEEN
Strathisla Guest House

★ ★ ★ ★ 71%

408 Gt Western Road AB10 6NR

☎ 01224 321026

email: elza@strathisla-guesthouse.co.uk

Dir: *A90 over Dee Bridge, over rdbt, on dual-
carriageway, over 2nd rdbt to lights, right
onto Great Western Rd*

Dogs: Bedrooms (Unattended) Exercise Area
(0.25m)

Resident Pets: Holly (Chocolate Labrador),
Diva (cat)

A comfortable granite-built terrace house on
the west side of the city, Strathisla has
attractive bedrooms, all individual and
inviting, with added touches such as alarm
clocks and a complimentary slice of cake with
the beverage facilities. Vegetarian options are
available at breakfast.

Rooms: 5rms en suite (1 fmly)
dble room £42 - £50*

Facilities: TV Cen ht Parking 1
Last d order 9.45pm

ABERDEEN
Aberdeen Patio Hotel

★ ★ ★ ★ 77% HL

Beach Boulevard AB24 5EF

☎ 01224 633339 & 380000 ▤ 01224 638833

email: info@patiohotels.com

www.patiohotels.com

Dir: *from A90 follow signs for city centre,*
then for sea. On Beach Blvd, turn left at lights,
hotel on right

Dogs: Bedrooms (Unattended) Exercise Area
(100yds)

This modern, purpose-built hotel lies close to
the seafront. Bedrooms come in two different
styles - the retro-style Classics and spacious
Premiers. A new building, the Platinum Club,
offers 44 superb high spec bedrooms that
have their own bar/lounge/dinner/breakfast
room and reception. The restaurant and
Atrium bar is housed in the main building.

Rooms: 168rms en suite (8 fmly) (22 GF)
dble room £70 - £175*

Facilities: TV STV Lift Licensed TVL
Parking 172 ☜

EDINBURGH
Galloway Guest House

★ ★ ★ 63% GH

22 Dean Park Crescent EH4 1PH

☎ 0131 332 3672 ▤ 0131 332 3672

email: galloway_theclarks@hotmail.com

Dir: *Off A90, 0.5m from W end of Princes St*

Dogs: Bedrooms (Unattended) Public Areas
(except dining room) Exercise Area (0.5km)
Located in a peaceful residential area,
conveniently situated for both the shops and
bistros north of the city centre, this guest
house provides smart, thoughtfully equipped
bedrooms. Breakfasts featuring a
comprehensive selection of starters and
hot dishes are served in the ground floor
dining room.

Rooms: 10rms 6 en suite (6 fmly) (1 GF)
dble room £45 - £70

Facilities: TV Cen ht Last d order 9.30pm

EDINBURGH
Best Western Kings Manor
★★★ 78% HL
100 Milton Road East EH15 2NP
☎ 0131 669 0444 & 468 8003
🖹 0131 669 6650
email: reservations@kingsmanor.com
www.kingsmanor.com
Dir: *A720 E to Old Craighall junct, left into city, right att A1/A199 junct, hotel 200yds on right*
Dogs: Bedrooms Public Areas (except dining areas) Garden Exercise Area (on site)
Resident Pets: Guide Dogs for the Blind Association use as residential training centre. Lying on the eastern side of the city, this hotel is popular with business guests, tour groups and for conferences. It boasts a fine leisure complex and a bistro, which complements the creative cooking in the main restaurant.
Rooms: 95rms en suite (8 fmly) (13 GF)
dble room £96 - £160
Facilities: TV STV Lift Licensed
Parking 100 🍽

EDINBURGH
Garfield Guest House
★★★ 56% GH
264 Ferry Road EH5 3AN
☎ 0131 552 2369
email: enquiries@garfieldguesthouse.co.uk
www.garfieldguesthouse.co.uk
Dogs: Bedrooms Exercise Area (50yds) Friendly hospitality and good value, no-frills accommodation offering modern comfortable bedrooms. Well situated within easy striking distance of the centre of Edinburgh and well serviced by a regular bus service.
Rooms: 7rms 6 en suite (1 GF)
dble room £45 - £100*
Facilities: TV Modem/Fax Cen ht

GLASGOW

Kelvin Private Hotel ★★★ 61% GH

15 Buckingham Terrace Great Western Road
Hillhead G12 8EB

☎ 0141 339 7143 📄 0141 339 5215

email: enquiries@kelvinhotel.com

www.kelvinhotel.com

Dir: *M8 junct 17, A82 Kelvinside/Dumbarton,*
1m on right before Botanic Gardens

Dogs: Bedrooms Garden Exercise Area
(0.25m)

Two substantial Victorian terrace houses on
the west side of the city have been combined
to create this friendly establishment close to
the Botanical Gardens. The attractive
bedrooms are comfortably proportioned and
well equipped. The dining room on the first
floor is the setting for hearty traditional
breakfasts served at individual tables.

Rooms: 21rms 9 en suite (5 fmly) (2 GF)
dble room £48 - £62

Facilities: TV Cen ht Parking 5
Last d order 9.30pm

GLASGOW

Quality Hotel Glasgow ★★★ 68% HL

99 Gordon Street G1 3SF

☎ 0141 221 9680 📄 0141 226 3948

email: enquiries@quality-hotels-
glasgow.com

www.quality-hotels-glasgow.com

Dir: *M8 junct 19, left into Argyle St and left*
into Hope St

Dogs: Bedrooms (Unattended) Public Areas
(except in restaurant)

A splendid Victorian railway hotel, forming
part of Central Station. It retains much
original charm combined with modern
facilities. Public rooms are impressive and
include a recently transformed bar area and a
modernised reception. Bedrooms continue to
be upgraded and are generally spacious and
well laid out.

Rooms: 222rms en suite (8 fmly)
dble room £115 - £135*

Facilities: TV STV Modem/Fax Lift
Licensed TVL 🕯

CITY OF GLASGOW

CITY OF GLASGOW

GLASGOW

Kelvingrove Hotel ★ ★ ★ ★ 76% GA

944 Sauchiehall Street G3 7TH

☎ 0141 339 5011 🖹 0141 339 6566

email: kelvingrove.hotel@business.ntl.com

www.kelvingrove-hotel.co.uk

Dir: *M8 junct 18, 0.5m along road signed Kelvingrove Museum, on left*

Dogs: Bedrooms Garden

Exercise Area (1 mins' walk)

This friendly, well-maintained establishment is in a terrace just west of the city centre, and easily spotted in summer with its colourful floral displays. Bedrooms, including several rooms suitable for families, are well equipped and have smart, fully tiled en suite bathrooms. There is a bright breakfast room, and the reception lounge is open 24 hours.

Rooms: 22rms en suite (5 fmly) (3 GF) dble room £50 - £80*

Facilities: TV Cen ht Last d order 10pm

GLASGOW

Langs Hotel ★ ★ ★ ★ 77% ◉ ◉ HL

2 Port Dundas Place G2 3LD

☎ 0141 333 1500 & 352 2452

🖹 0141 333 5700

email: reservations@langshotels.co.uk

www.langshotels.co.uk

Dir: *M8 junct 16, follow signs for George Square. Hotel immediately left after Concert Square car park*

Dogs: Bedrooms Public Areas (except restaurants)

A sharply styled, modern city centre hotel offering a choice of restaurants for dinner. Oshi has a spacious split-level Euro fusion style, whilst Aurora has award-winning food in a more formal dining environment. Bedrooms have good facilities and some feature interesting duplex suites. State of the art spa facilities ensure guests can relax.

Rooms: 100rms en suite (4 fmly) dble room £100

Facilities: TV STV Modem/Fax Lift Licensed

GLASGOW

The Merchant Lodge ★ ★ ★ 56% GA

52 Virginia Street G1 1TY

☎ 0141 552 2424 📄 0141 552 4747

email: themerchant@ukonline.co.uk

www.merchantlodgehotel.com

Dir: *Off George Sq onto North Hanover St, towards Ingram St, onto Virginia Place & Virginia St*

Dogs: Bedrooms (Unattended)
Exercise Area (0.5m)
Set within The Merchant City and close to Argyle St, this former home of a tobacco lord features a cobbled courtyard and stone turnpike stair. The house, on five floors, has been fully modernised with pine floors, pine furniture and pleasant understated decor. Breakfast is fully self-service in a bright and cheerful lower level room.

Rooms: 40rms en suite (8 fmly) (6 GF)
dble room £62 - £80*

Facilities: TV Cen ht

TILLICOULTRY

Westbourne House ★ ★ ★ ★ 71%
BB

10 Dollar Road FK13 6PA

☎ 01259 750314

email: info@westbournehouse.co.uk

www.westbournehouse.co.uk

Dir: *A91 to St Andrews. Establishment on left just past minirdbt*

Dogs: Bedrooms Garden Exercise Area (200yds)

Resident Pets: Brock (Border Collie)
This former mill-owner's home, set in wooded gardens on the edge of the village, is adorned with memorabilia gathered by the owners during their travels abroad. They offer a friendly welcome and an excellent choice is offered at breakfast.

Rooms: 3rms 2 en suite (1 fmly) (1 GF)
dble room £50 - £54

Facilities: TV Modem/Fax TVL Cen ht
Parking 3 Last d order 8.30pm

AUCHENCAIRN
Balcary Bay Hotel
★★★ 85% ®® HL
Castle Douglas DG7 1QZ
☎ 01556 640217 & 640311 ▤ 01556 640272
email: reservations@balcary-bay-hotel.co.uk
www.balcary-bay-hotel.co.uk
Dir: *on the A711 between Dalbeattie and Kirkcudbright, hotel on Shore road, 2m from village*
Dogs: Bedrooms (Unattended) Garden Exercise Area (beach) Pet Food/Bowls
Resident Pets: Rusty (Irish Red Setter)
Taking its name from the bay on which it lies, this hotel has lawns running down to the shore. The larger bedrooms enjoy stunning views over the bay, whilst others overlook the gardens. Comfortable public areas invite relaxation. Imaginative dishes feature at dinner, accompanied by a good wine list.
Rooms: 20rms en suite (1 fmly) (3 GF) dble room £120 - £150
Facilities: TV Licensed Parking 50
Last d order 8.30pm

CASTLE DOUGLAS
Imperial Hotel ★★ 68% HL
35 King Street DG7 1AA
☎ 01556 502086 ▤ 01556 503009
email: david@thegolfhotel.co.uk
www.thegolfhotel.co.uk
Dir: *exit A75 at sign for Castle Douglas, hotel opposite library*
Dogs: Bedrooms (Unattended) Public Areas (except eating areas) Garden Exercise Area (100yds)
Situated in the main street, this former coaching inn, popular with golfers, offers guests well-equipped and cheerfully decorated bedrooms. There is a choice of bars and good-value meals are served either in the foyer bar or the upstairs dining room.
Rooms: 12rms en suite (1 fmly)
Facilities: TV Licensed Parking 29

CASTLE DOUGLAS

Craigadam ★★★★ 83% GH

Craigadam DG7 3HU

☎ 01556 650233 & 650100 📄 01556 650233

email: inquiry@craigadam.com

www.craigadam.com

Dir: *From Castle Douglas E on A75 to*
Crocketford. In Crocketford turn left on A712
for 2m. House on hill

Dogs: Bedrooms (Unattended) Sep Accom
(kennel) Garden Exercise Area (field next
door)

Resident Pets: Craig (Collie), Ted & Jet
(Black Labradors), Highland cattle

Set on a working farm, this elegant country
house offers gracious living in a relaxed
environment. The large bedrooms, most set
around a courtyard, are strikingly individual in
style. Public areas include a billiard room
with honesty bar and the panelled dining
room features a magnificent 15-seater table,
the setting for Celia Pickup's delightful meals.

Rooms: 10rms en suite (2 fmly) (7 GF)

Facilities: TV Licensed Cen ht Parking 12

GRETNA

Days Inn Gretna Green ⌂ BUD

Welcome Break Service Area DG16 5HQ

☎ 01461 337566 📄 01461 337823

email: gretna.hotel@welcomebreak.co.uk

www.daysinn.com

Dir: *between junct 21/22 on M74 -*
accessible from both N'bound & S'bound
carriageway

Dogs: Bedrooms Garden Exercise Area
(adjacent)

This modern building offers accommodation
in smart, spacious and well-equipped
bedrooms suitable for families and business
travellers, and all with en suite bathrooms.
The lodge has just undergone a full
refurbishment. Continental breakfast is
available and other refreshments may be taken
at the nearby family restaurant.

Rooms: 64rms en suite (54 fmly) (64 GF)
dble room £45 - £55*

Facilities: TV STV Parking 60

DUMFRIES & GALLOWAY

DUMFRIES & GALLOWAY

GRETNA

Barrasgate ★★★ 64% GA

Millhill DG16 5HU

☎ 01461 337577 & 07711 661938

🖷 01461 337577

email: info@barrasgate.co.uk

www.barrasgate.co.uk

Dir: *M74 junct with A6071 signed Longtown. From S follow A6071 1m take 2nd left signed Gretna Green establishment on left. From N follow signs for Longtown, Barrasgate House on right 1m from motorway*

Dogs: Bedrooms Garden Exercise Area (on site & 0.5m) Pet Food/Bowls dried food
Resident Pets: Cookie (Whippet) & Megan (Lurcher)

This detached house lies in attractive gardens in a rural setting yet is convenient for the motorway. Bedrooms are well presented and there is a cosy lounge where breakfasts and light suppers are served around the one table.

Rooms: 4rms en suite (1 fmly) (1 GF)
Facilities: TV Modem/Fax TVL Cen ht
Parking 8 Last d order 8.30pm

KIRKCUDBRIGHT

Arden House Hotel ★★ 67% HL

Tongland Road DG6 4UU

☎ 01557 330544 🖷 01557 330742

Dir: *off A57 Euro route Stranraer, 4m W of Castle Douglas onto A711. Signed for Kirkcudbright, crossing Telford Bridge. Hotel 400m on left*

Dogs: Bedrooms (Unattended) Public Areas (except restaurant) Exercise Area (50yds) Pet Food/Bowls bowls on request

Set well back from the main road in extensive grounds on the northeast side of town, this spotlessly maintained hotel offers attractive bedrooms, a lounge bar and adjoining conservatory serving a range of popular dishes, which are also available in the dining room. It boasts an impressive function suite in its grounds.

Rooms: 9rms 8 en suite (7 fmly)
Facilities: TV Licensed TVL Parking 70
Last d order 9.30pm

LOCKERBIE
Ravenshill House Hotel

★★ 67% HL

12 Dumfries Road DG11 2EF

☎ 01576 202882 📠 01576 202882

email: aaenquiries@ravenshillhotellockerbie.co.uk

www.ravenshillhotellockerbie.co.uk

Dir: *from A74M Lockerbie junct onto A709.
Hotel 0.5m on right*

Dogs: Bedrooms Garden Exercise Area
(nature reserve nearby & woodland walks)
Set in spacious gardens on the fringe of the
town, this friendly, family-run hotel offers
cheerful service and good value, home-
cooked meals. The bedrooms are generally
spacious and comfortably equipped, including
an ideal two-room family unit.

Rooms: 8rms 7 en suite (2 fmly)
dble room £70 - £80*

Facilities: TV Licensed Parking 35

MOFFAT
Barnhill Springs Country Guest
House ★★ 56% GA

DG10 9QS

☎ 01683 220580

Dir: *A74M junct 15, A701 towards Moffat,
Barnhill Rd 50yds on right*

Dogs: Bedrooms (Unattended) Public Areas
(except dining room) Garden Exercise Area
(on site) Pet Food/Bowls 1.5 acres of
grounds

Resident Pets: Kim (Collie cross)
This former farmhouse has a quiet rural
location south of the town and within easy
reach of the M74. Bedrooms are well
proportioned; none have bathrooms en suite,
though one room on the ground floor has a
private shower room. There is a comfortable
lounge and separate dining room.

Rooms: 5rms 0 en suite (1 fmly) (1 GF)
dble room £54 - £56

Facilities: TVL Cen ht Parking 10

DUMFRIES & GALLOWAY

DUMFRIES & GALLOWAY

MOFFAT

Hartfell House ★★★★ 71% GH

Hartfell Crescent DG10 9AL

☎ 01683 220153 📄 01683 220153

email: enquiries@hartfellhouse.co.uk

www.hartfellhouse.co.uk

Dir: *Off High St at war memorial onto Well St & Old Well Rd, Hartfell Crescent on right*

Dogs: Bedrooms Garden Exercise Area (100yds)

Built in 1850, this impressive Victorian house is in a peaceful terrace high above the town, having lovely views of the surrounding countryside. Beautifully maintained, its bedrooms offer high quality and comfort. There is an inviting first-floor lounge and attractive dining room, where delicious breakfasts and evening meals are served. A computer with broadband and WiFi is now also available for guests use.

Rooms: 9rms 7 en suite (2 fmly) (2 GF)

Facilities: TV Licensed Cen ht Parking 6

MOFFAT

Limetree House ★★★★ 75% GA

Eastgate DG10 9AE

☎ 01683 220001

email: info@limetreehouse.co.uk

www.limetreehouse.co.uk

Dir: *Off High St onto Well St, left onto Eastgate, house 100yds*

Dogs: Bedrooms Public Areas (but never unattended) Exercise Area (100yds)

Resident Pets: Mike, Sully & Beatrice (cats)

A warm welcome is assured at this well-maintained guest house, quietly situated behind the main high street. Recognisable by its colourful flower baskets in season, it provides an inviting lounge and bright cheerful breakfast room. Bedrooms are smartly furnished in pine and include a large family room.

Rooms: 6rms en suite (1 fmly) (1 GF)

Facilities: TV Cen ht Parking 3

Last d order 9.30pm

GULLANE

Greywalls Hotel

★ ★ ★ 85% ◉ ◉ ◉ HL

Muirfield EH31 2EG

☎ 01620 842144 🖹 01620 842241

email: hotel@greywalls.co.uk

www.greywalls.co.uk

Dir: *A198, hotel signposted at E end of village*

Dogs: Bedrooms (Unattended) Garden
Exercise Area (adjacent) a very warm welcome
to well behaved dogs

A dignified but relaxing Edwardian country
house designed by Sir Edwin Lutyens;
Greywalls overlooks the famous Muirfield Golf
Course and is just a half hours' drive from
Edinburgh. Delightful public rooms look onto
beautiful gardens and freshly prepared cuisine
may be enjoyed in the restaurant. Stylish
bedrooms, whether cosy singles or spacious
master rooms, are thoughtfully equipped. A
gatehouse lodge is ideal for golfing parties.

Rooms: 23rms en suite (9 GF)

dble room £240 - £285*

Facilities: TV STV Licensed Parking 40

Last d order 9.30pm

ABERDOUR

The Cedar Inn ★ 64% SHL

20 Shore Road KY3 0TR

☎ 01383 860310 🖹 01383 860004

email: enquiries@cedarinn.co.uk

www.cedarinn.co.uk

Dir: *in Aberdour village turn right off A921
into Main St then right into Shore Rd. Hotel
100yds on left*

Dogs: Bedrooms (Unattended) Public Areas
(except dining area) Garden Exercise Area
(20yds) Pet Food/Bowls

Lying between the village centre and the
beach, this small hotel has three character
bars, one dedicated to malt whiskies, and
impressive bar and dinner menus.
Bedrooms offer a mix of standards but all
are well equipped.

Rooms: 9rms en suite (2 fmly)

dble room £60 - £70*

Facilities: TV Modem/Fax Licensed
Parking 12

EAST LOTHIAN/FIFE

FIFE

ANSTRUTHER

The Spindrift ★ ★ ★ ★ 81% GA

Pittenweem Road KY10 3DT

☎ 01333 310573 📄 01333 310573

email: info@thespindrift.co.uk

www.thespindrift.co.uk

Dir: *Entering town from W on A917, 1st building on left*

Dogs: Bedrooms (Unattended) Garden Exercise Area (2 mins) Pet Food/Bowls beds & blankets

This immaculate Victorian villa stands on the western edge of the village. The attractive bedrooms offer a wide range of extra touches; the Captain's Room, a replica of a wood-panelled cabin, is a particular feature. The inviting lounge has an honesty bar, while imaginative breakfasts, and enjoyable home-cooked meals by arrangement, are served in the cheerful dining room.

Rooms: 8rms 7 en suite (2 fmly)

dble room £55 - £76

Facilities: TV Modem/Fax Licensed Cen ht Parking 12 Last d order 9.30pm

DUNFERMLINE

Pitbauchlie House Hotel

★ ★ ★ 75% HL

Aberdour Road KY11 4PB

☎ 01383 722282 📄 01383 620738

email: info@pitbauchlie.com

www.pitbauchlie.com

Dir: *M90 junct 2, onto A823, then B916. Hotel 0.5m on right*

Dogs: Bedrooms (Unattended) Garden

This hotel is set in landscaped gardens a mile south of the town centre. A stylish foyer and cocktail lounge catch the eye; the latter overlooking the garden, as does the restaurant and separate bar/bistro. The modern bedrooms are well equipped, the deluxe rooms having CD players and videos.

Rooms: 50rms en suite (3 fmly) (19 GF)

dble room £108 - £118*

Facilities: TV STV Licensed Parking 80 Last d order 9.30pm

LADYBANK

Fernie Castle ★ ★ ★ 74% HL

Letham KY15 7RU

☎ 01337 810381 📄 01337 810422

email: mail@ferniecastle.demon.co.uk

www.ferniecastle.demon.co.uk

Dir: *M90 junct 8 take A91 E Tay Bridge/St Andrews to Melville Lodges rdbt. Left onto A92 signed Tay Bridge. Hotel 1.2m on right*

Dogs: Bedrooms (Unattended) Public Areas Garden Exercise Area (woodland) Pet Food/Bowls

Resident Pets: Cinders (Great Dane), Buttons (Chihuahua), Apollo (Dalmatian), cows, chickens

An historic, turreted castle set in seventeen acres of wooded grounds in the heart of Fife, is a popular venue for weddings. Bedrooms range in size. There is an elegant restaurant or guests can eat in the bar and bistro.

Rooms: 20rms en suite (2 fmly)

dble room £130 - £198*

Facilities: TV Licensed TVL Parking 80 Last d order 9pm

NEWBURGH

The Abbey Inn ★ ★ ★ 55% INN

East Port KY14 6EZ

☎ 01337 840761 📄 01337 842220

email: drew@lindoresabbey.co.uk

www.theabbeyinn.com

Dir: *On A913 High St*

Dogs: Bedrooms (Unattended) Public Areas (only in bar) Garden Exercise Area

Situated at the east end of the village, the Abbey Inn offers comfortable good value accommodation. The bright, well-appointed bedrooms are on the first floor and are all en suite. There is a popular public bar and home-made meals are served in the lounge bar.

Rooms: 3rms en suite dble room £50 - £60

Facilities: TV Licensed Cen ht

FIFE

HIGHLAND

BALLACHULISH
Lyn-Leven Guest House
★★★★ 77% GH
West Laroch PH49 4JP
☎ 01855 811392 📄 01855 811600
email: macleodcilla@aol.com
www.lynleven.co.uk
Dir: *Off A82 signed on left West Laroch*
Dogs: Bedrooms Exercise Area
Genuine Highland hospitality and high standards are part of the appeal of this comfortable guest house. The attractive bedrooms vary in size, are well equipped, offering many thoughtful extra touches. There is a spacious lounge and a smart dining room where delicious home-cooked evening meals and breakfasts are served at individual tables.
Rooms: 12rms en suite (3 fmly) (12 GF)
Facilities: TV Licensed TVL Cen ht
Parking 12

CARRBRIDGE
The Pines Country House ♦♦♦ 55%
Duthil PH23 3ND
☎ 01479 841220 📄 01479 841220 *51
email: Lynn@thepines-duthil.fsnet.co.uk
www.thepines-duthil.fsnet.co.uk
Dir: *2m E of Carrbridge in Duthil on A938*
Dogs: Bedrooms (Unattended) Garden
Exercise Area (on site) Pet Food/Bowls
Resident Pets: Corrie (English Springer Spaniel), Rhea (Golden Labrador)
A warm welcome is assured at this comfortable home in the Cairngorms National Park. The bright bedrooms are traditionally furnished and offer good amenities. Enjoyable home-cooked fare is served around a communal table. You can relax watching squirrels feed in the nearby wood from the conservatory-lounge.
Rooms: 4rms en suite (1 fmly) (1 GF)
dble room £45 - £46*
Facilities: TV STV Modem/Fax Cen ht
Parking 5

DRUMNADROCHIT
Clunebeg Lodge Guest House

★★★ 63% GH

Clunebeg Estate IV63 6US

☎ 01456 450387 ▤ 01456 450152

email: info@clunebeg.com

www.clunebeg.com

Dir: *Off A82 S of Drumnadrochit signed Bunloit. 100yds next right up private track to Clunebeg Estate*

Dogs: Bedrooms Public Areas (except meal times) Garden Exercise Area (set in 27 acres)
At the end of a long track into Glen Urquhart, this guest house is handy for walkers and cyclists as the Great Glen Way passes its doorstep. A modern single storey building, its bedrooms are well equipped. The spacious dining room has a lounge area with wide-screen TV, DVD and video; also internet access. An apartment is also available.

Rooms: 6rms en suite (6 GF)

dble room £55 - £72*

Facilities: TV Licensed TVL Cen ht
Parking 6

INVERNESS
Moyness House ◆◆◆◆◆ 86%

6 Bruce Gardens IV3 5EN

☎ 01463 233836 ▤ 01463 233836

email: stay@moyness.co.uk

www.moyness.co.uk

Dir: *Off A82 Fort William road, almost opp Highland Regional Council headquarters*

Dogs: Bedrooms (Unattended) Garden Exercise Area (nearby) Pet Food/Bowls
Situated in a quiet residential area just a short distance from the city centre, this elegant Victorian villa dates from 1880 and offers beautifully decorated, comfortable bedrooms and well-appointed bathrooms. There is an attractive sitting room and an inviting dining room, where traditional Scottish breakfasts are served. Guests are welcome to use the secluded and well-maintained back garden.

Rooms: 7rms en suite (1 fmly) (2 GF)

dble room £64 - £80

Facilities: TV Cen ht Parking 10

HIGHLAND

HIGHLAND

INVERNESS

Fraser House ★★★ 66% GA

49 Huntly Street IV3 5HS

☎ 01463 716488 📄 01463 716488

email: fraserlea@btopenworld.com

www.fraserhouse.co.uk

Dir: *A82 W over bridge, left onto Huntly St, house 100yds*

Dogs: Bedrooms Exercise Area (50yds) Situated on the west bank of the River Ness, Fraser House has a commanding position overlooking the city, and is within easy walking distance of the central amenities. Bedrooms, all en suite, vary in size and are comfortably furnished and well equipped. The ground-floor dining room is the setting for freshly cooked Scottish breakfasts.

Rooms: 5rms en suite (2 fmly)

dble room £50 - £60

Facilities:

KINGUSSIE

The Osprey ★★★★★ 85% GA

Ruthven Road PH21 1EN

☎ 01540 661510 📄 01540 661510

email: jmbseil@aol.com

www.ospreyhotel.co.uk

Dir: *At S end of the main street*

Dogs: Bedrooms (Unattended) Exercise Area (300 yds)

Resident Pets: Jessie (Basset Hound) This smart, cosy house in the village centre is now under attentive new ownership. Dinner is an enjoyable and casual affair emphasising local produce, while hearty breakfasts should set you up to pursue many of the activities available within the Cairngorms National Park.

Rooms: 8rms en suite (2 GF)

dble room £55 - £65*

Facilities: TV Modem/Fax Licensed TVL Cen ht Last d order 9pm

MALLAIG

West Highland Hotel ★★ 70% HL

PH41 4QZ

☎ 01687 462210 📄 01687 462130

email: westhighland.hotel@virgin.net

www.westhighlandhotel.co.uk

Dir: *from Fort William turn right at rdbt then 1st right up hill, from ferry left at rdbt then 1st right uphill*

Dogs: Bedrooms Garden Exercise Area (adjacent) Pet Food/Bowls
Originally the town's station hotel the original building was destroyed by fire and the current hotel built on the same site in the early 20th century. Fine views over to Skye are a real feature of the public rooms which include a bright airy conservatory, whilst the attractive bedrooms are thoughtfully equipped and generally spacious.

Rooms: 34rms en suite (6 fmly)
dble room £70 - £78*

Facilities: TV FTV Licensed Parking 40
Last d order 9pm

MUIR OF ORD

Ord House Hotel ★★ 71% ◉ HL

IV6 7UH

☎ 01463 870492 📄 01463 870297

email: admin@ord-house.co.uk

www.ord-house.co.uk

Dir: *off A9 at Tore rdbt onto A832. 5m, through Muir of Ord. Left towards Ullapool still A832. Hotel 0.5m on left*

Dogs: Bedrooms (Unattended) Sep Accom (kennel) Public Areas (except restaurant) Garden Exercise Area (large gardens & woodlands) Pet Food/Bowls

Resident Pets: Tatty (Black Labrador)
Dating back to 1637, this country-house hotel is situated in wooded grounds and offers brightly furnished accommodation. Day rooms reflect the character and charm of the house, with inviting lounges, a cosy snug bar and an elegant dining room where wide-ranging, creative menus are offered.

Rooms: 12rms en suite (3 GF)
dble room £80 - £120*

Facilities: Licensed TVL Parking 30

HIGHLAND

HIGHLAND

NEWTONMORE
Crubenbeg House ★★★★ 82%
Falls of Truim PH20 1BE
☎ 01540 673300
email: enquiries@crubenbeghouse.com
www.crubenbeghouse.com
Dir: *4m S of Newtonmore. Off A9 for*
Crubenmore, over railway bridge & right,
signed
Dogs: Bedrooms Public Areas Garden
Exercise Area (50yds) Pet Food/Bowls
Resident Pets: Rajah (Saluki-Alsatian)
Set in a peaceful rural location, Crubenbeg
House has stunning views and is well located
for touring the Highlands. The bedrooms are
well equipped, and the ground-floor bedroom
provides easier access. There is an inviting
lounge. Breakfast features the best of local
produce. Irene England was a top-twenty
finalist for AA Landlady of the Year 2006.
Rooms: 4rms 3 en suite (1 GF)
dble room £50 - £75
Facilities: TV Modem/Fax Licensed
Cen ht Parking 10 Last d order 8.30pm

SCOURIE
Scourie Hotel ★★ 78% HL
Sutherland IV27 4SX
☎ 01971 502396 📠 01971 502423
email: patrick@scourie-hotel.co.uk
www.scourie-hotel.co.uk
Dir: *N'bound on A894. Hotel in village on left*
Dogs: Bedrooms (Unattended) Public Areas
(except dining areas) Garden Exercise Area
(0.25m)
Resident Pets: Molly (Springer Spaniel),
Jessie & Clemmie (cats), Minstrel & Angus
(horses)
This well-established hotel is an angler's
paradise with extensive fishing rights
available on a 25,000-acre estate. Public
areas include a choice of lounges, a cosy bar
and a smart dining room offering wholesome
fare. The bedrooms are comfortable and there
is a relaxed and friendly atmosphere.
Rooms: 20rms 19 en suite (2 fmly) (5 GF)
dble room £100 - £120*
Facilities: Modem/Fax Licensed
Parking 30 Last d order 9.30pm

SPEAN BRIDGE

Smiddy House ★★★★ 82% ◎◎ GH

Roy Bridge Road PH34 4EU

☎ 01397 712335 📠 01397 712043

email: enquiry@smiddyhouse.co.uk

www.smiddyhouse.co.uk

Dir: *In village centre, A82 onto A86*

Dogs: Bedrooms Exercise Area (0.5m)

Resident Pets: Cara (King Charles Cavalier)

Set within the Great Glen, which stretches from Fort William to Inverness, this was once the village smithy, and is now a friendly guest house. The attractive bedrooms, which are named after Scottish places and whiskies, are comfortably furnished and well equipped. Delicious evening meals are served in the Russell's Bistro, which has achieved two AA Rosettes. A new residents lounge is planned for 2007.

Rooms: 4rms en suite (1 fmly)

dble room £60 - £75*

Facilities: TV Licensed Parking 15

Last d order 8pm

TAIN

The Glenmorangie Highland Home at Cadboll ★★ 85% ◎◎ CHH

Cadboll Fearn IV20 1XP

☎ 01862 871671 📠 01862 871625

email: relax@glenmorangieplc.co.uk

www.theglenmorangiehouse.co.uk

Dir: *from A9 onto B9175 towards Nigg. Follow tourist signs*

Dogs: Bedrooms (Unattended) Garden Exercise Area (0.25m) Pet Food/Bowls

This establishment balances top class service with the intimate customer care of an historic highland home. Evenings are dominated by the highly successful 'house party' where guests are introduced in the drawing room, sample whiskies then take dinner together around one long table. Stylish bedrooms are divided between the traditional main house and some cosy cottages in the grounds.

Rooms: 9rms en suite (4 fmly) (3 GF)

dble room £320 - £390*

Facilities: TV Modem/Fax Licensed TVL Parking 60 Last d order 8pm

HIGHLAND

HIGHLAND

TONGUE

Ben Loyal Hotel ★★ 74% ❀ HL

Main Street IV27 4XE

☎ 01847 611216 🖹 01847 611212

email: benloyalhotel@btinternet.com

www.benloyal.co.uk

Dir: *at Junct of A838/A836. Hotel by Royal Bank of Scotland*

Dogs: Bedrooms (Unattended) Public Areas (bar only, not at meal times) Garden Exercise Area (adjacent)

Resident Pets: Jasper (Cocker Spaniel), Beanie (cat)

Enjoying a super location close to Ben Loyal and with views of the Kyle of Tongue, this hotel often marks the welcome completion of a stunning highland drive. Bedrooms are well equipped and brightly decorated. There is a traditional dining room and a cosy bar. Extensive menus use quality local ingredients and ensure there's something for everyone.

Rooms: 11rms en suite dble room £70 - £80*

Facilities: TV Modem/Fax Licensed Parking 20 Last d order 8.30pm

WHITEBRIDGE

Whitebridge Hotel ★★ 68% HL

Stratherrick IV2 6UN

☎ 01456 486226 🖹 01456 486413

email: info@whitebridgehotel.co.uk

www.whitebridgehotel.co.uk

Dir: *off A9 onto B851, follow signs to Fort Augustus. Off A82 onto B862 at Fort Augustus*

Dogs: Bedrooms (Unattended) Public Areas (except restaurant) Garden Exercise Area (adjacent)

Close to Loch Ness and set amid rugged mountain and moorland scenery this hotel is popular with tourists, fishermen and deerstalkers. Guests have a choice of more formal dining in the restaurant or lighter meals in the popular cosy bar. Bedrooms are thoughtfully equipped and brightly furnished.

Rooms: 12rms en suite (3 fmly)

dble room £55 - £60*

Facilities: TV Licensed Parking 32 Last d order 9.30pm

ROSLIN
The Original Roslin Inn
★★★ 64% INN

4 Main Street EH25 9LE

☎ 0131 440 2384 ▤ 0131 440 2514

email: enquiries@theoriginalhotel.co.uk

www.theoriginalhotel.co.uk

Dir: *Off city bypass at Straiton for A703, Inn is close to Roslin Chapel*

Dogs: Bedrooms Garden Exercise Area (10yds) Pet Food/Bowls

Whether you find yourself on the Da Vinci Code trail or in the area on business, this delightful village inn is within easy distance of the famous Roslin Chapel which is well worth the visit. Offers well-equipped bedrooms with upgraded en suites. Four of the rooms have four-poster beds. The newly refurbished "The Grail" restaurant opened in 2006. The lounge and conservatory offer a range of bar meals.

Rooms: 6rms en suite (2 fmly)

dble room £70 - £85*

Facilities: TV STV Licensed Cen ht

Parking 8 Last d order 10.00pm

KILWINNING
Montgreenan Mansion House Hotel ★★★ 75% HL

Montgreenan Estate KA13 7QZ

☎ 01294 850005 ▤ 01294 850397

email: reservations@montgreenhotel.com

www.montgreenanhotel.com

Dir: *hotel signs 4m N of Irvine on A736 & on A737*

Dogs: Bedrooms (Unattended) Public Areas (must be well behaved) Garden Exercise Area (20yds)

Resident Pets: Toots (Golden Retriever)

In a peaceful setting of 48 acres of parkland and woods, this 19th-century mansion retains many of its original features. There is a splendid drawing room, a library, a club-style bar and a restaurant. Accommodation ranges from compact modern rooms to the classical rooms of the original house.

Rooms: 21rms en suite (1 fmly)

dble room £159 - £219*

Facilities: TV STV Modem/Fax Licensed

Parking 50 Last d order 9.45pm

MIDLOTHIAN/NORTH AYRSHIRE

NORTH LANARKSHIRE

CUMBERNAULD
The Westerwood Hotel

★★★★ 74% HL

1 St Andrews Drive Westerwood G68 0EW

☎ 01236 457171 ▤ 01236 738478

email: westerwood@qhotels.co.uk

www.qhotels.co.uk

Dogs: Bedrooms (Unattended) Garden Exercise Area (on site) Pet Food/Bowls
This stylish, contemporary hotel enjoys an elevated position within 400 acres at the foot of the Camspie Hills. Accommodation is provided in spacious, bright bedrooms, many with super bathrooms, and day rooms include sumptuous lounges, an airy restaurant and extensive golf, fitness and conference facilities.

Rooms: 100rms en suite (14 fmly) (35 GF) dble room £85 - £180

Facilities: TV STV Modem/Fax Lift Licensed TVL Parking 200
Last d order 10pm ☜

CUMBERNAULD
Castlecary House Hotel

★★ 84% HL

Castlecary Road Castlecary G68 0HD

☎ 01324 840233 ▤ 01324 841608

email: enquiries@castlecaryhotel.com

www.castlecaryhotel.com

Dir: *off A80 onto B816 between Glasgow and Stirling, the hotel is by the Castlecary Arches*

Dogs: Bedrooms (Unattended) Garden Exercise Area (100yds)
Close to the Forth Clyde Canal and convenient for the M80, this popular hotel provides a versatile range of accommodation, within purpose-built units in the grounds and also in an extension to the original house. The attractive and spacious restaurant offers a short fixed-price menu, and enjoyable meals are also served in the busy bars.

Rooms: 60rms 55 en suite (2 fmly) dble room £65 - £85

Facilities: TV Lift Licensed Parking 100

CRIEFF

Comely Bank Guest House

★★★★ /1%

32 Burrell Street PH7 4DT

☎ 01764 653409 ▤ 01764 654309

email: marion@comelybank.demon.co.uk

www.comelybank.demon.co.uk

Dir: *On A822 near Meadow Inn*

Dogs: Bedrooms Garden
Exercise Area (0.5m)

Resident Pets: Cassy (Persian cat)
Centrally located, Comely Bank offers
comfortable, bright airy bedrooms with
attractive soft furnishings. There is a ground-
floor bedroom with easier access, which is
next to the inviting lounge. Breakfasts and by
arrangement evening meals are served at
individual tables in the peaceful dining room.

Rooms: 5rms 3 en suite (2 fmly) (1 GF)
dble room £40 - £48*

Facilities: TV Modem/Fax TVL Cen ht
Last d order 9.30pm

KINROSS

Green Hotel ★★★★ 75% ❀ HL

2 The Muirs KY13 8AS

☎ 01577 863467 ▤ 01577 863180

email: reservations@green-hotel.com

www.green-hotel.com

Dir: *M90 junct 6 follow Kinross signs, onto
A922, hotel on this road*

Dogs: Bedrooms Public Areas (except
Basil's restaurant) Garden Exercise Area (on
site) Pet Food/Bowls

Resident Pets: Samantha & Shuna (Cocker
Spaniels)
A long-established hotel offering a wide range
of indoor and outdoor activities. Public areas
include a classical restaurant, a choice of bars
and a well-stocked gift shop. The comfortable,
well-equipped bedrooms, most of which are
generously proportioned, boast attractive
colour schemes and modern furnishings.

Rooms: 46rms en suite (4 fmly) (14 GF)
dble room £150 - £165*

Facilities: TV STV Modem/Fax Licensed
Parking 60 Last d order 9pm ☙

PERTH & KINROSS

PERTH & KINROSS

KIRKMICHAEL

Kirkmichael Hotel ★★★ 62% INN

Main Street Blairgowrie PH10 7NT

☎ 01250 881769 📄 01250 881779

email: info@kirkmichaelhotel.co.uk

www.kirkmichaelhotel.co.uk

Dir: *In village centre on A924*

Dogs: Bedrooms (Unattended) Sep Accom
Public Areas (except dining room) Garden
Exercise Area (50yds) Pet Food/Bowls

Resident Pets: Brodie (English Springer
Spaniel)

This friendly establishment is the hub of the
village. Hearty, well-prepared meals are
served in the restaurant or in the bar with its
cosy snug, and the spacious bedrooms are
well equipped and smartly furnished.

Rooms: 5rms en suite (1 fmly)

Facilities: TV Licensed Cen ht Parking 8
Last d order 9.30pm

PERTH

Quality Hotel ★★★ 71% HL

Leonard Street PH2 8HE

☎ 01738 624141 📄 01738 639912

email: reservations@hotels-perth.com

www.hotels-perth.com

Dir: *Follow signs for Railway station, Hotel
adjacent*

Dogs: Bedrooms Garden Exercise Area
(300yds)

Situated beside the railway station this
substantial Victorian hotel has undergone a
full refurbishment. Public rooms are well
proportioned; whilst the well-equipped
accommodation includes some massive
bedrooms.

Rooms: 71rms en suite (4 fmly)
dble room £94 - £129*

Facilities: TV STV Modem/Fax Lift
Licensed TVL Parking 100

PERTH

Westview Guest House

★★★★ 76% BB

49 Dunkeld Road PH1 5RP

☎ 01738 627787 ▤ 01738 447790

email: angiewestview@aol.com

Dir: *On A912 0.5m NW from town centre opp Royal Bank of Scotland*

Dogs: Bedrooms Garden
Exercise Area (5 mins' walk)

Resident Pets: William Wallace & Flora McDonald (Yorkshire Terriers)

Expect a warm welcome from enthusiastic owner Angie Livingstone. She is a fan of Victoriana, and her house captures that period, one feature being the teddies on the stairs. Best use is made of available space in the bedrooms, which are full of character. Public areas include an inviting lounge and a dining room.

Rooms: 5rms 3 en suite (1 fmly) (1 GF)
dble room £46 - £52*

Facilities: TV STV TVL Cen ht Parking 4
Last d order 8.30pm

PITLOCHRY

Green Park Hotel ★★★ 85% ◉ CHH

Clunie Bridge Road PH16 5JY

☎ 01796 473248 ▤ 01796 473520

email: bookings@thegreenpark.co.uk

www.thegreenpark.co.uk

Dir: *turn off A9 at Pitlochry, follow signs 0.25m through town*

Dogs: Bedrooms (Unattended) Garden
Exercise Area (20yds)

Guests return year after year to this lovely hotel that is situated in a stunning setting on the shores of Loch Faskally. Most of the thoughtfully designed bedrooms, including a splendid new wing, the restaurant and the comfortable lounges enjoy these views. Dinner utilises fresh produce, much of it grown in the kitchen garden.

Rooms: 51rms en suite (16 GF)
dble room £124 - £174*

Facilities: TV Licensed Parking 51
Last d order 8pm

PITLOCHRY
Balrobin Hotel ★★ 75% HL
Higher Oakfield PH16 5HT
☎ 01796 472901 📠 01796 474200
email: info@balrobin.co.uk
www.balrobin.co.uk
Dir: *leave A9 at Pitlochry junct, continue to town centre and follow brown tourists signs to hotel*
Dogs: Bedrooms Exercise Area (200yds)
A welcoming atmosphere prevails at this family-run hotel, which, from its position above the town, enjoys delightful countryside views. Public rooms include a relaxing lounge, a well-stocked bar and an attractive restaurant offering traditional home-cooked fare. The bedrooms are comfortable and many enjoy the fine views.
Rooms: 14rms en suite (2 fmly) (4 GF)
dble room £68 - £84*
Facilities: TV Licensed Parking 15
Last d order 9pm

ST FILLANS
The Four Seasons Hotel
★★★ 82% ❀❀ HL
Loch Earn PH6 2NF
☎ 01764 685333 📠 01764 685444
email: info@thefourseasonshotel.co.uk
www.thefourseasonshotel.co.uk
Dir: *on A85, towards W of village facing Loch*
Dogs: Bedrooms (Unattended) Public Areas (except restaurants) Garden Exercise Area (on site) Pet Food/Bowls
Resident Pets: Sham (Münsterlander)
Set on the edge of Loch Earn, this welcoming hotel and many of its bedrooms benefit from fine views. There is a choice of lounges, including a library, warmed by log fires during winter. Local produce is used to good effect in both the Meall Reamhar restaurant and the more informal Tarken Room.
Rooms: 18rms en suite (7 fmly)
dble room £106 - £126
Facilities: TV Licensed Parking 40
Last d order 7.30pm

BROUGHTON
The Glenholm Centre

★★★ 68% GA

ML12 6JF

☎ 01899 830408 ▪ 01899 830408

email: info@glenholm.co.uk

www.glenholm.dircon.co.uk

Dir: *2m S of Broughton. Off A701 to Glenholm, on right before cattle grid*

Dogs: Bedrooms (Unattended - ground floor rooms only) Garden Exercise Area (Adjacent) Pet Food/Bowls Areas of farm available for dog walking

Resident Pets: Tarry & Minty (Bearded Collies)

This former schoolhouse, surrounded by farmland, has a distinct African theme. The home-cooked meals have received much praise and are served in the spacious lounge-dining room. The bright bedrooms are well equipped. Computer courses are available.

Rooms: 4rms en suite (1 fmly) (1 GF)
dble room £48 - £53*

Facilities: TV Licensed TVL Cen ht Parking 14 Last d order 9.15pm

GALASHIELS
Kingsknowes Hotel ★★★ 73% HL

Selkirk Road TD1 3HY

☎ 01896 758375 ▪ 01896 750377

email: enq@kingsknowes.co.uk

www.kingsknowes.co.uk

Dir: *off A7 at Galashiels/Selkirk rdbt*

Dogs: Bedrooms (Unattended) Public Areas (except meal times) Garden Exercise Area (on site)

Resident Pets: Isla & Hector (Labradors)

An imposing turreted mansion, this hotel lies in attractive gardens on the outskirts of town close to the River Tweed. It boasts elegant public areas and many spacious bedrooms, some with excellent views. There is a choice of bars, one with a popular menu to supplement the restaurant.

Rooms: 12rms en suite (2 fmly)
dble room £90 - £110*

Facilities: TV STV Licensed Parking 50

SCOTTISH BORDERS

SCOTTISH BORDERS

GALASHIELS

Over Langshaw ★★ 52% FH

Langshaw TD1 2PE

☎ 01896 860244 📠 01896 860668

email: bergius@overlangshaw.fsnet.co.uk

www.overlangshaw.com

Dir: *3m N of Galashiels. A7 N from
Galashiels, 1m right signed Langshaw, right
at T-junct into Langshaw, left signed Earlston,
Over Langshaw 1m, signed*

Dogs: Bedrooms Garden Exercise Area
There are fine panoramic views from this
organic hillside farm. It offers two comfortable
and spacious bedrooms, one en suite on the
ground floor, and one upstairs with a private
bathroom. Hearty breakfasts are provided at
individual tables in the lounge and a friendly
welcome is guaranteed.

Rooms: 2rms en suite (1 fmly) (1 GF)

Facilities: TVL Cen ht Parking 4

Last d order 9pm

PEEBLES

Park Hotel ★★★ 74% HL

Innerleithen Road EH45 8BA

☎ 01721 720451 📠 01721 723510

email: reserve@parkpeebles.co.uk

www.parkpeebles.co.uk

Dir: *in town centre opposite filling station*

Dogs: Bedrooms (Unattended) Public Areas
(except when food is served) Garden
Exercise Area (on site) Pet Food/Bowls
This hotel offers pleasant, well-equipped
bedrooms of various sizes - those in the
original house are particularly spacious.
Public areas enjoy views of the gardens and
include a tartan-clad bar, a relaxing lounge
and a spacious wood-panelled restaurant.
Guests can use the extensive leisure facilities
on offer at the sister hotel, The Hydro.

Rooms: 24rms en suite

dble room £161 - £201*

Facilities: TV STV Lift Licensed
Parking 50

LERWICK

Glen Orchy House ★★★★ 72% GH

20 Knab Road ZE1 0AX

☎ 01595 692031 📄 01595 692031

email: glenorchy.house@virgin.net

www.guesthouselerwick.com

Dir: *Next to coastguard station*

Dogs: Bedrooms (Unattended) Garden
Exercise Area (20yds)

This welcoming and well-presented hotel lies
above the town with views over the Knab, and
is within easy walking distance of the town
centre. Bedrooms are modern in design and
there is a choice of lounges with books and
board games, one with an honesty bar.
Breakfasts are as substantial as dinner,
chosen from the daily-changing menu.

Rooms: 24rms en suite (4 fmly) (4 GF)
dble room £74*

Facilities: TV STV FTV Licensed Cen ht
Parking 10 Last d order 9pm

AYR

Savoy Park Hotel ★★★ 77% HL

16 Racecourse Road KA7 2UT

☎ 01292 266112 📄 01292 611488

email: mail@savoypark.com

www.savoypark.com

Dir: *from A77 follow A70 Holmston Road for
2m, through Parkhouse Street, left into
Beresford Terrace, 1st right into Bellevue
Road*

Dogs: Bedrooms Garden Exercise Area
(adjacent) Pet Food/Bowls

This hotel retains many of its traditional
values including attentive service. Public
rooms feature impressive panelled walls and
ornate ceilings. The restaurant is reminiscent
of a Highland shooting lodge and offers a
wide ranging menu to suit all tastes. The large
superior bedrooms retain a classical elegance
while others are smart and modern.

Rooms: 15rms en suite (3 fmly)
dble room £95 - £115

Facilities: TV STV Licensed Parking 60
Last d order 10pm

SHETLAND/SOUTH AYRSHIRE

SOUTH AYRSHIRE/SOUTH LANARKSHIRE

TURNBERRY
The Westin Turnberry Resort

★ ★ ★ ★ ★ 77% ❀ ❀ HL

KA26 9LT

☎ 01655 331000 📠 01655 331706

email: turnberry@westin.com

www.westin.com/turnberry

Dir: *from Glasgow take A77/M77 S towards Stranraer, 2m past Kirkoswald, follow signs for A719/Turnberry. Hotel 500yds on right*

Dogs: Bedrooms Public Areas (foyer only) Garden Exercise Area (500yds) Pet Bowls dog sitting service, 'heavenly dog bed', vet on call This famous hotel enjoys views over to Arran, Ailsa Craig and the Mull of Kintyre. Facilities include a world-renowned golf course, the Colin Montgomerie Golf Academy, a spa and outdoor pursuits. In the main hotel there are elegant bedrooms and suites; lodges provide spacious, well-equipped accommodation.

Rooms: 219rms en suite (9 fmly) (16 GF) dble room £395*

Facilities: TV STV Modem/Fax Lift Licensed Parking 200 🐾

ABINGTON
Days Inn Abington ⌂ BUD

Biggar ML12 6RG

☎ 01864 502782 📠 01864 502759

email: abington.hotel@welcomebreak.co.uk

www.welcomebreak.co.uk

Dir: *M74 junct 13, accessible from N'bound and S'bound carriageways*

Dogs: Bedrooms (Unattended) Public Areas (must be kept on lead) Garden Exercise Area (adjacent) welcome snack pack on arrival This modern building offers accommodation in smart, spacious and well-equipped bedrooms, suitable for families and business travellers, and all with en suite bathrooms. Continental breakfast is available and other refreshments may be taken at the nearby family restaurant.

Rooms: 52rms en suite (50 fmly) dble room £35 - £55*

Facilities: TV STV Parking 100 Last d order 8.45pm

SOUTH LANARKSHIRE/STIRLING

BIGGAR
Shieldhill Castle
★★★ 80% ❀❀ CHH

Quothquan ML12 6NA

☎ 01899 220035 🖷 01899 221092

email: enquiries@shieldhill.co.uk

www.shieldhill.co.uk

Dir: *A702 onto B7016 Biggar to Carnwath road, after 2m left into Shieldhill Road. Hotel 1.5m on right*

Dogs: Bedrooms (Unattended) Garden Exercise Area (within grounds) Pet Food/Bowls

Resident Pets: Mutley (Springer/Cocker Spaniel)

Food and wine are an important focus at this imposing fortified country mansion dating back almost 800 years. Public rooms include the classical Chancellor's restaurant, oak-panelled lounge and the Gun Room bar that offers its own menu. Bedrooms, many with feature baths, are spacious and comfortable.

Rooms: 16rms en suite

dble room £100 - £248*

Facilities: TV Modem/Fax Licensed TVL Parking 50 Last d order 10pm

KILLEARN
Black Bull Hotel ★★★ 72% SHL

2 The Square G63 9NG

☎ 01360 550215 🖷 01360 550143

email: sales@blackbullhotel.com

www.blackbullhotel.com

Dir: *N from Glasgow on A81, through Blanefield just past Glengoyne Distillery, take A875 to Killearn*

Dogs: Bedrooms (Unattended) Public Areas (only in bar) Garden Exercise Area (park behind hotel) Pet Food/Bowls

Resident Pets: Archie (Scottish Terrier), Penny (West Highland Terrier)

This long established village inn is an ideal destination for those wishing to enjoy the scenic splendour of the nearby Trossachs. The public areas boast a public bar, a popular bistro, and a spacious conservatory restaurant overlooking the attractive gardens.

Rooms: 12rms en suite (2 fmly)

dble room £90 - £95*

Facilities: TV STV Licensed Parking 100 Last d order 8.30pm

STIRLING/BRIDGEND

STRATHYRE
Creagan House

★★★★★ 91% ◎◎ RR

Callander FK18 8ND

☎ 01877 384638 📄 01877 384319

email: eatandstay@creaganhouse.co.uk

www.creaganhouse.co.uk

Dir: *0.25m N of Strathyre on A84*

Dogs: Bedrooms (Unattended) Sep Accom (kennel) Garden Exercise Area (Queen Elizabeth Forest nearby) Pet Food/Bowls

Resident Pets: Budd (Gordon Setter), Raffles (African Grey Parrot)

Originally a farmhouse dating from the 17th century, the Creagan House has operated as a restaurant with rooms for many years. The baronial-style dining room provides a wonderful setting for sympathetic cooking. Warm hospitality and attentive service are the highlight of any stay.

Rooms: 5rms en suite (1 fmly) (1 GF)

Facilities: Licensed Parking 26

Last d order 10pm

BRIDGEND
Days Inn Cardiff West ⌂ BUD

Sarn Park Services CF32 9RW

☎ 01656 659218 📄 01656 768665

email: sarnpark.hotel@welcomebreak.co.uk

www.welcomebreak.co.uk

Dir: *M4 junct 36*

Dogs: Bedrooms Garden Exercise Area (adjacent)

This modern building offers accommodation in smart, spacious and well-equipped bedrooms, suitable for families and business travellers, and all with en suite bathrooms. Continental breakfast is available and other refreshments may be taken at the nearby family restaurant.

Rooms: 40rms en suite (39 fmly) (20 GF) dble room £35 - £55*

Facilities: TV STV Parking 40

Last d order 9.45pm

CARDIFF
Copthorne Hotel Cardiff - Caerdydd

★ ★ ★ ★ 68% ● HL

Copthorne Way Culverhouse Cross CF5 6DA

☎ 029 2059 9100 ▤ 029 20599080

email: reservations.cardiff@mill-cop.com

www.copthone.com

Dir: *M4 junct 33, A4232 for 2.5m towards Cardiff West. Then A48 W to Cowbridge*

Dogs: Bedrooms Public Areas (except restaurant) Garden Exercise Area (hotel's lakeside area) Pet Bowls

A comfortable, popular and modern hotel, conveniently located for the airport and city. Bedrooms are a good size and some have a private lounge. Public areas are smartly presented with features including a gym, pool, meeting rooms and a comfortable restaurant with views of the adjacent lake.

Rooms: 135rms en suite (14 fmly) (27 GF) dble room £59 - £247.50*

Facilities: TV STV Modem/Fax Lift Licensed Parking 225 ☖

CWMDUAD
Neuadd-Wen Guest House

★ ★ ★ 67% GH

Carmarthen SA33 6XJ

☎ 01267 281438 ▤ 01267 281438

email: goodbourn@neuaddwen.plus.com

Dir: *On A484, 9m N of Carmarthen, towards Cardigan*

Dogs: Bedrooms (Unattended) Public Areas (except dining room) Garden Exercise Area (field adjacent)

Excellent customer care is assured at this combined Post Office and house situated in pretty gardens in an unspoiled village. Bedrooms are filled with thoughtful extras and there is a choice of lounges. One bedroom is in a carefully renovated Victorian toll cottage across the road. There is an attractive dining room that serves imaginative dinners using fresh local produce.

Rooms: 9rms 7 en suite (2 fmly) (2 GF) dble room £42 - £50

Facilities: TV Licensed TVL Cen ht Parking 12 Last d order 8.30pm

CEREDIGION

ABERPORTH

Ffynonwen ★ ★ ★ ★ 75% GH

Cardigan SA43 2HT

☎ 01239 810312 📄 01239 814910

email: ffynon.wen@tesco.net

www.cardiganshirecoastandcountry.com/ffynonwen.htm

Dir: *A487 N from Cardigan, 2nd left signed Aberporth B4333. Continue 0.5m & Ffynonwen signed to the left. Follow lane 0.5m & Ffynonwen on right*

Dogs: Bedrooms Public Areas (except dining areas) Garden Exercise Area (surrounding farmland)

Resident Pets: Trusty, Elly & Sian (dogs), Misty (Welsh Cob Pony), 4 cats, chicken, peacocks

Located in 20 acres of grounds one mile from the sea, this 17th-century former farmhouse provides homely bedrooms, including a two-bedroom family suite. Spacious public areas include a dining room and a bar. There are fishing lakes and a clay pigeon shoot.

Rooms: 4rms en suite (1 fmly)

Facilities: TV Licensed Cen ht Parking 11

LLANDYSUL

Plas Cerdin ★ ★ ★ ★ 79% BB

Ffostrasol SA44 4TA

☎ 01239 851329

www.plascerdin.co.uk

Dir: *4.5m NW of Llandysul. Off A486 N, right onto private road*

Dogs: Bedrooms Garden Exercise Area (paddock adjacent)

Resident Pets: Sam (cat), Suzie (parrot)

The very well-maintained modern house stands in lovely gardens north of the town on an elevated position with stunning views of the Cerdin Valley and the Cambrian Mountains. One of the homely bedrooms is ideal for a family, and a lounge is also available.

Rooms: 3rms en suite (1 fmly) (1 GF) dble room £46 - £50*

Facilities: TV TVL Cen ht Parking 4

BYLCHAU

Hafod Elwy Hall ★ ★ ★ ★ 79% FH

Denbigh LL16 5SP

☎ 01690 770345

email: enquiries@hafodelwyhall.co.uk

www.hafodelwyhall.co.uk

Dir: *A5 onto A543, 5.5m right onto track signed Hafod Elwy Hall*

Dogs: Bedrooms (Unattended) Sep Accom (kennel & pens) Public Areas (sun room available for dogs only) Garden Exercise Area (60-acre grounds) Pet Food/Bowls

Resident Pets: dogs, cats, birds, tortoises, horses, ram

A warm welcome awaits you at this charming house, which originates from the 14th century. Overlooking the surrounding countryside, the peaceful property is located on a 60-acre sheep and pig-rearing holding. Rooms are well equipped and have thoughtful extras.

Rooms: 3rms 2 en suite (1 GF)

dble room £55 - £90

Facilities: TV STV TVL Cen ht Parking 4

COLWYN BAY

Cabin Hill Private Hotel

★ ★ 53% GH

College Avenue Rhos-on-Sea LL28 4NT

☎ 01492 544568

Dir: *1.5m NW of Colwyn Bay in Rhos-on-Sea. Off seafront Marine Dr onto College Av*

Dogs: Bedrooms (Unattended) Public Areas (except dining room) Garden Exercise Area (5 mins' walk)

Resident Pets: Eddie & Franky (Boxers)

Cabin Hill lies in a quiet residential area within walking distance of the seafront and local shops. Bedrooms are neatly decorated and thoughtfully furnished and equipped. Ground floor areas include an attractive spacious dining room and a lounge.

Rooms: 9rms 7 en suite (2 fmly)

Facilities: TV TVL Cen ht Parking 2

Last d order 8.30pm

CONWY

CONWY

CONWY
Sychnant Pass House
★ ★ ★ ★ ★ 86% GA
Sychnant Pass Road LL32 8BJ
☎ 01492 596868 📄 01492 585486
email: bre@sychnant-pass-house.co.uk
www.sychnant-pass-house.co.uk
Dir: *1.75m W of Conwy. Off A547 Bangor Rd
in town onto Mount Pleasant & Sychnant
Pass Rd, 1.75m on right near top of hill*
Dogs: Bedrooms (Unattended) Public Areas
(except restaurant) Garden Exercise Area
(Snowdonia park opposite) Pet Food/Bowls
Resident Pets: Morris, Peter & Wellington
(cats), Nellie, Molly, Maisie & Millie (dogs)
This Edwardian house is set in landscaped
grounds. Bedrooms, including suites and four
poster rooms, are individually furnished.
Lounges are comfortable. Imaginative dinners
and suppers are served in the dining room.
Rooms: 10rms en suite (3 fmly) (2 GF)
dble room £90 - £170*
Facilities: TV Modem/Fax Licensed
Cen ht Parking 30 Last d order 8pm 🐾

CONWY
The Old Rectory Country House
★ ★ ★ ★ ★ 87% ◉◉◉ GA
Llanrwst Road Llansanffraid Glan
Conwy LL28 5LF
☎ 01492 580611 📄 01492 584555
email: info@oldrectorycountryhouse.co.uk
www.oldrectorycountryhouse.co.uk
Dir: *0.5m S from A470/A55 junct on left, by
30mph sign*
Dogs: Bedrooms (Unattended - Coach house
only) Exercise Area (adjacent)
This very welcoming accommodation has fine
views over the Conwy estuary and towards
Snowdonia. The elegant day rooms are
luxurious and home-baked afternoon teas are
available in the lounge. Bedrooms share the
delightful views and are thoughtfully
furnished, and the genuine hospitality creates
a real home from home.
Rooms: 6rms en suite
dble room £99 - £159*
Facilities: TV Licensed Parking 10

LLANDUDNO

Sunnymede Hotel ★★ 74% HL

West Parade LL30 2BD

☎ 01492 877130 ◻ 01492 871824

email: sunnymedehotel@yahoo.co.uk

www.smoothound.co.uk/hotels/sunnymede.html

Dir: *from A55 follow Llandudno & Deganwy signs. At 1st rdbt after Deganwy take 1st exit towards sea. Left at corner, then 400yds*

Dogs: Bedrooms (Unattended by prior arrangement) Public Areas (except restaurant & library) Exercise Area (10yds) Pet Food/Bowls

Resident Pets: Sassy, Candy & Radar (rescue dogs)

Sunnymede is a friendly family-run hotel on the town's West Shore. Many rooms have views over Conwy Estuary and Snowdonia. The modern, attractive bedrooms are well equipped. Comfortable bar and lounge areas.

Rooms: 15rms en suite (3 fmly) (4 GF) dble room £94 - £117*

Facilities: TV Licensed Parking 18 Last d order 8pm

LLANDUDNO

Epperstone Hotel ★★ 80% SHL

15 Abbey Road LL30 2EE

☎ 01492 878746 ◻ 01492 871223

email: epperstonehotel@btconnect.com

www.epperstone-hotel.co.uk

Dir: *A55-A470 to Mostyn Street. Left at rdbt, 4th right into York Rd. Hotel on junct of York Rd & Abbey Rd*

Dogs: Bedrooms Public Areas (except restaurant) Garden Exercise Area (on doorstep)

This delightful hotel is located in wonderful gardens in a residential area, within easy walking distance of the seafront and shops. Bedrooms are attractively decorated and thoughtfully equipped. Two lounges, a non-smoking room and a Victorian-style conservatory are available. A daily changing menu is offered in the bright dining room.

Rooms: 8rms en suite (5 fmly) (1 GF) dble room £54 - £79*

Facilities: TV STV Licensed Parking 8

CONWY

CONWY/DENBIGHSHIRE

LLANDUDNO
The Quinton Bed & Breakfast

♦♦♦ 64%

36 Church Walks LL30 2HN

☎ 01492 876879 📄 01492 876879

Dir: *A546 N towards pier, left onto Church Walks*

Dogs: Bedrooms Public Areas Garden Exercise Area

Resident Pets: Barney (West Highland Terrier)

The Quinton is convenient for the town centre and both beaches. Personally run by the same owners for over 25 years, it provides friendly hospitality and value for money. Bedrooms are well equipped and include one on the ground floor.

Rooms: 9rms en suite (3 fmly) (1 GF)

Facilities: TV Licensed TVL Cen ht Parking 12 Last d order 9.30pm

CORWEN
Bron-y-Graig ★★★★★ 85% GH

LL21 0DR

☎ 01490 413007 📄 01490 413007

email: business@north-wales-hotel.co.uk

www.north-wales-hotel.co.uk

Dir: *On A5 on E edge of Corwen*

Dogs: Bedrooms Public Areas (except restaurant) Garden Exercise Area (30yds) Pet Food/Bowls

Resident Pets: Jodie (Labrador), Tiptoes (cat)

A short walk from the town centre, this impressive Victorian house retains many original features including fireplaces, stained glass and a tiled floor in the entrance hall. Bedrooms, with luxurious bathrooms, are thoughtfully furnished; two are in a renovated coach house. Public rooms include a dining room and a comfortable lounge. A warm welcome and imaginative food is assured.

Rooms: 10rms en suite (3 fmly)

Facilities: TV STV Modem/Fax Licensed Cen ht Parking 15

BARMOUTH

Llwyndu Farmhouse ★★★★ 77% GA

Llanaber GWYNEDD LL42 1RR

☎ 01341 280144

email: Intouch@llwyndu-farmhouse.co.uk

www.llwyndu-farmhouse.co.uk

Dir: *A496 towards Harlech where street lights end, on outskirts of Barmouth, take next right*

Dogs: Bedrooms (Unattended) Garden Exercise Area

Resident Pets: Juke (Jack Russell), Lampshade & Suzy (cats), Holly & Melody (horses)

This converted 16th-century farmhouse retains many original features including inglenook fireplaces and beams. There is a cosy lounge and meals are enjoyed in the character dining room. Bedrooms are modern and well equipped, and some have four-poster beds. Four rooms are in nearby buildings.

Rooms: 7rms en suite (2 fmly)
dble room £76 - £80*

Facilities: TV Modem/Fax Licensed TVL Cen ht Parking 10 Last d order 10pm

DOLGELLAU

Fronoleu Country Hotel ★★ 67% HL

Tabor LL40 2PS

☎ 01341 422361 & 422197 📠 01341 422023

email: fronoleu@fronoleu.co.uk

www.fronoleu.co.uk

Dir: *A487/A470 junct, towards Tabor opposite Cross Foxes & continue for 1.25m. From Dolgellau take road for hospital & continue 1.25m up the hill*

Dogs: Bedrooms (Unattended) Public Areas Garden

Resident Pets: Patch (Jack Russell)

This 16th-century farmhouse lies in the shadow of Cader Idris. Carefully extended, it retains many original features. The bar and lounge are located in the old building where there are exposed timbers and open fires, and the restaurant attracts a large local following. Most of the bedrooms are in a modern extension.

Rooms: 11rms en suite (3 fmly)

Facilities: TV Licensed Parking 60

GWYNEDD

FFESTINIOG

Ty Clwb ★★★★ 78% BB

The Square LL41 4LS

☎ 01766 762658 📄 01766 762658

email: tyclwb@talk21.com

www.tyclwb.co.uk

Dir: *On B4391 in of Ffestiniog, opp church*

Dogs: Bedrooms (Unattended) Public Areas (except dining room) Garden Exercise Area (100yds)

Resident Pets: Ben (Lurcher/Old English Sheepdog cross), Caspar (Border Collie) Located opposite the historic church, this elegant house has been carefully modernised and is immaculately maintained throughout. Bedrooms are thoughtfully furnished and in addition to an attractive dining room, a spacious lounge with sun patio provides stunning views of the surrounding mountain range.

Rooms: 3rms en suite dble room £46 - £52

Facilities: TVL Cen ht

FFESTINIOG

Morannedd ★★★ 70% GA

Blaenau Road LL41 4LG

☎ 01766 762734

email: morannedd@talk21.com

www.morannedd-guesthouse.co.uk

Dir: *At edge of village on A470 towards Blaenau Ffestiniog*

Dogs: Bedrooms Public Areas (except dining room) Garden Exercise Area (surrounding countryside) Pet Food/Bowls

Resident Pets: Tessa (cat)

This guest house is set in the Snowdonia National Park and is well located for touring north Wales. A friendly welcome is offered and the atmosphere is relaxed and informal. Bedrooms are smart and modern and a cosy lounge is available. Hearty home cooking can be enjoyed here.

Rooms: 4rms en suite dble room £40 - £46*

Facilities: TV Cen ht Last d order 8.45pm

LLANBEDR

Ty Mawr Hotel ★ ★ 68% SHL

LL45 2NH

☎ 01341 241440 ⓘ 01341 241440

email: tymawrhotel@onetel.com

www.tymawrhotel.org.uk

Dir: *from Barmouth A496 Harlech road. In Llanbedr turn right after bridge, hotel 50yds on left, brown tourist signs on junct*

Dogs: Bedrooms (Unattended) Public Areas (except dining room) Garden Exercise Area (100yds) Pet Food/Bowls

Resident Pets: Carlo (Welsh Sheepdog), Chelly (Border Collie), Tara (Sheepdog), Lola (rabbit), Dolce (budgie)

Located in a picturesque village, this family-run hotel has a relaxed atmosphere. There is a popular beer garden opposite the River Artro. The bar offers a selection of food and a more formal menu is available in the restaurant. Bedrooms are smart and brightly decorated.

Rooms: 10rms en suite (2 fmly)

Facilities: TV STV Licensed TVL Parking 30 Last d order 9.30pm

AMLWCH

Lastra Farm Hotel ★ ★ 76% HL

Penrhyd Anglesey LL68 9TF

☎ 01407 830906 ⓘ 01407 832522

email: booking@lastra-hotel.com

www.lastra-hotel.com

Dir: *after 'Welcome to Amlwch' sign turn left. Straight across main road, left at T-junct on to Rhosgoch Rd*

Dogs: Bedrooms (Unattended) Public Areas (except restaurant) Garden Exercise Area (200yds) Pet Food/Bowls

This 17th-century farmhouse offers pine-furnished, colourfully decorated bedrooms. There is also a comfortable lounge and a cosy bar. A wide range of good-value food is available either in the restaurant or Granary's Bistro. The hotel can cater for functions in a separate purpose built suite.

Rooms: 8rms en suite (1 fmly) (3 GF) dble room £65 - £73*

Facilities: TV Modem/Fax Licensed Parking 40

GWYNEDD/ISLE OF ANGLESEY

MONMOUTHSHIRE/NEATH PORT TALBOT

MONMOUTH

Church Farm Guest House

★★ 53% GH

Mitchel Troy NP25 4HZ

☎ 01600 712176

www.churchfarmmitcheltroy.co.uk

Dir: *2m S of Monmouth. A40 onto B4293, left into Mitchel Troy*

Dogs: Bedrooms Public Areas (except dining room) Garden Exercise Area (100yds)
Located in the village of Mitchel Troy, this 16th-century former farmhouse retains many original features including exposed beams and open fireplaces. There is a range of bedrooms and a spacious lounge, and breakfast is served the traditionally furnished dining room. Dinner is available by prior arrangement.

Rooms: 9rms 7 en suite (3 fmly)

dble room £48 - £56

Facilities: TVL Cen ht Parking 12

Last d order 9.30pm

PORT TALBOT

Best Western Aberavon Beach Hotel ★★★ 72% HL

Swansea Bay SA12 6QP

☎ 01639 884949 📠 01639 897885

email: sales@aberavonbeach.com

www.aberavonbeach.com

Dir: *M4 junct 41/A48 & follow signs for Aberavon Beach & Hollywood Park*

Dogs: Bedrooms (Unattended) Public Areas (except restaurant) Garden Exercise Area (100yds to beach)
This friendly, purpose-built hotel enjoys a prominent position on the seafront overlooking Swansea Bay. Bedrooms, many of which have sea views, are comfortably appointed and thoughtfully equipped. Public areas include a leisure suite with swimming pool, open-plan bar and restaurant and a selection of function rooms.

Rooms: 52rms en suite (6 fmly)

dble room £78*

Facilities: TV FTV Lift Licensed Parking 150 Last d order 9.15pm 🛥

HAVERFORDWEST

Hotel Mariners ★★ 67% HL

Mariners Square SA61 2DU

☎ 01437 763353 📄 01437 764258

Dir: *follow town centre signs, over bridge, up High St, 1st turning on right, hotel at the end*

Dogs: Bedrooms Exercise Area (1m)
Located a few minutes walk from the town centre, this privately owned and friendly hotel is reputed to date back to 1625. The bedrooms are equipped with modern facilities and are soundly maintained. A good range of food is offered in the popular bar, which is a focus for the town. The restaurant offers a more formal dining option. Facilities include a choice of meeting rooms.

Rooms: 28rms en suite (5 fmly)
dble room £79 - £87.50

Facilities: TV STV Licensed Parking 50
Last d order 8.30pm

MANORBIER

Castle Mead Hotel ★★ 69% HL

SA70 7TA

☎ 01834 871358 📄 01834 871358

email: castlemeadhotel@aol.com

www.castlemeadhotel.com

Dir: *A4139 towards Pembroke, turn onto B4585 into village & follow signs to beach & castle. Hotel on left above beach*

Dogs: Bedrooms Garden Exercise Area (100yds to beach)

Resident Pets: Rosie (Border Collie), Max & Polly (cats)
Benefiting from a superb location with views of the bay, the Norman church and Manorbier Castle, this family-run hotel is welcoming. Bedrooms, which include some in a converted former coach house, are generally spacious with modern facilities. There is a restaurant, bar and lounge, and an extensive garden.

Rooms: 8rms en suite (2 fmly) (3 GF)
dble room £82*

Facilities: TV Licensed Parking 20

PEMBROKESHIRE

PEMBROKESHIRE/POWYS

SOLVA
Lochmeyler Farm Guest House

★ ★ ★ ★ ★ 85% FH

Llandeloy Solva St David's SA62 6LL

☎ 01348 837724 📠 01348 837622

email: stay@lochmeyler.co.uk

www.lochmeyler.co.uk

Dir: *From Haverfordwest A487 St Davids Rd to Penycwm, right to Llandeloy*

Dogs: Bedrooms Sep Accom (kennels) Garden Exercise Area

Resident Pets: George (Labrador), Patch (Collie), Sooty (Cocker Spaniel)

Located on a 220-acre dairy farm in an Area of Outstanding Natural Beauty, this farmhouse provides high levels of comfort. The spacious bedrooms, some in converted outbuildings, are equipped with a wealth of extras and four have private sitting rooms. There's a dining room and two sumptuous lounges.

Rooms: 11rms en suite (11 fmly) (5 GF) dble room £55 - £80

Facilities: TV Licensed TVL Cen ht Parking 11

BRECON
Borderers Guesthouse ★ ★ ★ 63% GH

47 The Watton LD3 7EG

☎ 01874 623559

email: ian@borderers.com

www.borderers.com

Dir: *200yds SE from town centre on B4601, opp church*

Dogs: Bedrooms (Unattended) Garden Exercise Area (300yds)

Resident Pets: Heather & Ella (Black Labradors)

This guest house was originally a 17th-century drovers' inn. The courtyard, now a car park, is surrounded by many of the bedrooms, and pretty hanging baskets are seen everywhere. The non-smoking bedrooms are attractively decorated with rich floral fabrics. A room suitable for easier access is available.

Rooms: 9rms 8 en suite (2 fmly) (4 GF) dble room £50 - £50*

Facilities: TV Cen ht Parking 6 Last d order 9.30pm

BRECON
The Felin Fach Griffin

★ ★ ★ ★ 78% @ @ INN

Felin Fach LD3 0UB

☎ 01874 620111 📄 01874 620120

email: enquiries@eatdrinksleep.ltd.uk

www.eatdrinksleep.ltd.uk

Dir: *4m NE of Brecon on A470*

Dogs: Bedrooms (Unattended) Public Areas (except dining room) Garden Exercise Area (on site)

This delightful inn stands in an extensive garden at the northern end of Felin Fach village. The public areas have a wealth of rustic charm and provide the setting for the excellent food. Service and hospitality are commendable. The bedrooms are carefully appointed and have modern equipment and facilities.

Rooms: 7rms en suite (1 fmly)
dble room £97.50 - £125*

Facilities: Modem/Fax Licensed Cen ht Parking 61 Last d order 9.30pm

CRICKHOWELL
Bear Hotel ★ ★ ★ 78% @ @ HL

NP8 1BW

☎ 01873 810408 📄 01873 811696

email: bearhotel@aol.com

www.bearhotel.co.uk

Dir: *on A40 between Abergavenny & Brecon*

Dogs: Bedrooms Public Areas (except restaurant) Garden Exercise Area (5 mins' walk) Pet Food/Bowls cooked chicken as a treat

Resident Pets: Magic (Cat)

A favourite with locals as well as visitors, the character and friendliness of this 15th-century coaching inn are renowned. The bar and restaurant are furnished in keeping with the style of the building and provide comfortable areas in which to enjoy some of the very popular dishes that use the finest locally-sourced ingredients.

Rooms: 34rms en suite (6 fmly)
dble room £80 - £150*

Facilities: TV Licensed TVL Parking 45

POWYS

POWYS

CRIGGION

Brimford House ◆◆◆◆ 83%

Shrewsbury SY5 9AU

☎ 01938 570235 📄 01938 570235

email: info@brimford.co.uk

www.brimford.co.uk

Dir: *Off B4393 W of Crew Green, on left after pub*

Dogs: Bedrooms Public Areas Garden Exercise Area (surrounding fields)

Resident Pets: Emma (Black Labrador), Cally (Golden Labrador)

This elegant Georgian house stands in lovely open countryside and is a good base for touring central Wales and the Marches. Bedrooms are spacious, and thoughtful extras enhance guest comfort. A cheery log fire burns in the lounge during colder weather and the hospitality is equally warm, providing a relaxing atmosphere throughout.

Rooms: 3rms en suite dble room £50 - £70*

Facilities: TV TVL Cen ht Parking 4

ERWOOD

Hafod-y-Garreg ★★★★ 74% BB

LD2 3TQ

☎ 01982 560400

email: john-annie@hafod-y.wanadoo.co.uk

www.hafodygarreg.co.uk

Dir: *1m S of Erwood. Off A470 at Trericket Mill, sharp right, up track past cream farmhouse towards pine forest, through gate*

Dogs: Bedrooms (Unattended) Public Areas Garden Exercise Area (adjacent)

Resident Pets: Ginger (cat), Rosie (goat)

This remote Grade II listed farmhouse dates in part from 1401 and is the oldest surviving traditional house in Wales. It has tremendous character and has been furnished and decorated to befit its age, while the bedrooms have modern facilities. There is an impressive dining room and a lounge. Warm hospitality is another major strength here.

Rooms: 2rms en suite (1 fmly)

dble room £50 - £55.50

Facilities: TV Cen ht Parking 6

Last d order 9pm

MONTGOMERY

Dragon Hotel ★★ 79% ⬤ HL

SY15 6PA

☎ 01686 668359 📄 0870 011 8227

email: reception@dragonhotel.com

www.dragonhotel.com

Dir: *behind town hall*

Dogs: Bedrooms (Unattended) Public Areas
(except in dining areas) Garden Exercise
Area (local countryside)

This fine 17th-century coaching inn stands in
the centre of Montgomery. Beams and timbers
from the nearby castle, which was destroyed
by Cromwell, are visible in the lounge and
bar. A wide choice of soundly prepared,
wholesome food is available in both the
restaurant and bar. Bedrooms are well
equipped and family rooms are available.

Rooms: 20rms en suite (6 fmly)
dble room £87.50 - £97.50

Facilities: TV Licensed TVL Parking 21
Last d order 9.30pm ♨

PONTYPRIDD

Llechwen Hall Hotel ★★★ 73% HL

Llanfabon CF37 4HP

☎ 01443 742050 & 743020 📄 01443 742189

email: llechwen@aol.com

www.llechwen.com

Dir: *A470 N towards Merthyr Tydfil, then
A472, then A4054 for Cilfynydd. After 0.25m,
left at hotel sign*

Dogs: Bedrooms (Unattended) Garden
Exercise Area (on site)

Resident Pets: Charles & William (Cavalier
King Charles Spaniels)

Set on top of a hill with a stunning approach,
this establishment has served many purposes
in its 200-year-old history, which includes a
private school and a magistrates' court.
Bedrooms are individually decorated and well
equipped, and some are situated in the coach
house nearby. The Victorian-style public areas
are attractively appointed.

Rooms: 20rms en suite (11 fmly) (4 GF)

Facilities: TV Modem/Fax Licensed TVL
Parking 100 Last d order 9pm

POWYS/RHONDDA CYNON TAFF

WREXHAM/DOWN

LLANARMON DYFFRYN CEIRIOG
The Hand at Llanarmon ★★ 76% SHL

Llangollen LL20 7LD

☎ 01691 600666 📠 01691 600262

email: reception@thehandhotel.co.uk

www.thehandhotel.co.uk

Dir: *Turn off A5 at Chirk onto B4500 signed Ceiriog Valley, continue for 11m*

Dogs: Bedrooms (Unattended) Sep Accom (kennels) Public Areas (except restaurant) Garden Exercise Area (adjacent)

Resident Pets: Toodles (Sussex Spaniel) This small, pleasant, privately owned and run hotel is located in the village centre and has a wealth of charm and character. Apart from warm and friendly hospitality, it provides a variety of bedroom styles, including rooms on ground floor level and two in a separate annexe building. A very good choice of competently prepared food is provided.

Rooms: 13rms en suite (4 GF)

dble room £70 - £100*

Facilities: TV Licensed Parking 18

NEWTOWNARDS
Edenvale House ★★★★★ 93% GH

130 Portaferry Road Co Down BT22 2AH

☎ 028 9181 4881 📠 028 9182 6192

email: edenvalehouse@hotmail.com

www.edenvalehouse.com

Dir: *2m S of Newtownards on A20*

Dogs: Bedrooms Sep Accom (pens) (not in field with farm animals) Garden Exercise Area (on site) Pet Food/Bowls

Resident Pets: Pip (Jack Russell), Biscuite (Shetland pony), 3 cats

A genuine warm welcome is provided at this beautifully restored Georgian house, set in grounds and furnished with antiques. Bedrooms are decorated in period style and feature many extras. One of the elegant lounges has views across Strangford Lough. Breakfast, served around a communal table, is a selection of home-made and local produce.

Rooms: 3rms en suite (2 fmly)

dble room £70 - £80*

Facilities: TV Cen ht Parking 15

Last d order 10pm

AGHADOWEY
Brown Trout Golf & Country Inn

★★ 76% HL

209 Agivey Road BT51 4AD

☎ 028 7086 8209 ▤ 028 7086 8878

email: bill@browntroutinn.com

www.browntroutinn.com

Dir: *at junct of A54 & B66 junct on road to Coleraine*

Dogs: Bedrooms (Unattended) Public Areas Garden Exercise Area (Golf course on site)

Resident Pets: Muffin (Chocolate Labrador)

Set alongside the Agivey River and featuring its own 9-hole golf course, this welcoming inn offers a choice of accommodation. Comfortably furnished bedrooms are situated around a courtyard area whilst the cottage suites also have lounge areas. Home-cooked meals are served in the restaurant and lighter fare is available in the charming lounge bar which has entertainment at weekends.

Rooms: 15rms en suite (11 fmly)

dble room £70 - £90*

Facilities: TV Licensed TVL Parking 80

KILRUSH
Bruach-na-Coille ♦♦♦ 69%

Killimer Road

☎ 065 9052250 ▤ 065 9052250

email: clarkekilrush@hotmail.com

www.clarkekilrush.com

Dir: *From Kilrush left at Shannon Side Insurance onto Moore St, right at Mace supermarket onto N67 Killimer Rd*

Dogs: Bedrooms Public Areas Garden Exercise Area (across road)

Resident Pets: Lady (Terrier)

This house, overlooking Kilrush Forest, offers accommodation with views of the Shannon Estuary. All rooms are well equipped and you can look forward to a warm welcome, an enjoyable breakfast, and helpful information about the area.

Rooms: 4rms 2 en suite (1 fmly)

Facilities: TV TVL Cen ht Parking 8

CORK

BANDON
Glebe Country House ◆◆◆◆
Ballinadee

☎ 021 4778294 📄 021 4778456

email: glebehse@indigo.ie

web: http://indigo.ie/🌐glebehse/

Dir: *Off N71 at Innishannon Bridge signed Ballinadee, 8km along river bank, left after village sign*

Dogs: Bedrooms Garden Exercise Area (Large garden)

Resident Pets: Tarka (Dalmatian)

This lovely guest house stands in well-kept gardens, and is run with great attention to detail. Antique furnishings predominate throughout this comfortable house, which has a lounge and an elegant dining room. An interesting breakfast menu offers unusual options, and a country-house style dinner is available by arrangement.

Rooms: 4rms en suite (2 fmly)

dble room £100 - £110

Facilities: TVL Cen ht Parking 30 Last d order 8.30pm

BLARNEY
Ashlee Lodge ◆◆◆◆◆ 93%
Tower

☎ 021 4385346 📄 021 4385726

email: info@ashleelodge.com

www.ashleelodge.com

Dir: *4km from Blarney on R617*

Dogs: Bedrooms Garden Exercise Area (adjacent Garden)

Ashley Lodge is a purpose-built guest house, in the village of Tower, close to Blarney and local pubs and restaurants. Bedrooms are comfortable and elegant, some with whirlpool baths, and one room has easier access. The breakfast menu is memorable for Ann's home baking. There is a sauna and an outdoor hot tub. Transfers to the airport and railway station can be arranged, and tee times can be booked at the nearby golf courses. AA Guest Accommodation of the Year for Ireland 2006.

Rooms: 10rms en suite (2 fmly) (6 GF)

dble room £140 - £240

Facilities: TV STV Modem/Fax Licensed TVL Cen ht Parking 12

CLONAKILTY

Desert House ♦♦ 49%

Coast Road

☎ 023 33331 ▤ 023 33048

email: deserthouse@eircom.net

Dir: *1km E of Clonakilty. Signed on N71 at 1st rdbt, house 500 metres on left*

Dogs: Bedrooms (Unattended) (except dining & sitting room) Garden Exercise Area (adjacent)

Resident Pets: Holly & Sophie (Golden Cockers), Tess (Sheepdog)

This comfortable Georgian farmhouse overlooks Clonakilty Bay and is within walking distance of the town. The estuary is of great interest to bird watching enthusiasts. It is a good base for touring west Cork and Kerry.

Rooms: 5rms 4 en suite

Facilities: TV Cen ht Parking 10

Last d order 9pm

ROSSNOWLAGH

Sandhouse Hotel ★★★ 85% ⊛ HL

☎ 071 9851777 ▤ 071 9852100

email: info@sandhouse.ie

www.sandhouse.ie

Dir: *from Donegal on coast road to Ballyshannon. In centre of Donegal Bay*

Dogs: Bedrooms Garden Exercise Area (beach by hotel) guests are requsted to bring own dog basket/blanket

The Sandhouse is perched over Rossnowlagh sandy beach, which is a haven for surfers. It offers very comfortable lounges with open fires, restaurant, cocktail bar and Surfers bar. The spacious bedrooms are well appointed and most enjoy the splendid sea views. Known for its hospitality, good food and service in relaxing surroundings.

Rooms: 55rms en suite (6 fmly)

dble room £180 - £280*

Facilities: TV STV Lift Licensed TVL

Parking 42 Last d order 9.30pm

CORK/DONEGAL

GALWAY

CLIFDEN
Ardagh Hotel & Restaurant

★★★ 73% ◉ ◉ HL

Ballyconneely Road

☎ 095 21384 📄 095 21314

email: ardaghhotel@eircom.net

www.ardaghhotel.com

Dir: *N59 Galway to Clifden, signed to Ballyconneely*

Dogs: Bedrooms Public Areas (except bar and restaurant) Garden Exercise Area (on site) Situated at the head of Ardbear Bay, this family-run hotel makes full use of the spectacular scenery in the area. The restaurant is renowned for its cuisine, which is complemented by friendly and knowledgeable service. Many of the spacious and well-appointed bedrooms have large picture windows and plenty of comfort.

Rooms: 19rms en suite (2 fmly) dble room £150 - £175*

Facilities: TV Licensed Parking 35 Last d order 9.15pm

GALWAY
Ardilaun House Hotel Conference Centre & LC ★★★★ 76% ◉ HL

Taylor's Hill

☎ 091 521433 📄 091 521546

email: info@ardilaunhousehotel.ie

www.ardilaunhousehotel.ie

Dir: *N6 to Galway City West, then follow signs for N59 Clifden, then N6 towards Salthill, hotel on this road*

Dogs: Bedrooms Garden Exercise Area (0.25m)

Located on five acres of private grounds and landscaped gardens, the original Ardilaun House was built in 1840 and converted to a hotel over 40 years ago. The bedrooms are well equipped and pleasantly furnished. Public areas include an elegant restaurant overlooking the garden, lounges and a bar, and there are banqueting and leisure facilities.

Rooms: 125rms en suite (7 fmly) (8 GF) dble room £110 - £320*

Facilities: TV STV Modem/Fax Lift Licensed TVL Parking 320 ☞

GALWAY

Atlantic Heights ★ ★ ★ ★ 76%

2 Cashelmara Knocknacarra Cross Salthill

☎ 091 529466 & 528830

email: info@atlanticheightsgalway.com

www.atlanticheightsgalway.com

Dir: *2km W of city centre. 1km from Salthill promenade in upper Salthill on R336*

Dogs: Bedrooms (Unattended) Garden Exercise Area (on site) Pet Food/Bowls

Resident Pets: Susie (Brehony Spaniel) Enthusiastic hosts Robbie and Madeline Mitchell take great pride in their fine balconied house with views of Galway Bay. The bedrooms have many thoughful extras, and the extensive breakfast menu, served late if required, features home baking. Laundry service available.

Rooms: 6rms en suite (3 fmly)
dble room £70 - £100

Facilities: TV STV Modem/Fax Cen ht Parking 6

KYLEMORE

Kylemore House ★ ★ ★ ★ 72%

Connemara

☎ 095 41143 📄 095 41143

email: kylemorehouse@eircom.net

www.connemara.net/kylemorehouse

Dir: *Off N59 from Galway onto R344 at Recess*

Dogs: Bedrooms Public Areas Garden Exercise Area
Standing on the shores of Lake Kylemore, protected by the Twelve Pins Mountains, this comfortable house has fishing rights on three lakes in a very scenic area of Connemara. Owner Mrs Naughton takes pride in her cooking and serves evening meals by arrangement.

Rooms: 6rms en suite (1 fmly) (1 GF)
dble room £68 - £76

Facilities: Modem/Fax Licensed TVL Cen ht Parking 8 Last d order 9pm

RECESS
Lough Inagh Lodge Hotel
★★★ 81% ❀ CHH
Inagh Valley
☎ 095 34706 & 34694 📄 095 34708
email: inagh@iol.ie
www.loughinaghlodgehotel.ie
Dir: *from Recess take R344 towards Kylemore*
Dogs: Bedrooms (Unattended) Sep Accom Public Areas Garden Exercise Area (field) Pet Food/Bowls
Resident Pets: Rex (Springer Spaniel), Sasha (cat)
This 19th-century, former fishing lodge is akin to a family home where guests can enjoy the peace. It nestles between the Connemara Mountains, fronted by a good fishing lake. Bedrooms are smart and comfortable, there is a choice of lounges and a bar. The delightful restaurant serves local lamb and fish.
Rooms: 12rms en suite (4 GF)
dble room £178 - £213*
Facilities: TV STV Licensed Parking 16

ATHY
Coursetown Country House ◆◆◆◆◆
Stradbally Road
☎ 059 8631101 📄 059 8632740
email: coursetown@hotmail.com
www.coursetown.com
Dir: *N78 at Athy onto R428, 3km from Athy*
Dogs: Bedrooms Garden Exercise Area (270 acres surrounding property)
Resident Pets: Casper, Millicent & Leopold (cats)
This charming Victorian country house stands on a 100-hectare tillage farm and bird sanctuary. It has been extensively refurbished, and all bedrooms are furnished to the highest standards. Convalescent or disabled guests are especially welcome, and Iris and Jim Fox are happy to share their knowledge of the Irish countryside and its wildlife.
Rooms: 5rms en suite (1 GF)
dble room £110 - £120
Facilities: TV TVL Cen ht Parking 22

ACHILL ISLAND
Gray's Guest House ♦♦♦♦ 76%

Dugort

☎ 098 43244 & 43315

Dir: *11km NW of Achill Sound. Off R319 to Doogort*

Dogs: Bedrooms Garden Exercise Area
Resident Pets: Cuddles (Corgi), Huggy Bear & Phoebe (cats)

This welcoming guest house is in Doogort, on the northern shore of Achill Island, at the foot of the Slievemore mountains. There is a smart conservatory and various lounges, the cosy bedrooms are well appointed, and dinner is served nightly in the cheerful dining room. A self-contained villa, ideal for families, is also available.

Rooms: 15rms en suite (4 fmly) (2 GF)
Facilities: TV Licensed TVL Cen ht Parking 30 Last d order 10pm

ROSCOMMON
Gleesons Townhouse & Restaurant

62% RR

Market Square

☎ 090 6626954 📄 090 6627425

email: info@gleesonstownhouse.com

www.gleesonstownhouse.com

Dogs: Bedrooms (Unattended) Sep Accom (kennels) Garden Exercise Area
Resident Pets: Millie (Cavalier King Charles Spaniel)

This 19th-century cut-limestone town house has been very tastefully restored. The bedrooms and suites are decorated and furnished to a high standard. Dinner is served nightly in the Manse Restaurant and there is an extensive lunch and afternoon tea menu in the cafe or in the beautifully landscaped front courtyard. Conference facilities and secure car parking are available.

Rooms: 19rms en suite (1 fmly)
Facilities: TV STV Modem/Fax Licensed TVL Parking 25

MAYO/ROSCOMMON

WATERFORD/WICKLOW

DUNGARVAN
The Castle Country House ♦♦♦♦♦

Millstreet Cappagh

☎ 058 68049 📄 058 68099

email: castlefm@iol.ie

www.castlecountryhouse.com

Dir: *13km NW of Dungarvan. Off N72 onto R671 N to Millstreet*

Dogs: Bedrooms (Unattended) Garden Exercise Area (adjacent)

This delightful house is in the west wing of a 15th-century castle. Guests are spoiled by host Joan Nugent who loves to cook and hunt out antiques for her visitors to enjoy. She is helped by her husband Emmett who enjoys showing off his high-tech dairy farm and is a fount of local knowledge. Bedrooms are spacious and enjoy lovely views. There is a river walk and a beautiful garden to relax in.

Rooms: 5rms en suite (1 fmly)

dble room £90 - £100*

Facilities: TV Licensed Cen ht Parking 11

DUNLAVIN
Tynte House ♦♦♦♦   73%

☎ 045 401561 📄 045 401586

email: info@tyntehouse.com

www.tyntehouse.com

Dir: *N81 at Hollywood Cross, right at Dunlavin, follow finger signs for Tynte House, past market house in town centre*

Dogs: Bedrooms Garden Exercise Area

Resident Pets: Suki (Maltese), Sasha (West Yorkshire Terrier)

The 19th-century farmhouse stands in the square of this quiet country village. The friendly hosts have carried out a lot of restoration resulting in comfortable bedrooms and a relaxing guest sitting room. Breakfast is high light of a visit to this house, which features Caroline's home baking.

Rooms: 7rms en suite (2 fmly)

dble room £70 - £90

Facilities: TV Modem/Fax TVL Cen ht Parking 16